Bridge Street from the north, 1923. Note deep bridged gully bordering the street.

Main residential section, about 1911. Lee Street, looking north. Patterson home on left midway of block with fancy gingerbread bordering eaves. New Hesperian School on hill overlooking town. Old school moved to the left. Rigdon home, second house on right. (Courtesy Paul Squibb)

The old Coast Road over Leffingwell property much as it appeared in 1870. Today it provides private access to the former Leffingwell holdings.

Where the Highway Ends -

Cambria, San Simeon and the Ranchos

by Geneva Hamilton

The colorful history of Spanish explorers,
Indians, Whaling, Life on the Ranchos,
Chinese, Quicksilver mines, Fires, Floods,
Swiss dairies, Hearst ranches, and
Early California pioneers.

Padre Lachlan P. MacDonald, Editor & Publisher
Productions
P.O. Box 1275
San Luis Obispo, CA 93406

Contents

*Note: p. 35 Josephine Marquart should read Anna Marquart;
p. 77 Young Luis; p. 83 Dubost; caption following
p. 106 Ulric Music.*

Additional copies of this book may be obtained at your bookstore or
by mail from the Publisher, Padre Productions, P.O. Box 1275, San
Luis Obispo, California 93406

Top: Bridge and Main Streets, probably 1868. Cambria Hill with coast road descending from south to Santa Rosa Creek. Bridge Street crosses creek from left to right, entering between larger buildings. Included at left were Cosmopolitan Hotel under construction, Proctor and Davis blacksmith shop and Jerry Johnson livery stable; Campbell livery stable under construction. Right: two-story Grant, Lull and Co. store also housing "San Simeon" post office; other buildings included J. P. Lewelling, Thaddeus Sherman, Price's Hotel and Ott, who were establishing themselves opposite the livery stables.

Bottom: Bridge Sreet looking north from corner of Center Street, 1908. At left: blacksmith shop, Stacey's jewelry, butchershop, Cambria Hotel; right: Guerra's Hotel, restaurant and saloon; IOOF hall with Lull Store, and Anderson Store on further corner. IOOF building was later destroyed by fire originating in Guerra Hotel.

Some well known pioneers and old residents of the area appearing in the book. Facing page, left to right: Wm. Gillespie, Samuel A. Pollard, F. F. Letcher; George Lingo, Job E. Apsey, Geo. W. Ramage; A. M. Hardie, James C. McFerson, Elmer S. Rigdon; José de Jésus Pico, J. C. Baker, Wm. Leffingwell, Sr. Above, left to right: Wm. Leffingwell, Jr., Tom Stilts, Wm. M. Lyons; Emma Foster Leffingwell (Aunt Em), Caroline Gillespie Leffingwell (Aunt Carlie); W. W. Warren, George Steiner, Joaquin Soto.

Preface

This history is especially timely, when so many California communities are disappearing under pavement and under the rising tide of immigration from other states.

Until the writing of the chapters that form this book, no generous and competent effort has ever been made to tell the story of Cambria, the first Anglo town of San Luis Obispo County.

Members of the San Luis Obispo County Historical Society have collected much information and many photographs which have been gladly turned over to Mrs. Hamilton for her careful verification and incorporation in this interesting history.

Mrs. Hamilton has shown energy, patience and tact in reporting conflicting stories of old-timers and professional skill in uncovering remains of Indian, Mexican and Anglo civilization.

Her careful checking of County, State and National records has made the book a valuable contribution to San Luis Obispo County history.

PAUL SQUIBB
Past President of the
San Luis Obispo County Historical Society

Second fire cart in Cambria. Put together by John Eubanks, blacksmith, this cart was pulled by volunteers who formed a bucket brigade. Still preserved and in the care of Paul Squibb of Cambria. (Ralph Morgan photo)

Introduction

This history is an outgrowth of a series of newspaper articles I contributed to various county editions for several years. They are now combined and enlarged upon by popular demand of local residents to preserve for posterity some of the pioneer names, places and events, as well as a way of life which is gone.

After more than 100 years the population, which associates itself under the name of Cambria, still contains a large number of pioneer descendents and people attracted by the remaining flavor of its former rugged nature. These chapters are devoted, not only to the area known as Cambria, but to all areas and elements which contributed to the formation and support of the town. County histories have touched but briefly upon the north coastal area of San Luis Obispo County and, in many instances, information came exclusively from personal interviews among local inhabitants without verification of facts. It has been the sincere endeavor of the author to compare information received through her own interviews with recorded data whenever possible, knowing the unconscious tendency for facts to become distorted when given from memory. Information obtained through interview is usually mentioned in conjunction with the name of the contributor. Cooperation of old residents of the area made this book possible; invaluable leads to authentic information came from them, as well as the bits of human interest which personalizes a work of this kind.

Following are but a few of the people who have generously contributed information and help toward the creation of this book: the late Miss Helen Ballard, daughter of Edward B. Ballard, an early county pioneer; Lindy Bonomi, present owner of that portion of Rancho San Simeon on which the outpost of Mission San Miguel was located; the late Deville Bovee, pioneer of the upper reaches of San Simeon Creek and a nephew to Joseph Johnson, pioneer lumberman of Cambria; Miss Mabel Bright and her sister, Mrs. Neva Williams, descendents of some of Cambria's earliest pioneers, the Woods; the late Albert "Slim"

Cunha, a fisherman who lived at San Simeon Whaling Station after its closure, who contributed his knowledge of whaling and the history of San Simeon Point after the whaling station was closed; Mrs. Peter Fiscalini, who provided invaluable information and pictures concerning the Fiscalini family and early Swiss settlers, as well as Hearst activities in Green Valley; the late Caroline Hale Fitzhugh, daughter of Joseph Hale, an early pioneer in the upper reaches of the San Simeon and Santa Rosa Creek area, gave highlights of mountain life as a homesteader, having been born in the area 100 years ago. The late Hazel VanGorden Gamboni and Helen Hafley contribued to the history of the VanGorden family; Carl Hansen, C. L. Mitchell, and Mrs. Morris Salmina supplied history of the Harmony Valley Creamery Association; Rocco Rava, Joaquin Soto, Nick Storni and the late Willian M. Lyons contributed incidents of human interest, and much history relative to the area shortly after the turn of the century; the late George "Jack" Steiner, a native of Cambria, was a never-ending source of information covering the entire area. His experience in every conceivable local enterprise and endeavor over a period of 80 years, and his affiliation with the county as local constable, Justice of the Peace, and Judge of San Simeon District before its consolidation with the Morro Bay area were valuable as a source of human interest stories.

William "Bill" Warren, 91-year-old son of the pioneer, Albert Warren, and his uncle, the late Tom Stilts, contributed much information about early homesteaders, mining and general ranch life. Others of the Warren family giving information include Florence Porte Warren, George Warren, Forrester Warren and Mary O'Neill Warren. Lois Trace Webster, daughter of Professor Trace, a pioneer teacher in the Cambria high school, cleared up many details concerning Cambria school life. Isabelle Patterson Wineman and Lela Martin Andrews, elderly daughters of San Simeon Creek homesteaders; Gladys Kester Smithers of the Leffingwell properties; the late Miss Frances Olmsted, daughter of Green Valley pioneers; Tony and J. C. Sebastian of San Simeon; Mrs. H. R. Stiles, daughter of Reverend Henry C. Thomson, D.D., pastor during the 1890's at the Cambria Presbyterian

Church; the late Mrs. Mabel Estrada Somers, granddaughter of Don Julian Estrada; Lorin V. Thorndyke, son of Captain L. V. Thorndyke, first keeper at Piedras Blancas Lighthouse, and Paul Squibb, local collector of historical artifacts and documents. Still others who helped are Mrs. Irma Music Jones, granddaughter of B. F. Music; the late Delfino Molinari of Harmony Valley; the late Constantine Fiscalini; How Wong, elderly Chinese pioneer; Mrs. George Brunner, keeper of the records and artifacts stored in the warehouses of the Hearst property; the late Grace Junge; Ralph Morgan, editor of *The Cambrian*; Clay Morss, and Phoebe Maggetti Storni. Appreciation is extended to personnel in the many departments of the San Luis Obispo County Court House, Bancroft Library, San Luis Obispo County libraries, San Luis Obispo County Museum, various Federal and State Government offices which answered numerous letters of inquiry, and to Helen Belknap for her guidance in editing and spelling.

It has been suggested that the pronounciation of the name of Cambria as accepted and officially recorded by the Cambria Chamber of Commerce be brought to the attention of the readers at this point. The soft *a* is used and pronounced as in man.

Throughout the book the name of *San Carpoforo Creek* has been used as a compromise in preference to San Carpojo as is shown on most recent maps for the following reason: According to the 1889 *Coast Pilot* the name of the creek was first known to mariners as *El Karpophorus,* a Greek word meaning "fruit bearer." The creek received this name because of the famous fruit orchards planted there by the early pioneers and San Antonio de Padua Mission Fathers who used the area as a route to the coast for fresh fish. Though most of the orchards are now gone, some of the old homesteads are still called by the name of their once productive orchards rather than by the name of the people who homesteaded them. Uninformed map makers have, without research, endeavored to standardize names and corrupted *El Karpophorus* to *San Carpoforo,* then, still later, to *San Carpojo,* neither of which has any connection to either a Saint or Spanish.

GENEVA HAMILTON

Main Street of Cambria in the early 1920's. (Courtesy Paul Squibb)

Part I Cambria

Chapter 1

Cambria: 1866-1889

It is now the concensus of opinion that the town of Cambria, located on the banks of Santa Rosa Creek two miles from the ocean in the central coast area of San Luis Obispo County, California, had its official beginning late in the year of 1866. This peaceful, quaint little town, nestled in a forest of Monterey Pine, once vied with San Luis Obispo for first place in the county and, in its early days was often called Santa Rosa, Rosaville or San Simeon before its inhabitants could decide upon a name suitable to both the locality and the government post office.

As early as 1863 the farming area along Santa Rosa Creek was frequently referred to simply as "Santa Rosa" in the San Luis Obispo County Board of Supervisors' meetings, the community being so closely knit together by common bonds of industry and isolation. Further, to emphasize the solidarity of the area, in August of 1866 a petition was received by the Board from "the citizens of Santa Rosa." The name was, at this time, simply an early indication of the desire of the community to be known as a co-ordinated unit. The acceptance of this use on the county level was proof that the desire was acknowledged by the county government.

Several enterprising individuals visiting the San Simeon—Santa Rosa Creek area foresaw the junction of the public road serving the upper reaches of the Santa Rosa Creek Valley with the coast route from San Luis Obispo to San Simeon Bay as an ideal location for a town site. This junction was the halfway point between the two heaviest populated areas on the north coast.

1

This junction was, moreover, located on a small stretch of relatively level though heavily wooded valley land. However, the junction was on part of the large Mexican grant known as Rancho Santa Rosa and, prior to September of 1866, it was not for sale to the public.

In 1862, H. Phillip Kaetzel, age 21, joined a wagon train from Ohio and headed for California. He had several years of apprenticeship as a bucket and tub maker and some solid knowledge of wagon building. He stayed in the San Joaquin Valley as a homesteader for three years but tired of the area and settled in San Luis Obispo County in 1865. He discovered 160 acres of unclaimed land adjacent to Santa Rosa Rancho, just north of the creek and within 1000 feet of the junction of the afore mentioned roads. Snuggled into this small "corner," Kaetzel was in an ideal position to serve a community which was obviously destined to arise at the road junction before long.

Kaetzel stocked his property with cattle and set up business as a wheelwright and wagon maker. Soon he was approached by two business men who had taken up homesteads as a business speculation in the vicinity of the Nacimiento River in 1862. Eventually realizing the Nacimiento location was a mistake, and observing the rapid influx of settlers to the San Simeon-Santa Rosa area, they decided to obtain an early foothold; not in acreage but in the business of merchandising, a field in which they were better qualified than that of farming. These two men were William Grant and George W. Lull, both originally from San Francisco. Grant, the financier, had strong business connections in San Francisco and preferred to maintain his home there. Lull, his junior partner who came to the county in 1858 at the age of 27, was delegated to pioneer the business.

Representing the partnership, Lull soon secured a lease from Kaetzel with an option to purchase a small portion of the homestead where it bordered the Santa Rosa Creek road. Lull immediately proceeded to erect a small, two-story building from virgin lumber being cut at Leffingwell Saw Mill, located deep in the pine forest about two miles distant on the county road.

Lull designed the lower story of his building for use as a general merchandise store. The upper floor provided him with bachelor quarters. Wooden bins held beans and other staples while shelving provided room for packaged commodities. Redwood siding brought to the Leffingwell beach landing by schooner was added to the outside of the building to enhance its appearance as well as to add strength and insure against attack of the elements and general dampness of the area. The store was completed well before the end of 1865.

Prior to this time Domingo Pujol, a wealthy Spaniard and California lawyer, purchased all but 1500 acres of Santa Rosa Rancho from the Spanish-Mexican grantee, Don Julian Estrada, as a land investment. It was not until 1866, however, that he received clear title to the property and had the land surveyed into large plots of varying size. These properties were then placed on sale. Until this time, Pujol had managed to keep the entire land transaction from general public knowledge.

John Myers and William M. Gillespie were Pujol's first clients. They purchased 195 acres of heavily timbered bottom land in the extreme northwest corner of the rancho on September 22, immediately after the land was placed on sale. With the backing of Gillespie, Myers established a saw mill operation in competition with the Leffingwell concern which, at this time, had been in business for three years.

The following month, on October 12, George Long bought 2094 acres of the rancho in three different parcels. One parcel of 1010 acres comprised all of the rancho situated to the north and west of Santa Rosa Creek, bordering Kaetzel on the west.

Long immediately proceeded to sell portions of this land in amounts which would accommodate the purchasing power of people who wished smaller plots than could be secured from Pujol. These plots were sold on a mete and bound basis. At the same time Long joined partners with Samuel A. Pollard, also a land speculator.

The Myers-Gillespie partnership operated with a portable steam saw mill which was considered more practical than the establishment of a permanent mill site. The first timbers they processed were used to construct housing for the two partners and their families, and for the building of several sheds and outbuildings necessary to the business.

Mr. Pollard was undoubtedly the first customer of the mill for he purchased enough material to build a general store at the northeast corner of the road junction (Bridge and Main Streets), the first building to be placed on Long property. Establishment of this store, in competition with Grant, Lull and Company, was the first of a rapid series of buildings to be erected within the next few months.

The next business establishment was a blacksmith shop erected by John Hector, who purchased a piece of land adjoining the Pollard store to the east. Hector employed his two grown sons, Harrison and G. Wilson, to help him. They were kept busy from the first day they opened their doors.

At the same time short, plump and bald Rufus Rigdon and his wife, India Scott, daughter of Greenup Scott, purchased 150 acres along Santa Rosa Creek, west of the junction. Rigdon established his home on the property, which he farmed as it was cleared of timber. He also acted as notary and Justice of the Peace. The Rigdons had several children of school age when they settled on their farm.

Santa Rosa Creek road, which ended at its junction with the coast road, was now continued past the Rigdon property and the Myers-Gillespie saw mill to the ocean, with Long, W. Coffee and P. A. Forrester as "viewers," to accommodate settlers who were buying small pieces of land from the saw mill owners as they cleared it of timber.

In three short months after buying their property Myers and Gillespie had realized a substantial profit from their holdings. They sold the balance of the property, together with the saw mill operation, to F. F. Letcher from Virginia, and J. W. Ford on December 24, 1866. The mill was named Pacific Saw Mill and, while competing with Leffingwell, had all the work it could handle. Many of the structures in the vicinity of the junction were put up in such haste that slabs with bark still remaining on them were often used. The rough appearance of the town immediately brought into use the nickname of "Slab Town" which continued as a colloquial term for some time.

George W. Proctor and George S. Davis, as partners, were the third ones to buy property from Long near the junction.

They bought land to the north of the continuation of Santa Rosa Creek Road and opposite Rigdon.

With the sale of property to Proctor and Davis, it may be said that the "founding of Cambria" had become a reality, with eight of the previously mentioned people constituting the founding nucleus: Kaetzel, Lull, Long, Pollard, Hector, Rigdon, Proctor and Davis. The area occupied by the saw mill, though it played an important part in the founding, did not come within the bounds of the town until approximately 1930.

Pollard was the husband of Josefa Dana, the former wife of the late Henry Tefft, who had been a prosperous real estate broker and land speculator in the county. Josefa was a wealthy woman in her own right, both through inheritance from her Dana connections, and through the death of her former husband. Pollard apparently used some of her money in making local investments, following much the same pattern Tefft had used in other areas. Besides being active in county politics and civic affairs, Pollard was also part owner of the short lived county newspaper, *San Luis Obispo Democrat*.

Rigdon came to the community in company with his brother, Elmer, who was more interested in mining and prospecting than in the building of a town and, without a family, lived on the mining properties with which he became closely associated. As Kaetzel became more involved as a wheelwright, he abandoned farming to devote his time to mending and building of carriages and wagons. He sold his farm, with the exception of a few acres, to Greenup Scott, father of Mrs. Rigdon. Mr. Scott established his home on Santa Rosa Creek Road below the dome-like rock which received his name and is known to all Cambrians as Scott Rock.

Both Proctor and Davis, who arrived in the county from Maine in 1861, were blacksmiths prior to establishing themselves in the new community. Since they were preceded by John Hector and his two sons as blacksmiths, they devoted their time to other interests until an increase in business permitted the profitable establishment of a second blacksmith shop in the town. Davis erected a small hotel which operated under the name of Davis Hotel.

In 1867 many other people arrived who soon became prominent. Among them were George Washington Lingo, a county resident since 1861, who erected the well patronized Cosmopolitan Hotel adjacent to the Pollard store on the north; Jerry Johnson of Ohio, who settled, first on the Gauman ranch in Santa Rosa Valley with J. M. Buffum in 1859, then established the first livery stable; Thaddeus Sherman, another wheelwright and carriage maker, arrived with his wife, Lilla, and James Campbell who, arriving late in the year, prepared to open a second livery stable. Fred Ott, a shoemaker, built a two story establishment on Main street, the upper floor of which served as a meeting hall. The newspaper also notes another lodging place called Price's Hotel, Mr. Price being one of the petitioners for the continuation of Main Street to the coast, thus connecting his hotel, Rigdon, a blacksmith shop and Gillespie's mill.

The first physician, Dr. J. W. Frame, also arrived early in the year. Dr. Frame was a native of Scotland but recently arrived from Australia, who became general practitioner for the whole coastal area including the still existent Indian settlement located near Bain's store on Old Creek below what is now known as Cayucos. Dr. Frame, in spite of the large territory he covered, usually on horseback, also found time to act as general news correspondent for the San Luis Obispo weekly newspaper until he died suddenly in 1869 at the Bain's store during a diphtheria epidemic.

As the town grew, Santa Rosa Creek Road became known as Main Street because more travel occurred on it than over the coast road from the south to San Simeon Bay. Within the town the coast road was referred to as Bridge Street, an outgrowth of a reference to "the street with the bridges." These bridges were numerous due to the fact that after crossing Santa Rosa Creek the road to the north of the junction paralleled a deep gully formed by a small spring-fed creek, and necessitated the building of many small bridges as access to business houses and residences fronting the street on the west side. A large wooden bridge was built to cover the intersection when Main Street was continued westward beyond the coast road. This was covered with a layer of soil and gave the appearance of solid ground. Eventually the entire gully was bridged. Proctor Lane between Center and Main Streets, as well as Center Street, were established about this time, these divisions constituting the hub of the business section.

Probably the most important event in 1867 was the establishment of a United States Post Office on October 2 in the Grant, Lull and Company store, located on the southwest corner of Main and Bridge Streets, with store clerk Winfield S. Whittaker as postmaster. At this same time the town became officially known as San Simeon.

Prior to this date, citizens of the town had agreed upon the name of Santa Rosa to match the name of the creek beside which it was located. The post office department, however, required three names be submitted at the time of application for an office in the event one or another was found unsuitable. The names Santa Rosa, Rosaville and San Simeon were chosen for the application, the people little dreaming that neither of the first two names would be acceptable. Both were rejected on the grounds that other California post offices existed with these names. The local people never liked the name of San Simeon after adoption by the postal system and continued to refer to themselves as Santa Rosans.

The installation of a post office necessitated regular transport of mail. J. P. Lewelling, constable and general law officer of San Luis Obispo, obtained the mail contract and established the first stage service between San Luis Obispo and "San Simeon" carrying the mail, Wells Fargo and Company freight, and packages for Pacific Union Express, as well as occasional passengers. A cumbersome spring wagon made the run to "San Simeon" every Saturday. The "stage" gave such little comfort or protection to the passengers from dust and weather that most people preferred to travel by saddle horse or in their own, faster buggies when road conditions permitted. The rut-worn road was extremely dusty and rough in the summer, and almost impassable from mud in the winter.

Lewelling sold the stage run to R. A. Minor before the end of his first year. Minor, too, soon tired of the run and found other local business more to his liking. In a few months he sold to D. S. Miller, an experienced stage driver. Miller took a real interest in his newly acquired enterprise and quickly increased the runs to twice, then three times a week. The "stage" left "San Simeon" on Mondays, Wednesdays and Fridays at 7:00 A.M. and arrived in San Luis Obispo at 3:00 P.M., returning on alternate days.

In the meantime, Mr. Letcher bought out his partner, Ford, and became the sole owner of the Pacific Steam Saw Mill. He continued selling five and ten acre plots of the mill holdings as they were cleared or, on occasion, with the timber still standing but with timber rights reserved. He also purchased timber rights from others who wished their lands cleared.

Every family within a radius of 20 miles of the new town became vitally interested in its growth and welfare. They immediately associated themselves with the activities of the village in spite of the many difficult miles often lying between it and their homes. The town meant not only a close center for the reception of mail formerly distributed at San Luis Obispo and picked up at the Bay of San Simeon on the arrival of steamers or schooners, but a center for organized social and political activities for which the isolated people were starved. The majority of these early pioneers were comparatively well educated. Many of them had grown or nearly grown children who also needed the social contacts a town provided.

When George Hearst, who had recently acquired a portion of Rancho Piedra Blanca about San Simeon Bay, started subdivision of the beach frontage into small lots and secured a franchise for building of a pier on San Simeon Point, Santa Rosans and the entire area decided to do something about the name of the town. A committee was immediately appointed for the selection and adoption of a name that would be acceptable to both the people and the postal authorities.

Further business and social changes within the town were instigated at the time, due not only to Hearst's proposed plans but to an increased tempo in the quest for cinnabar in adjacent hills, and the beginning of actual mining operations on already established claims. In 1869 Samuel Pollard sold his store to J. L. Chamblin, to devote himself more fully to the details of increased land transactions and timber sales. Mr. Lull negotiated with Hearst and Captain Joseph Clark of the San Simeon whaling station for a partnership in construction of the pier with the added right to build and maintain a warehouse and store to operate in conjunction with the pier when it was completed.

Socially, the first fraternal order in the town was organized by the Masons who formed San Simeon Lodge 198 and received their charter in November of 1869. Lodge meetings were scheduled for moonlight nights, not for romantic purposes but to obtain the advantages of bright moonlight while driving buggy or riding horse over rough roads and trails on the homeward journey to distant farms.

George Lull, also in need of larger quarters, took advantage of a chance to acquire a small lot on the southwest corner of Main and Bridge Streets, opposite the Chamblin store. He negotiated with the new lodge for a partnership erection of a two story building. When completed the upper floor belonged "lock, stock, and barrel" to the Masons while the lower half remained the exclusive property of Grant, Lull and Company.

The committee for renaming "San Simeon" failed to turn in a prompt report and, with pier construction slated to begin in the early part of 1869, pressure was brought to bear upon the members. In the summer of 1869, with the pier now under construction, the committee agreed to have a final meeting "to end all meetings," at which time they vowed to continue until a suitable name was selected. Unfortunately, no minutes of the meeting survived, but the men who were gathered together were a desperate and weary bunch. It is said that as the discussion continued very late into the night, they found themselves no nearer a solution than they had been early in the evening. Finally, according to a newspaper report of the time, a recess was called for refreshments and stretching of tired legs. During this break, and in the course of a casual conversation, P. A. Forrester, an engineer engaged in local mining interests and recently returned from a trip east, remarked that while in his home state of Pennsylvania he was in a small settlement by the name of *Cambria* which lay in a setting similar to "San Simeon," and which was also the hub of a local mining industry.

When the meeting reconvened the name of Cambria was proposed. After a brief discussion, it was quickly accepted, apparently because of the similarities existent between the two places. Whether the choice was influenced by the lateness of the hour or whether the committee seriously considered the name before adopting it will never be known.

Post office authorities were immediately notified of the desired change, and the San Luis Obispo weekly newspaper noted in August of 1869:

> Until three years prior to this date Cambria has always gone by a variety of names. When the place was founded it was called *Rosaville* and *Santa Rosa* and all along it has been called, by some, by the name of *San Simeon.*
>
> The present name used by the post office is down in the lists as *San Simeon* . . . A public meeting of the citizens has been held at which time it was determined to call the town *Cambria.* The post office authorities were memorialized to alter the name in conformity . . .
> (italics by author).

Since that time some, unaware of the facts, have given credit to John P. "Chino" Lewelling (sometimes spelled Lewellyn), former stage driver and at the time of the decision, a carpenter in Cambria, for suggesting the new name because it was he who first placed the name of Cambria above his establishment. Lewelling came to the county of San Luis Obispo from Kentucky in the 1850's, and married Senora Maria Josefa Rodriquez. He served as guard at the county jail and as sheriff and constable for several years before taking the stage contract. On quitting the stage run he purchased property from F. F. Letcher and settled here as a carpenter. His action immediately following the naming of Cambria appears to have been a serious effort on his part to expedite the adoption of the new name by the citizenry. The name of Cambria was finally accepted and recorded by the United States postal system on January 10, 1870.

Further expansion marked the year of 1870. Mr. and Mrs. George Lingo arrived in "Rosaville" in 1868 and soon purchased property from Pollard. In this year, 1870, he erected the Cosmopolitan Hotel, at which time he was also serving as constable for the area.

The Odd Fellows' Hesperian Lodge was organized, and the first church was started. Pioneer cattleman, Jeffrey Phelan, whose properties joined those of Hector, Chamblin and Lingo, donated a small piece of land on October 14 to the Reverend Father Amat of Mission San Luis Obispo for a Catholic Mission Church. Enthusiastic San Luis Obispo women held several fund-raising affairs to aid in financing construction of the small church building which circumstances indicate was erected in 1871 though mission records fail to note the date of construction.

Again the Pacific Saw Mill changed hands but not until it had gained county wide reputation for its lumber. This time the mill, with only three acres of land, was sold to Joseph Johnson and T. C. Hayes, who was related by marriage to several of the early settlers of the area. These two men continued operation under the name of Johnson Saw Mill.

George Davis, a better blacksmith than hotel manager, turned over operation of the hotel to his partner, George Proctor who, in turn, placed his wife in charge while he, with Davis, opened another blacksmith shop at the southwest corner of Bridge and Main Streets. Besides running their business the two men continued to buy more property from others wishing to subdivide their holdings or to sell out. They soon became relatively large property holders within the town. Other streets located and named at this time were West, Lee, and Wall Streets.

Property gained in value daily, especially along Bridge, Main and Center streets where lots were divided and redivided, some residential ones being as small as 25 by 50 feet.

The Cambria stage line changed hands again this year. This time it was purchased by Juan Castro of Piedra Blanca Rancho and his partner, Mr. Brown of San Luis Obispo. As a partnership the two men were already owners of an elaborate livery stable in San Luis Obispo. Their first move was to replace the clumsy spring wagon, still in use, with comfortable stage coaches pulled by fast horses. They also instituted a daily stage service. These greatly improved conditions appealed to the Cambrians who immediately began using the stage as a regular means of travel to and from San Luis Obispo. Fare was considered reasonable at $3 per one-way trip.

P. A. Forrester was not only a good mining engineer but was considered as a qualified surveyor, often employed by the county to survey and plot numerous of the early "roads" in the north coastal area. When he came to Cambria in 1868 he immediately became active in the growth of the community. He purchased property on the corner of Bridge and Center Streets where he built his home and lived for a number of years. He was also active in the Masons and Odd Fellows.

By the time he arrived in Cambria the town had grown to such proportions that it was deemed expedient to have an accurate survey which would delineate property lines and streets, the boundaries of which had heretofore been described entirely on a mete and bound basis without benefit of survey.

Forrester was engaged to conduct a thorough survey and provide an accurate map. Using the United States survey post No. 7 of Rancho Santa Rosa as a datum point, he carefully mapped each piece of property according to surveyors' measurements of chains, links and feet, and he noted the compass angle of all property lines. These findings were recorded on a map which became known as "Forrester's Plat." For many years after the survey all property sales contained the reference, "according to Forresters' Plat." Unfortunately, there is no record of this survey ever having been recorded in the San Luis Obispo County court house recorder's office. At the present time there appears to be no copy of the Plat in existence though some say it may have been recorded elsewhere and, as yet, undiscovered.

The loss of this map has caused no end of trouble to property owners of Cambria in the past 50 years as modern surveys fail to conform to the original property lines or deed descriptions, and many hard feelings have developed because of these nonconformities.

Horse racing in the county suddenly became popular after 1870. Prosperous Cambrians and adjacent ranchers were among the first to participate in the county events, regularly taking top prizes with their excellent riding and buggy horses. They also formed their own organization known as the Cambria Jockey

Club with a local track situated on an outlying ranch where purses of $100 and $150 were not unusual and competiton was "open to all horses in the county." James D. Campbell, owner of Cambria's largest livery stable, was one of the most active participants.

James D. Campbell, "one of Cambria's most prominent figures," had five children—three girls: Mary, Catherine and Alice; and two boys: James D., Jr., and Archie. James D., Sr., was afflicted with dyspepsia in his later years. George Warren, born in Cambria in 1879, recalls him as always taking handfuls of baking soda. ". . . could hardly eat anything without getting an upset stomach." He was a heavy, fat man, "full of tricks which he played on the kids" who hung around the livery stable. His two sons were the same. James had boxing gloves for the youngsters to practice with and, as George said, "A whole raft of kids gathered there," (including himself).

Young J. D. assisted his father at the stable and had a good home near the business section of Cambria, on Main Street. Before his father's death in the late 1880's, he was already involved in local affairs and carried a great deal of influence in civic matters.

During this time the Cambria Hall building was purchased by E. Taylor and D. Parker who refitted it for a restaurant and hotel. It was located near the corner of Lee and Main Streets.

By 1873, reflecting the prosperity of the new town and a swing toward refinement in the construction of homes, Johnson Saw Mill advertised "battings, boardings, scantlings, siding and fencing" as the chief products of his mill. Imported redwood and Douglas fir were also sold. These were used freely in the construction of finer parts of the buildings, while some of the homes of the wealthier business men were constructed almost entirely of redwood. Many cypress hedges were planted about the buildings and kept neatly trimmed.

The Phoenix Livery Stable and Paint Shop opened on the corner of Wall and Main Streets. And the Patrons of Husbandry, Grange No. 25, was formed. This organization immediately became active, and in 1874 gained the reputation of "never doing things by halves." As a major project, they took over the responsibility of the annual Fourth of July program and celebration, which was already a yearly event attended by people from many parts of the country.

During 1874 George Davis dissolved partnership with Proctor, and John Hackney, another blacksmith, joined Proctor in the Bridge and Main Street shop; and the Davis Hotel became known as the Proctor House. Joseph Johnson bought out his partner, T. C. Hayes, and changed the name of the mill to Pacific Saw Mills after adding another rig.

As an outgrowth of Protestant Sunday School meetings held at various places in the country around Cambria (beginning first in 1865), the Presbyterian Church of Cambria was organized on September 20, 1874. Services were conducted with the Reverend R. S. Symington as pastor. Land was purchased on north Bridge Street from Henry Williams and a church erected. First services were held in the new church in May of 1875.

Cambria was now advertised as the "City of Cinnabar and 1000 Pines," for many of the nearby mines were at peak production, and business in the town was brisk. Board walks were built in front of the more prosperous establishments which accommodated foot traffic. Other stores had raised platforms three and four steps from the ground to facilitate the loading and unloading of merchandise from delivery wagons. A stream of freight wagons hauling furnace wood and other supplies to the mines churned up a continuous cloud of dust from the dirt streets or created a sea of mud according to the season; and a flow of late evening shoppers and patrons of the saloons stumbled about with only the aid of dim lanterns. Also, a familiar sight on the Cambria streets were droves of hogs and cattle being driven to market on foot.

In September of this year Judge Steele of San Luis Obispo, approaching Cambria from the south, met with a near accident on the steep grade entering Cambria (via Bridge Street-Santa Rosa Creek crossing). "He met the 4-horse stage going up grade from Cambria. His buggy was upset by his spirited team but the (stage) driver was quick to rescue the horses and prevent a run-away."

The same year, in July, E. Peter Smith, a temporary resident of Cambria who was mining in the area, "mysteriously disappeared during the night while staying at Lingo's Cosmopolitan Hotel." He was noted to have gone out but not to return though he had an appointment to meet friends the following day for a "prospecting trip into the hills. He was of good character and possessed of property in the county." Sixteen men hunted for him, fearing something serious had happened. Two weeks later a notation in the paper states that Smith ". . . believed taken to Stockton as insane. P. A. Forrester wrote asking for information." His clothes still remained at the hotel and there was no local information accounting for his disappearance, also, no confirmation of his being in Stockton.

A coarse and sometimes lawless element came with the mining boom. The San Luis Obispo *Tribune* reported:

Robbers broke into a house on Santa Rosa Creek, then San Simeon. They made a family get up and get supper for them (3 men). They are reported to be a. remnant of the Vasquez gang—tall, dark, long straight black hair and 'more cheek than an army mule'."

Among other things, W. Truewell had his horse stolen.

Some of the miners were a rough lot, and in 1875 George Lingo decided the town was too wild for him and he "feared the harmful influence they (the miners) would have on his two teen-age daughters." As a consequence, he sold the Cosmopolitan Hotel to Job Apsey and moved to San Luis Obispo.

The population of Cambria was variously noted as being between 1000 and 2000 people; but these estimates were based on the total area which the town served. Actual resident population of the surveyed town was approximately 300. Nevertheless, Cambria was the second largest town of the county, outranked only by San Luis Obispo, the county seat. Every inhabitant of the hills and coastline depended heavily on Cambria for supplies and the transaction of business.

Due to this undivided support of the people, the town was able to boast of a sizeable business section which consisted of four large general merchandise stores, two drug stores, two or four hotels (some establishments classed as hotels may have only been extra rooms behind a bar or in a residence), a paint and carpenter shop, two doctors, a dentist, lawyer, shoe shop, three blacksmith establishments, two livery stables, two carriage shops, a butcher shop, several saloons, Wells Fargo and Western Union offices as well as several other small concerns less permanently situated and supported chiefly by the mines and their employees.

San Simeon Bay served as the focal point for tri-weekly steamship service to San Francisco. Other unscheduled ships also arrived there or touched at the newly constructed Leffingwell Wharf located one and a half miles above the town toward San Simeon Bay. So, in conjunction with the stage, the people of the area were relatively less "off the beaten track" to the rest of the world than in later days when all passenger transportation depended upon private vehicles.

Between 1874 and 1880 the names of many new business men became household words. These included Abraham Gans who arrived with his wife, Johanna, and George Rothschild, his partner, to start one of the general merchandise stores. Rothschild committed suicide three months after his marriage and the opening of the new business. He was greatly mourned by the local people who were already very fond of him.

Following Rothchild's death, Gans went in partnership with Samuel Frank from Westphalia, Germany, to form the Samuel Frank and Company general merchandise and trading business.

G. W. Ramage also opened a general merchandise store. Like others, he found time to engage in local social activities and was liked well enough to be selected Supervisor of the San Simeon District. In May of 1875 the *Tribune* reported Ramage as a partner with E. N. Conway, noting that the old store occupied by Ramage had been torn down and a new one "in the process of construction" two stories high and extending from Main to Bridge Street, with a front 35 feet high and 50 feet wide, of tenon and mortise construction. The upstairs, 25 by 40 feet, was to be occupied by the IOOF.

The Manderscheid brothers, Otto and Mr. C., were pharmacists from Germany and especially liked because of their sympathetic and quiet manners. They built a two story home on Main Street now owned and occupied by Mr. and Mrs. Gordon

Howard. George M. Cole, saddler and harness maker, soon had a thriving business; and J. H. Janssen developed a reputation for his skill as a furniture and cabinet maker.

P. A. Forrester became wealthy through his connection with the Bonanza Mine and retired from active participation as a surveyor and engineer to become a real estate broker and to campaign for state office. In 1877 he sold his Cambria property and moved to San Luis Obispo where his ambitions had more play. There he became mayor in 1878 and remained active in civic affairs until 1883 at which time he was appointed State Commissioner of Immigration and moved to San Francisco.

Grant, Lull and Company continued to retain first position in the community. In 1871-72 the company established and ran a store on San Simeon Point in conjunction with the newly completed Clark-Hearst pier located 300 feet from the point extremity. As a store, it lasted until 1873 when the building was used exclusively as a warehouse. Late in 1874 it was again opened as a store under the ownership of Mr. Hearst and with Adam Leffingwell in charge. Sometime in 1875 the store, proving unprofitable, was again closed.

In 1875 Lull hired Frank "Brick Top" Taylor to raise the company store on the corner of Bridge and Main Streets "three feet, goods and all, above the former level," and he bought 105 feet more of frontage along Bridge Street, thus extending the length of the property to 140 feet. He widened the Main Street side of the store to 40 feet and extended its length to 70 feet, "Not more than sufficient to afford convenience for the amount of business they have been doing in the past year."

Lull, who was soon considered one of the richest men in town, courted and won Mary Leah Inman, a widow with two daughters. He built a pretentious home (now the central structure of the Bluebird Motel) in keeping with his position as leading business man on property he purchased from Rufus Rigdon. The villagers considered Lull to be very dignified. He was an impeccable dresser though stocky of build and somewhat bald, and in all outward respects, a real gentleman.

Mrs. Lull's daughters were Mrs. Josephine Waterman Somers and Mrs. Elinor Minor, wife of R. A. Minor, previously mentioned. Josephine had several children, among them were two sons from her last marriage who resided in the Lull household after the death of their father, James Somers. Young George Somers became a great favorite in the household and was formally adopted by Lull. However, during Lull's lifetime, George, who was considered a brilliant student by his school companions, gave his foster father a tremendous amount of trouble, both morally and financially. Being fully satiated with his behavior, Lull quietly deprived him of his inheritance by leaving him only one dollar in his will. The exclusion was a great surprise to the young man, age 21 at the time of Lull's death, April 16, 1899. George was then a member of the California Volunteers in the Spanish American War, stationed in Manila.

LeRoy, the other Somers boy, always spelled his name as Summers. He married Mabel Estrada, granddaughter of Julian Estrada, and settled at San Simeon Bay as wharfinger for George Hearst.

Frances Olmsted wrote: "Lull was ill for two or three years before he died. He was very neat in his business suit and a derby on his head."

After Lull's death George attended Stanford University and became a prominent lawyer. He served as San Luis Obispo City Attorney for several years, then moved to San Francisco in 1917 where his reputation secured him the position of San Francisco District Attorney. His friends all considered him a likeable man, but his addiction to drink brought his life to an early end.

In 1879 Roma T. Jackson chose Cambria as the ideal place for a weekly newspaper and established the *Cambria Critic*, a publication which continued until the Great Fire of 1889.

San Lus Obispo bowed to the town of Cambria in 1880 when George Proctor erected the new Proctor Hotel on the site of the Proctor and Hackney blacksmith shop. It was a three story affair, the first of its kind in the county. As before, Mrs. Proctor was put in charge.

Cambria reached a peak in her growth about 1880 with little major change occurring in the town for nearly 10 years, at which time, October 1, 1889, the business section of the town was completely destroyed.

Samuel Guthrie home, corner of Lee and Center Sreets about 1890. Original Hesperian School may be seen on hill at upper left. Mr. and Mrs. Guthrie, Mrs. Charles Ott and Mrs. William Leffingwell, Jr. The three ladies are sisters—Sarah, Margaret and May Woods. (Courtesy Mabel Bright)

Home built on north Bridge Street by Adam Leffingwell the year he was killed (1882). Later occupied by his brother, William, and famiy, believed to be those pictured. (Courtesy Mabel Bright)

Bridge and Main Streets before the fire of October 1889. (Alice Phelan Nock collection)

Heavy rain, an overflowing creek and high tide combined to flood the town of Cambria in 1956. (Courtesy Ralph Morgan, editor of *The Cambrian*)

Chapter 2

The Great Fire and Minor Floods

In the late summer of 1889 B. F. Muma of San Simeon Bay remarked about the extreme dryness of the coastal area. In August several brush and forest fires were reported giving considerable trouble in various parts of the coastal range, many of them apparently started by spontaneous combustion. The whole area was noted as being "tinder dry." Not only was the ground dry, but the atmosphere contained much less moisture than normal for the season.

This condition continued into the fall, and on the night of September 30, or more correctly, the morning of October 1, the little town of Cambria made history by having the Great Fire which totally destroyed the business district of the community and tested the stamina and pioneering spirit of its people.

W. S. Rickey, traveling dentist, has probably given posterity the best eye witness account of the holocaust. Mr. Rickey was well acquainted with most of the residents of Cambria and with the town. It was his practice to periodically set up a temporary office at the Proctor House, the town's big three story hotel on the corner of Bridge and Main Streets. He always took two rooms, one of which he used as an office where he placed the portable tools of his trade and took care of those in need of dental attention. The other room he used as private quarters.

Mr. Rickey arrived in Cambria on Saturday, September 29, and established himself in the corner rooms, 1 and 2 of the second floor, overlooking the busy intersection. Sunday he "arranged the equipment in anticipation of the busy day ahead"

19

and was in the "process of securing a good night's sleep" when, at 2:20 A.M., he was suddenly awakened by Mrs. Proctor yelling "Fire! Fire!" in the rear portion of the same floor.

The Proctors occupied a second story room at the rear overlooking Proctor Lane. They had been roused by a flickering rosy glare shining into their window. On looking out they were amazed to see their back fence, shed, and three cords of recently delivered wood in full blaze "not more than 29 feet from the building."

A few men were already gathered at the fire, futilely attempting to get water from a 6,000 gallon tank close at hand, which had a single bottom spigot and a garden hose badly in need of repair. The fire was gaining rapidly in intensity and heat.

Mr. Rickey, apparently the only hotel guest, wrote that after his "first quick glance, the outside of the hotel caught fire in a matter of minutes." He raced to his rooms hoping to rescue some of his equipment and other valuables. With arms loaded he opened his door only to see flames coming up from below, encouraged by the drafty nature of the halls and stairwell. Quickly shutting the door he abandoned all thought of saving anything but himself. A yell brought help in the form of a hook and ladder which, when placed against the wall under his window, fell some distance short of it. Dangling by his hands in darkness lit only by the glare of increasing flames he relates that, by taking a desperate chance in his effort to escape he "finally maneuvered a toe hold on the ladder and made the safety of the ground."

At this time Cambria had a small hand-pulled fire cart with a few buckets and a small hook and ladder arrangement. One must also remember that high ceilings, at least 14 to 16 feet, were in vogue for many of the buildings at this time, the hotel being no exception. Presumably the first floor of the hotel had these high ceilings and the distance from the ground to the window was in excess of 20 feet, a long reach for the hook and ladder arrangement used in the 1870's and 1880's.

Within a few minutes after Mr. Rickey's escape the entire building was in flames. Shortly the Ramage building, directly across the street from the hotel, took fire, then the Lull store.

From that point on, progress of the flames went unrecorded due to the full concentration of everyone frantically working to save valued possessions.

As the roof of the hotel fell there was a terrific explosion. According to Mr. Rickey, members of the crowd looked at each other in astonishment "as no one could suggest a cause for it." Later he remembered a cylinder of compressed oxygen that he carried with his equipment, and which he presumed to have caused the loud report. The only thing saved from the Proctor House, he relates, was Mrs. Proctor's trunk.

George Ramage saved a small portion of his clothing stock; George W. Lull salvaged the company books and papers, and his safe was later found to have preserved some other valuables; Mr. G. M. Cole, saddler, rescued a portion of his harness stock by piling it in the street, to lose it shortly afterward by spontaneous combustion or a stray spark. Benjamin H. Franklin, owner of a general merchandise store, the Franklin Theater, and the Granger Saloon on the corner of Main and Lee Streets, was more fortunate than many. He had time to rescue about $1000 worth of merchandise. Max Fischer, druggist and photographer, saved a portion of his drug stock, but lost all of his photographic equipment and negatives. The contents of the local post office were preserved through frantic efforts of the postmaster and citizenry though it was located directly across Proctor Lane from the hotel.

Mr. Rickey viewed the scene as one of

> hopeless destruction, as there was no water for fighting
> fire and no means of tearing down or removing any-
> thing from the path of the fire, which burned until
> there was nothing more in reach.

In two and a half hours all that was left of the business district was smouldering ashes and stark chimneys.

Some others who lost their establishments were J. H. Janssen, a lumber mill and furniture store; Samuel Gross, general merchandise store; T. S. Morton, M.D., his offices; Robert Perry, business unknown; Ritner Dodson and H. E. McFadden, paints and equipment; Roma Jackson, owner and editor of the newspaper, *Cambria Critic*; Thaddeus Sherman, blacksmith; John

McCain and Mr. Music, a saloon, A. Citron, general merchandise store; B. C. Whitney and R. A. Minor, hardware store, J. D. Campbell, Sr., owner of the large livery stable; George W. Lull, Washington Saloon building, as well as the Grant, Lull and Company Store and G. Guerra, operator of the Washington Saloon. The Masonic Lodge occupying the upper floor of the Grant Lull building lost all of its records which included the burial records of the Masonic cemetery two miles north of town where most of Cambria's dead were interred.

A few of the firms were partially covered by insurance, but many of them suffered complete loss. Total damage was estimated at approximately $150,000, a moderate sum only because most of the buildings were considered of little value, all being of cheap construction and primarily of local wood.

Fortunately, there was no loss of human life and there is no record of serious injury, though James D. Campbell, who saved his buggies and other equipment as well as the horses from the livery stable, lost one horse which broke free and ran back into the blazing barn. Only six of the approximately 50 homes near the downtown area were lost. One belonged to Ed Lynn who, at the time of the fire, was too busy rescuing the contents of the post office to look after the safety of his own dwelling.

Monday morning more than one rancher, unaware of the disaster, was completely shocked at the sight before his eyes as he approached the town. Miss Frances Olmsted, a little girl of three at the time, vividly remembered the complete bewilderment of her parents, Mr. and Mrs. Herbert Olmsted, as they viewed the devastation from Cambria Hill grade on their way into the town area. The news had not reached them at their Green Valley home. Although Miss Olmsted remembered little about the remaining rubble of the town, the depth of the tragedy which was written on her parents' faces left its indelible impression on her young mind. Personally, according to her recounting of early events 75 years later, she was greatly concerned as she viewed the remains, fearing that her grandmother's house had also been destroyed.

George "Jack" Steiner, a young lad living at San Simeon Bay at the time, was impressed by the bright glow from the fire which was easily seen there as several people watched it from their homes with no end of speculation.

A week after the disaster William Leffingwell reported to the San Luis Obispo weekly newspaper that:

> . . . the fire actually seemed to lend new life to the town, though life savings and fortunes were swept away for many.

He also stated:

> Before the ground was cold B. H. Franklin was erecting a new building and G. W. Lull had, within the week, erected a temporary business structure on the site of the former Washington Saloon.

The Grant and Lull partnership seems to have dissolved at this time for Lull now joined with Samuel Guthrie. These two made plans for a new building to be erected in the early spring, this time it was to be built of brick and on the site of the old store. Abraham Gans, another merchant to suffer loss in the fire, also made plans to build in brick. J. M. Cole, not wishing to wait, purchased a nearby, unoccupied structure and moved it onto his lot. J. L. Chamblin, general merchandise merchant, cleared his lot and moved in lumber to build in this first week.

The partners, Merritt Utley and Ed Lynn, butchers, in whose building the post office had been located, were among the first to rebuild. G. W. Proctor sold the hotel lot the day after the fire to his friend, John H. Eubanks, another blacksmith, who erected a new smithy on the corner; Mrs. M. J. Terrill, milliner, and R. A. Minor and B. C. Whitney quickly re-established themselves.

Janssen and Ramage, probably suffering the greatest financial losses (in excess of $10,000 each), packed up and left town. Janssen, who had been the Wells Fargo agent, turned over the agency to Mr. Franklin, then in the process of rebuilding on his corner lot (northeast corner of Main and Lee Streets).

Guthrie and Lull cooperated with the Odd Fellows Lodge in the early spring of 1890 to erect a pretentious structure thereafter known as the Odd Fellows Building, the Lodge owning and occupying the upper floor. This "hall" soon became famous for the many social dinners served there by various of the town's organizations.

As an outgrowth of the fire, a volunteer fire department was organized, and new, more adequate fire fighting equipment secured. Many of the new business buildings were planned and constructed to resist fire, and better provision for water storage was made.

J. D. Campell, Jr., whose home had barely escaped the ravages of the fire, became intensely interested in water: water wells, water storage, and water service. He instituted a study of Cambria water problems and proceeded, privately, to develop the town's first water system, furnishing water to those whom he could persuade to buy at a time when every home had its own well. By 1913 his system included several storage cisterns scattered about town. These were kept full by pumping from a good well. The system provided pressure at various strategically located hydrants which became an asset in the fighting of fire and helped reduce the cost of fire insurance in the town. With most residents slow to accept modernization, the convenience and importance of an assured potable water supply was slow to take hold until the flood of January 1914 when wells and cesspools were filled to overflowing by unprecedented rains, and pure drinking water was at a premium.

A map made by the Sanborn Map Company for J. D. Campbell in 1913 notes that the prevailing wind at the town of Cambria was west, the town was practically level, the streets unimproved and all establishments lit by lamps. There were no city fire limits. The town had one hook and ladder truck, no steam, no hand engine, no independent hose cart. Water for fighting fire was furnished the town by hydrants from the J. D. Campbell water works, consisting of one well.

It was the improvement of this situation which became the obsession of Mr. Campbell. He was soon able to add notations to the map indicating the town had acquired a hand operated hose and ladder truck and gallon size chemical fire extinguishers kept at the Engine House on Main Street in Block 5 of a newly organized system for fighting fires.

Fully as exciting to many of the residents as the Great Fire, but fortunately lacking the tragic loss of substantial property and savings, have been two floods which partially inundated the business and residential district near Bridge and Main Streets, creating considerable but reparable havoc.

Situated as it is in a narrow valley along the banks of the Santa Rosa Creek, water from the surrounding hills drains downward toward the business district of Cambria. Under normal winter conditions natural gullies and creeks adequately handle run-off with no danger of flooding. But, during the winter of 1913-14 heavy rains continued falling for weeks without let-up, thoroughly saturating the soil. One morning in January Cambria citizens awakened to find the main streets deep in water, and cisterns and cesspools full. Every gully and stream was overflowing, and the rain continued in a heavy downpour.

Miss Mabel Bright gave an interesting account of her experience at this time. She lived on Bridge Street's upper end and did not realize the problems in the main part of the town a block away down the hill. She was employed at the post office under Postmaster Earl VanGorden and as she left her home for work she became so engrossed in the scene before her eyes that she completely forgot her job as she envisioned the minor disasters developing. She donned rain togs and dashed down to view the rising waters and hurried work of storekeepers hastily sandbagging their doorways in an effort to keep out the flood.

At noon Miss Bright suddenly remembered she was several hours late for work. Hurrying belatedly to her job she found Mr. VanGorden "at his wit's end," frantically trying to keep the post office from flooding and, at the same time, trying to wait on customers who, oblivious to flood conditions, were coming in for their mail. Needless to say, Miss Bright's sightseeing tour ended abruptly.

Mr. VanGorden was a painfully neat and fastidious person, and the threatened invasion of water into his domain was a major blow to the perfect order in which he kept the establishment. Not only was he worried about the post office but about his home, also situated in the path of the rising waters, for he had received a frantic message from his wife urging him to come home and help.

In spite of the water everywhere "business as usual" was the order of the day in such establishments as could be entered over the doorway obstructions. Homes bordering the creek suffered the most damage as rising water seeped over wooden floors and deposited its burden of silt.

Accompanying this storm and probably as momentous as the downtown flood was the unusual appearance of numerous large water spouts along the coast which, whirling shoreward, crashed heavily upon the sandy beaches near the mouth of Santa Rosa Creek. The late Hazel (VanGorden) Gamboni related seeing at least six of these awesome phenomena during the course of the day.

Again in 1956 heavy rains flooded the village which was actually less prepared for high water than 42 years previously. Ditches and gullies existing in 1914 had been replaced with culverts or bridged over thereby cutting down their capacity. The town had also grown, with several stores built on the low flats bordering the ocean a mile west of the "old" village site. Exceptionally heavy upland downpour rapidly swelled the creeks to overflowing, causing deep inundation of these lower flats, a not uncommon occurrence in the early days of the town. This flooding, combined with a high tide, flooded the stores of the lower flats with water pouring in at the windows. The older part of the town suffered less though water entered several homes with low foundations and sidewalks were buried beneath heavy layers of silt as the water receded.

Several lesser floods swept about the stores of the lower flats after 1956 but when the highway was changed to bypass Cambria a large amount of fill was hauled in to elevate the roadbed which ran between the river and the stores. The road, acting as a dike, now eliminates most of the flooding in the area.

Chapter 3

1889-1969

The fire of October 1, 1889, instead of retarding the community, gave impetus to latent pride and provided a challenge to its residents. Cambria not only rebuilt rapidly as indicated in Chapter II, but continued to increase in size. New arrivals soon became outstanding figures in its history and growth. One of these was Alexander Paterson, who moved to town from his San Simeon Creek ranch in 1889, purchased the large two-story Lee Street house of the former school teacher, F. E. Darke (now the home of Mr. and Mrs. Paul Squibb), and proceeded to use his many talents.

Paterson was originally attracted to the area by advertised offers of work in the quicksilver mines at $5 a day. However, he soon traded his mining job for the life of a homesteader and joined partners with John Kerr on 160 acres of range land near the top of the Santa Lucia mountains near the head of San Simeon Creek. He quickly saved enough to buy out his partner.

Being active in the limited social life of the area in 1878, he met and married Emma Gross, daughter of a neighboring rancher and businessman in Cambria, Franklin Gross. Paterson was soon elected as one of the trustees at the formation of the New Era School District which served the ranchers living on the upper reaches of San Simeon Creek.

Though doing well on his ranch land, he decided he could do better for himself and growing family with a town business. He leased the ranch to Antone Luchessa and moved into town with his wife and three children, Alex, Jr., Isabelle and Janie.

After making several substantial improvements on the Darke home he set up a business as an accomplished cabinet maker in the large adjoining barn. The community soon became dependent upon him for the manufacture of everything from handsome coffins to watering troughs, butter boxes, and interior decorations for the more fashionable homes, such as stair banisters and newel posts.

As coffin maker, it was only natural that he also act as undertaker, and as a third means of income, he set up a barley mill. Though entirely unrelated to his other business enterprises, the mill proved equally profitable.

After five years, when young Alex was old enough to help substantially in the shop, Paterson took back the operation of the ranch and, with young Alex as partner, continued to farm it for the next 15 years, carrying on his town businesses at the same time. He again rented the ranch, this time to Milton Mayfield, a second generation Cambrian, who finally purchased it in 1913 for a good price.

One of Mr. Paterson's early carpentry jobs was building the bell tower on the Santa Rosa Creek school house in 1890 which, together with the school, is now preserved as part of the area's historic past on grounds of the local Lions Club.

Prior to 1890 Cambria was already famous throughout the county for its periodic community picnics held in the pines at the "picnic ground" one-fourth mile back of the Hesperian School. The school was located on a bluff overlooking the town and facing toward Cambria Hill at the intersection of Lee and Main Streets. Biggest of all celebrations each year was on the Fourth of July when the blacksmiths fired their anvils with black powder and a town committee of able citizens organized a parade led by the Cambria band. Horse drawn floats and decorated carriages transporting the town's people paraded through the main streets to the picnic ground, followed by all the community, ranchers from miles around, and people from Cayucos and from other towns more distant who usually spent the night. George Steiner, a native Cambrian, recalling the early days said:

They sure had some roaring times in this community,

especially at the May Day festival, Fourth of July, and
Swiss Independence Day picnics. Flags were draped
everywhere and streets and stores were decorated with
many yards of red, white and blue bunting.
The numerous Swiss and Spanish from neighboring ranches
added further color to the celebrations. The men demonstrated
their horsemanship while the women were redundant in color-
ful costumes. It is not without nostalgia that old timers recall
these pleasant and exciting celebrations. They speak of the
deep-pit barbecues where whole beeves and hogs were roasted,
and the meals were free to all comers, the food being donated
by ranchers and townsmen.

Other recreational activities increased after 1890, and Joaquin
Cantua gained county-wide fame as "Master" of the barbecue.
It is still said that "no barbecue is better than the pit barbecues
over which he presided." During and following the meal, which
lasted for hours, there were speeches and many games continu-
ing until the last straggler left to do the evening chores. The
nights were filled wth dancing to the accompaniment of music
supplied by a traveling Spanish band from Jolon which came by
horseback over the mountains, guitars hanging from the saddle
horns. Joaquin Modesto "Jack'" Soto, founder of Soto's Market,
recalled his own participation as a small boy, proudly riding
with his own guitar tied in a flour sack fastened to the saddle.
His uncle was a member of the itinerant group and on special
occasions permitted young Joaquin to join them as they passed
his home in the mountains near Adelaida beyond the head-
waters of Santa Rosa Creek. The men all played by ear and the
music seldom stopped before time for the morning milking.

Jack Soto is a descendent of the early Spanish soldiering
Sotos of Monterey. His father, Yrculano Soto, was born in Mon-
terey in 1832, and his mother, Lola Dolores Grajalva, was from
San Francisco. After living in the vicinity of San Antonio Mis-
sion near Jolon for several years they moved to the mountains
between Adelaida and the Kláu Mine where Yrculano took up a
homestead and built an adobe house for his wife and growing
family. Here they raised cattle and goats which they butchered
and sold as fresh meat. Their livestock ranged over thousands

of acres of government land. Joaquin, youngest of the Soto boys, was born on the homestead in 1886.

While living near Jolon his parents had only Indian and Spanish speaking neighbors but on moving to the Adelaida area they were surrounded by English speaking families. Jack relates that his father never learned to speak good English because of his mature years when settling on the homestead.

Speaking of the Spanish band from Jolon, Jack said it was known as the San Antonio Band. Another oldtimer referring to the band said, "It was considered the last word in musical excellence." It was first introduced to the Cambria area by his father, who rode over with them from time to time. His father was a great joker. Once he hid all the musician's instruments in the various bars of the town. They were compelled to perform in each bar in order to redeem the instruments. At another time, because he disapproved of the dirty clothes the musicians were wearing, he caused their clothes to be badly burned as they dried on a log near a camp fire while they slept. Awaking in the morning they had only burned rags for clothes. On arrival in Cambria Yrculano told the sad tale of burned clothes to the local merchants with such pathos they were induced to supply the nearly naked men with new blue jeans.

Regular members of the band were Manuel Rosas, flute; Pedro Moreno, second violin; Celestino Garcia, guitar; and Jose Maria Caravajales, first violin. Occasionally they also had a cornetist. The men were always lodged free of charge at the local hotels. Jack always played guitar with the group whenever they came to the area. In later years he played with local musicians, the VanGorden boys, Frank Mayfield, George Allen and Francisco "Poncho" Estrada, continuing to do so for over 30 years.

After various jobs as a young man he went to work as a butcher for Ed Asevez, his brother-in-law, and Ed Hitchcock, who were partners operating as the Rocky Butte Cattle Company. They owned a butchershop in Cambria and Jack went to work there in 1915. He was able to buy the shop from them in 1917, eventually expanding to form Soto's Market. His brothers, Cipriano, Augustine and Bernardino, also established themselves in the area, primarily as ranchers and cattle men.

Young Elmer S. Rigdon, son of Rufus Rigdon, "loquacious but beloved by all," was usually selected as the main speaker of the day. Some say that the Fourth of July celebrations gave Elmer his education in oratory which eventually helped him win a seat in the Senate. Of Rufus Rigdon's five children, Elmer became the most famous, serving first as state assemblyman. Elmer has always been credited for the instigation and promotion of the coast highway from San Simeon to Monterey. Though it was not completed until 1937, Elmer won approval and appropriation of funds for the work in 1917 on the basis of its value as a military road for use in defense of California against invading forces, the appropriation being included in the so-called "Military Highway Bill."

Special hay rides on moonlight nights, ending in big picnics on the beach or at a favorite canyon glen, provided frequent social entertainment for the younger set; and occasional weekend campouts for unmarried eligibles were sponsored by understanding parents who loaded wagons with provisions and hauled the young people to the Morro Bay sand dunes for extended clam bakes, the girls sleeping in the safety of a tent while the young men camped under the stars.

With the institution of a private high school by Professor Merritt R. Trace late in 1890, young students from farm families boarded in town in order to attend. They, too, joined in these social activities. Many community entertainments were provided as the outgrowth of excellent school instruction, which developed highly talented young people. They graciously produced and performed musical entertainment, skits, and plays whenever called upon. Among these performers (of the 1890's) were Clara Cole and Blanche Franklin, daughter of Benjamin H. Franklin, who, with well trained voices, sang whenever the opportunity afforded. One year they organized a group of young people and some of the older members of the town to produce the cantata "Queen Esther" in the form of an opera. Elmer S. Rigdon and Benjamin H. Franklin (both good vocalists) were the leading men. The Reverend Doctor Henry C. Thomson, pastor of the Presbyterian Church (1893-1898) was the King and his little daughter, Ruth (Mrs. Homer Stiles), the cup bearer.

Many of the town's youngsters were used in the chorus. The affair, given in Ott's Hall, was attended by "throngs," according to some who participated.

The Trace family, consisting not only of the indomitable professor but his wife and three nearly grown, energetic children, was an acknowledged influence upon the town. Son Verne was an excellent carpenter and Mrs. Trace taught art. Gertrude and Lois, still of school age, participated in every activity that came along. All five members of the family sang in the church choir, and Gertrude played the organ as well. During their residence in Cambria young Verne built several of the better homes in the community, including the Presbyterian manse and two homes for the Evans family, one on their ranch property near Piedras Blancas Point (now part of Hearst property) and a two-story one on Lee Street, which was later purchased by the Rigdon family and is now owned by The Brambles Restaurant. He also erected several curved roof barns and numerous water tanks on outlying ranches.

Between 1890 and 1900 the old picnic ground was abandoned for a new area on the Phelan Ranch two miles north of town. Dubbed "Phelan Grove," the change made room for a baseball diamond and, later, a horse arena. Baseball became a popular sport and, like horse racing in the 1870's Cambrians went "all out" for the sport, organizing their own competition team, the *Cambria Kelp Eaters,* which gained considerable recognition in the county papers of the time.

The Hearst family often took an active interest in the Phelan Grove celebrations after 1900 by encouraging wild west show activities and parade entries, by donating beef, and by providing beautiful trophies for sweepstake winners. It was estimated that about 2,000 people usually attended these big free picnics.

The extension of the railroad into San Luis Obispo in 1894 caused a rapid decline in coastal shipping and Cambria, still isolated by mountains and bad roads at the turn of the century, ceased to be the second largest community as industry and transportation in other parts of the county improved. Accordingly, the life of each Cambrian became still more closely associated with that of his neighbor.

In a town less responsive to the welfare of the individual, little note would have been taken of the small incidents which residents later recalled as historic. For example: the first bathtub in the area was purchased by the Rigdon family in 1905; it was quickly followed by one in the Campbell household, thus marking them as the outstanding families of the community, the bathtub being a status symbol.

Then, one early morning a loud, though muffled explosion was heard throughout the town and particularly noted, as it was the result of cunning trickery to disclose a thief. This little event began when a family man noticed his corded stove wood was disappearing unusually fast. He loaded several sticks with black powder, sat back and waited. The explosion was his payoff. Then, there was the man who disliked the croaking of frogs. Hoping to diminish their numbers, he offered ten cents for each one the neighbor children would catch and bring him.

To some, the scent of fresh crushed mint growing in the deep ditches bordering Bridge Street marked a period in the town's history, as did the day when George Steiner, a volunteer fireman, running to a fire with a Foamite fire extinguisher, tripped and triggered the mechanism a full block from his destination.

Others recall more serious things as historic milestones: the cold-blooded murder of Tony Merrion by George Allen and witnessed by Henry Spain, following a hot argument over a misplaced fence line and a slapped face, the slapped face being all that saved Allen from prison; or the shooting to death of the town physician, Dr. Frieman, by jealous Rocha Daniels, the result of a love triangle.

The products of the saloons left their mark, too, in such tales as the following: A belligerent drunk who, after throwing a spitoon through the saloon window, ran for his team and wagon hoping to escape the constable hard on his heels. Unfortunately, he knocked himself cold as he collided with the back of his own wagon in the dark. Or the noisy but happily inebriated Mexican youths down from the mines who were jailed. Because of their earlier noisy state they were ignored when they continued to create quite a commotion in the jail situated on the bank of Santa Rosa Creek near the corner of Bridge and Center Streets, until smoke was seen coming from the little building in which they had been placed to sober up. It was then that the people learned their continued yells and cries had not been in fun, but for help. Another small turning point in the town's history was the enactment of a law in 1916 which prohibited cattle from wandering about the residential district.

It is of these inconsequential incidents that most of Cambria's later history is comprised, yet from such trivial things has developed the very character of the town which, today, is considered so unique.

Between the time the railroad came to the county and the automobile was placed on the market within reach of the average family, Cambrians were virtually isolated. Formerly they traveled frequently to distant points by boarding a ship at San Simeon. Now their movement was primarily restricted to infrequent visits to San Luis Obispo, for most of the year the road was difficult and barely usable. It was not uncommon for the trip to take 10 or 12 hours in bad weather. With the advent of the car it might be said that Cambria became its best customer.

When the horse drawn stage was discontinued in 1910, Orle Mayfield, a second generation Cambrian, took over the franchise and purchased two Packards. To his dismay, he soon discovered the majority of his passengers were Mexican laborers from the mines who piled, 20 at a time, into the cars which he also used for hauling freight.

Undoubtedly Cambria absorbed the car more rapidly than the urban areas, for it is interesting to note the abrupt changes that took place in spite of road conditions which could not have contributed to driving comfort. Trucking replaced the horse-drawn dray wagons; stores all became car dealers and installed gas pumps and repair parts; blacksmiths and livery stables advertised themselves as garages, and the ladies immediately changed their fashions to conform. Gone was the peace and quiet of the little village.

Car owners challenged each other to clip time from their trips to distant places. Off they were again to Los Angeles and San Francisco as well as other points of interest in spite of the uncertain mechanical idiosyncrasies of their new mounts.

When William M. Lyons arrived in Cambria in 1908, just prior to the car boom, he leased the Anderson Store, known for years after the fire as the Gans Building, located on the former site of the old Pollard, then Chamblin, store of 1866. Married to Josephine Marquart of the Adelaida area, and a former school teacher and principal of the Cayucos grammar school, Lyons soon became the leading merchant and sage of the town, a distinction he held for nearly 53 years. Just prior to World War I he moved to a new and larger brick store across the street which was called the Red and White. George Dickie, who had been operating a local hauling business, took over his old location. He found it more profitable to cater to the automobile trade and was one of the first to install gasoline pumps in conjunction with his merchandise store.

The aging and prosperous Mr. Paterson, Sr., retired in 1914 and moved to Los Angeles, leaving his business in the hands of his son. Young Alex, tall, handsome and well liked, was as efficient as his father and a hard worker, never knowing a day of ill health though said to be a heavy drinker, a failing which he tried several times to overcome but with little success.

About this time a private telephone service was started as the Cambria Telephone Company and operated by Anderson's Grocery on the northeast corner of Main and Bridge Streets. When George Dickie took over the store he continued the service until Will Warren purchased the company and established its headquarters in his home on Center Street. While he had it service was extended as far as the Klau mine and to Cayucos where the line could be connected with the regular Bell System for long distance calls. Both the Reghetti and Gezzi stores of Cayucos were hooked to the line.

Three operators at "central" were employed by Warren. Service, including a phone, the upkeep of lines and supplying of batteries, cost subscribers $1 per month. Those who had their own phone and did their own maintenance were charged 50 cents a month for hook-up service. The most unusual service breakdown occurred one fall when a long section of the line up Santa Rosa Creek went dead. It was found completely and heavily covered with caterpillars, which had caused a short circuit.

After four years of operation the company was sold to Alex Paterson, then Guerra, Fort, and finally the Bell System.

With the outbreak of World War I in Europe, mercury prices soared, old mines went into full scale production, and the prosperity of the town was again stimulated. As a result, in 1916 the citizens felt it was time for the town to have electricity. They agitated for electric power of their own until plans were formulated for the installation of a local generating plant at a cost of $1600. Due, however, to the gravity of the war as the United States became involved, these plans were postponed, never to be completed. As a result, Cambria remained without electricity until a public utility line was finally brought into the community in 1921, and into the adjacent valleys in 1923.

However, the lack of electricity did not slow prosperity. In 1917 a processing plant for fresh abalone was started by Jim Beckett, Ed Ellis and D. A. Monroe. While the market price was high they processed 150 pounds of abalone a day, continuing through the war, after which prices declined and, to economize, the plant was moved to a more central location in Morro Bay.

The citizens of Cambria, noted for their effusive patriotism, became active in all endeavors directed toward winning the war. The women of Cambria were among the first in the county to organize a Red Cross Chapter, and the young men became fearful lest they be rejected when they volunteered for military service. Many letters were written home for publication in the *Cambria Courier*, a new weekly paper started by C. A. Meacham on June 16, 1916.

More saloons and rowdy miners prompted action for a new jail, the third to be constructed since the town's first mining boom. In 1917 Bernardo Macagni and Louis Balaetti, local carpenters, were hired. Built of bridge timbers and heavy planks held together with bolts, and the heavy door fastened by a double bar, hand forged latch, it was constructed to withstand abuse from within and the ravages of time. This jail, unlike its predecessors located low on the bank of Santa Rosa Creek near its confluence with Bridge Street Creek, was placed above the creek where the post office parking lot is now located.

Rocco Rava, together with two of his companions, was the first to be locked in the new jail. As he told the story: Rava and three of his companions, Louis Batega, John Granuncelli and Enrico Balassi, were on a tour of inspection immediately after the jail was completed. The three first-named were inside when Enrico slammed the door shut, slipped the latch and quickly scampered to the nearest saloon. The three trapped men took the joke in stride but as time passed they became indignant, then alarmed. All attempts to escape were fruitless. After four hours had passed and night fallen, a chance passerby rescued them when he heard their yells. Rava said that was his first and last experience with a jail. The narrow, thinly padded bunk and the barren confines of the small cell left an unerasable impression.

Many months later a very intoxicated Mexican youth was locked in the jail to sober up. During the night frantic screams for help were heard by Pete Maggetti, a saloon owner who lived nearby. On going to the jail he found the Mexican had set his mattress afire while smoking in a half drunken stupor, and was nearing suffocation from smoke in the tightly constructed building. When released, it was also observed that he had severe burns on one arm where his coat had caught fire. That was the last time the wooden jail, now preserved by the Cambria Lions Club near the Pinedorado grounds, was ever used. As a result of the accident a regulation was passed which required someone in attendance whenever the jail was occupied. Later a cement jail was built on Rigdon Flat below town but was seldom used.

Cambria's first jail is said to have been constructed during the first mining boom. By 1884 it was no longer serviceable, at which time individual citizens donated various sums toward a new building. Following the Fourth of July celebration that year the profits of $100.50 were added to the donations and a small "coop" of beams and 1 x 6-inch planks was placed over the bank edge of Santa Rosa Creek. Cambrians boasted of having the "smallest and least used jail in America."

In 1917 Joaquin Soto, now grown and married, purchased the local meat market on Bridge Street where he had been employed as butcher for several years. Slowly he introduced a good line of groceries and eventually cornered the grocery trade to establish Soto's Market, still one of the leading grocery stores.

However, everything was not roses. The local lumber industry, at the peak of the war time boom, received a drastic set back. The saw mill was forced to cut its operations when it was discovered that second growth trees were of much poorer quality than the virgin timber cut up to this time. The industry, though hit hard, was never entirely abandoned. A small but regular demand continued for cheap building material.

In Cambria, as elsewhere, the flu epidemic hit and many people died. Young Alex was kept busy day and night building coffins and tending to burials, not once thinking about his own robust health. One trying day he awoke with the symptoms of a slight cold. With three burials scheduled for that day, he paid little attention to them other than to "hit the bottle" a few times. The following day he, too, died a victim of influenza. His wife, the former Amy Martin of the San Simeon Creek Martin family, and two daughters carried on the portions of business they could manage until Amy's application for postmaster was accepted and she became Cambria's first woman postmaster.

Mercury prices fell again after the war, the mines shut down, and Cambria proudly settled into the life of a snug, quiet farm village, apparently unconcerned with the loss of her standing as a leading community in former years. The basic economy of the town was secure, for it was built upon the prosperity of the surrounding dairies and farms. When a slump occurred, those who were the hurt the most were the business enterprises which had come with the boom.

An oiled and improved road into the town in 1924 eventually attracted land developers who formed the Cambria Development Company in 1927. They built a mountain lodge in the pine woods overlooking the village and subdivided a large tract of land surrounding it into small lots, which they believed would have immediate appeal to Americans dreaming of a vacation home in the mountains and trees bordering the sea. The subdivision was advertised by radio and print from coast to coast. At this time the nation was riding on a financial spending spree and the lots sold, sight unseen, to people in every state.

The lodge became a fashionable resort for those with money and time, though few of the visitors stayed to build a cabin or establish a residence so far from contact with the urban world. Marcus Waltz arrived in 1931 and was impressed with the possibilities of the town. He established the *Cambrian,* a weekly newspaper, and the third in the history of the town, for the *Courier* of 1916 had folded its doors after little more than a year of publication.

Then came the depression. Outsiders forgot their property holdings, though the mountain lodge continued to attract stray guests seeking a retreat from the trying problems of reality; and Waltz continued publication of the paper with the full support of the community behind him.

Finally, in 1950, the expanding population of California, looking for isolated recreational areas, rediscovered Cambria. Many summer homes were built among the pines and, for several months of each year, the village flourished; but it was not until 1958 when the State opened the late William Randolph Hearst home at San Simeon to the public that the tourist boom began.

Even during the quiet years there had been times of local excitement. Beginning in 1948, an annual Labor Day weekend celebration called Pinedorado was instituted in place of the former one-day Fourth of July picnics. Each year this gala four-day celebration attracted large crowds, with the citizens all dedicating their efforts toward a roaring success.

Whether the Pinedorado of 1954 triggered the unusual excitement that occurred September 2 on the eve of the celebration, or whether the event was entirely irrelevant will probably never be known, but the first bank robbery in more than 100 years of San Luis Obispo County history was perpetrated in Cambria that day. Brandishing revolvers, two unknowns garnered $5,600 in bank funds after binding and gagging the three employees, and escaped in a new car belonging to one of them. Constable Roy Evans gave chase, roads were blocked, police alerted and the FBI moved in, but to no avail. To this day, the perpetrators of the "Great Bank Robbery" have gone unpunished. By the next day, Cambrians recovering, the Pinedorado went on as scheduled.

In 1962 major changes in the highway between Morro Bay and Cambria were undertaken. Winding curves were removed and the roadbed widened. Driving time to San Luis Obispo was cut to 40 minutes and several people employed in the larger town moved to the suburban community, preferring to commute.

With tourist trade channeled through town on its way to San Simeon and the "Castle," and an increase in permanent residents, Cambria looked forward to a substantial rise in business. But prosperity was not so easily won. The following year the state began construction on Highway 1, an expressway by-pass which, when finished in 1964, completely diverted the tourist traffic, shuttling it directly to the Hearst Castle State Monument.

Still more financial bad luck followed. On the heels of an increase in tourism, the county imposed a steep rise in property taxes which forced numerous farmers and dairymen of the Cambria area to sell their land to speculators, curtailing farm activity, the basic economy on which the community had depended for three generations. With these combined changes, the town immediately became the victim of a drastic business slump. Cambrians, however, were determined to recover from these setbacks. As a by-passed community, they accepted the challenge and began master-planning their future, incorporating the quiet charm of the past with a new design for survival which marks the town as a "unique community expressing itself in a way of life not found in most areas of the United States." *

* Quote of Ned Rogoway
San Luis Obispo County Planning Commission

Remnant of quaint bridge crossing Arroyo del Pinal on old Coast Highway.

Bank of Cambria. George Dickie, Jim Stewart, bank manager, two unidentified trustees and Mrs. Stewart, who assisted her husband at the bank. About 1910. (Paul Squibb collection)

Bay View Hotel in 1910. Owned by William Gillespie for many years. Saloon downstairs was managed by John McCain, standing at far left. (Courtesy Mrs. Irma Jones)

Wm. M. Lyons General Merchandise Store about 1909. At site of former S. A. Pollard store. (Courtesy Paul Squibb)

L. V. Thorndyke and Co. Store (formerly the Frankl Store); Thorndyke Hotel, the former Ferrari-Righetti Hotel which was purchased by Frankl, and the Bay View Hotel owned by Gillespie as they appeared about 1904. (Courtesy Ralph Morgan, editor of *The Cambrian*)

Original Santa Rosa Catholic Church, little changed after 102 years. (Photo by author)

Santa Rosa School on bank of Santa Rosa Creek before relocation in Cambria. Bell tower and porch probably added in 1890.

First Presbyterian Church of Cambria, 1874. Tower contained bell until remodeling in 1906 added entryway and belfrey. (Picture from 75th church anniversary bulletin)

First Presbyterian Church of Cambria as it appeared in 1965. The original structure is contained within the main body of church. (Photo by author)

Santa Rosa School after rebuilding on bank of Santa Rosa Creek in 1881.

Abandoned San Simeon School at the bay of the same name.

Part II After the Dons

Chapter 4

Out of Log Schools, Statesmen

When California was admitted to the Union on September 9, 1850, San Luis Obispo County was among the 25 counties already formed. At this time the population of the county was composed primarily of Spanish speaking people and Indians, with a sprinkling of British and Europeans who had, in many instances, married into Spanish families. In 1854 it was estimated that not more than 40 children in the county could speak English, though most of the county business was transacted in English with an intermixture of Spanish words and phrases where the English equivalent failed. Education was supplied by private tutor or the Mission church school in San Luis Obispo.

About this time several new county employees, who knew very little Spanish, took office; and the recording of statistics and minutes of meetings became especially difficult because these men were at a loss to interpret or transcribe the Spanish they heard. As a result, records were often garbled or details simply omitted. In spite of this confusion many facts may be gleaned from early courthouse records and supplemented by contemporary records in private journals.

In September of 1855 Captain John Wilson, prominent in the county as a member of the Dana family, was elected Superintendent of Public Schools. However, no funds were designated for educational purposes and no public schools existed, the only school in the county being the church owned Catholic Mission School attended, primarily, by children of the Spanish Dons living near the town of San Luis Obispo. This same condition

41

prevailed when, in September of 1858, P. A. Forrester, county clerk, was elected to the office, replacing Wilson.

As more English speaking families moved into the county, especially on public domain in the San Simeon-Santa Rosa Creek area, the need for inexpensive local schooling conducted in English became urgent. Due to a general demand by these new citizens, on February 28, 1859, the County Board of Supervisors voted a county-wide five cent school tax for every hundred dollars of assessed valuation of property. Undoubtedly this demand was headed by Jeffrey Phelan, homesteader and pioneer in the San Simeon Creek area, for it was he who provided land for the erection of a small log school house on the banks of Whittaker Creek, which passed through his property. The location was convenient for families living on land adjacent to his holdings, and it also bordered the Coast Road from San Luis Obispo to the Bay of San Simeon.

The first little one-room county school was built of hand hewn pine logs and was simply designated as the Log School. Eight to thirteen children were in regular attendance. The first teacher was Miss Sarah Minerva Clark, daughter of Dr. Eleutheros A. Clark, a recent resident of San Simeon Creek. Her salary was $30 a month. Miss Clark, however, soon married C. W. Pinkham, another resident of the area, and her father took over the teaching.

Dr. Clark came to the county in 1858 and took up preemption land two and a half miles up San Simeon Creek, adjoining land occupied by Carolan Mathers, a relative of Mrs. Clark, and land of Harrison Dart, also related. He was well educated and his abilities soon became known, for he was elected supervisor from the north part of the county that same year.

After teaching for awhile, Dr. Clark asked permission to move the classes to his home as a convenience to himself and, probably, to several of the nearby families. Receiving permission, he continued to conduct the school within his home, with the result that the school was dubbed the Home School.

Records pertaining to these early country schools were not preserved. Therefore, most of the incidents relative to this school, as well as others in the area prior to 1874, are pieced together from bits of related history, records kept by private families and legend.

In the beginning, the county was designated as a single school district. On November 7, 1859, the Board of Supervisors divided the county into two townships, the northern portion being designated as the Township of San Simeon, roughly bounded on the south by Morro Creek, on the east by the high range of mountains, and on the north by the Monterey County line. The entire township was also designated as the San Simeon School District. However, the district, as such, was disregarded until 1861 when the Superintendent of Schools asked for an inventory of the Home School and its equipment for county records. It was the only public school in the county at this time. Its total value, including furnishings, was $160.

In 1863, still the only public school, it was again inventoried and its value set at $650, a figure which substantiates local claim that a new board and batten school had been constructed near the Clark home on the south bank of San Simeon Creek near the mouth of Whittaker Creek. At this inventory its name was officially recorded as the "Home School." Clark was still teaching but relinquished the job as he had become active in local and county affairs which required all the time he could spare from his ranching activities. He was serving on various road viewing boards in the north part of the county, presiding at elections, and was Justice of the Peace for the area. He had also developed an active interest in several new mining claims located in the hills near his homestead.

In July 1866 the district's south boundary was moved northward from Morro Creek to Villa Creek. In August of the same year "Citizens of Santa Rosa" successfully petitioned for a division of the large northern area into the San Simeon and Santa Rosa School Districts, with the dividing line being the ridge between the waters of San Simeon and Santa Rosa Creeks.

This division was instigated by James Cutler McFerson (also spelled McPherson) and by settlers along the borders of Santa Rosa Rancho who had already constructed a small log school building on the north bank of the creek. Immediately after the formation of the new district, the Santa Rosa Creek school house was designated by the supervisors as the official voting place for residents of the San Simeon supervisorial district instead of the Estrada adobe.

McFerson had recently arrived from Tulare County where he served as supervisor. He was interested not only in general schooling for the increased number of children, but was also active in religious schooling for both children and adults. After the erection of the school, he conducted regular Sunday School services there for some time prior to the organization of the First Presbyterian Church of Cambria in 1874, of which he was a charter member. Like many local residents McFerson was originally attracted to California by gold, though he did not participate in mining but in supplying wood to the quartz mills of General Fremont's estates in Mariposa.

Little is known concerning Santa Rosa School's early history though it is known the log school was abandoned within a few years and a more commodious frame building constructed. This was replaced in 1881 by a well constructed one-room school house used until all local school districts were consolidated during World War II, and the children from outlying areas transported by bus to a newly-built elementary school more centrally located in Cambria. The old school and the property on which it stood were purchased by D. V. Molinari, a rancher living in Harmony Valley. It remained unused until late in 1964 when the school house was donated by Mr. Molinari to the Lions Club of Cambria for use as a local museum. Early in 1965 it was moved from the banks of Santa Rosa Creek to Cambria where it was renovated and restored.

Typical history of most of the early schools of the area is the detailed account of the Olmstead School which was located in Green Valley. The facts were related by Miss Frances Olmsted, granddaughter of Rufus B. Olmsted, who proposed its erection and aided in its construction.

Mr. Olmsted settled on public domain bordering the eastern boundary of Rancho Santa Rosa at the head of what later became known as Green Valley (named for Samuel Green, who was an early settler there), late in 1860. He was the only English-American settler in a radius of several miles, close neighbors all being Indians and Spanish speaking people. His family of several children was nearly grown when he arrived. Previously he lived on the Foster Ranch in the wilderness area of San Marcos Creek on property belonging to his father-in-law, Judge A. T. Foster of San Jose. While living there he and his wife tutored their children at regular sessions, providing them with what was considered a good education for the time.

According to Herbert Olmsted, oldest of the Olmsted children, his father was continually aware of his responsibility for their education and consistently reminded them of the proper use of English by correcting them each time they spoke improperly, regardless of the situation.

The first English-speaking family to become neighbors was that of Alexander Cook, who located four miles to the south in what later became known as Harmony Valley. Mountainous terrain between the two valleys made visiting difficult and often entailed a major effort, but the advent of the Cook family with several chlidren was a real treat for Mrs. Olmsted

Soon afterward other families with children arrived, including the B. F. Music family. Mr. Olmsted became quite concerned about the education of these young children as the families were, in his estimation, neglecting instruction at home. He took the matter up with the County School Superintendent, offering to build a school himself. Permission was granted. With the help of his son, Herbert, who was just 21, and William Ogden, another neighbor, he began construction, assisted from time to time by other nearby families.

This first school was erected in a grove of sycamore trees on the bank of Harvey Creek. It was built of imported, dressed lumber hauled in by team from the beach at Leffingwell Landing north of Cambria where it had been delivered by schooner. The school was built on a stilt foundation four feet above ground. It had a small porch which faced the wagon road leading down from a small side canyon. Light was provided by six stylish, small-paned, sash windows. The rear of the building was of upright planks with battens covering the cracks, whereas the rest of the building was more neatly finished with horizontal boarding. The interior had a tongue and groove ceiling and was furnished with a sheet iron stove and, in the beginning, with sloping desks made by Herbert. Hats and coats were hung on nails at the front of the room. A blackboard with a big clock above it covered the back wall behind the teacher's desk. The entire building was unpainted, as paint was both expensive and difficult to obtain. Each morning a large pail was filled with water from a spring at the creek and brought to the building to serve as drinking water for the day.

Eventually the creek bank caved away, necessitating the building of a new school some distance from the creek but patterned after the old one. In the early days the pupils walked to school as there was no provision for hitching or sheltering a horse and, as the years passed by, walking to school became a tradition which new arrivals continued to follow.

Rufus Olmsted died from an accident in March of 1867, shortly after the school was successfully under way. The Olmstead School District, however, was not formed until May 4, 1868, when G. F. Shipp, D. G. Saunders, and 13 other family men petitioned the Board of Supervisors for a separate district. The school and district were named for Rufus Olmsted by the County School Superintendent as a memorial but his name was misspelled, a common practice in the early days, and it was recorded for posterity as the Olmstead School.

Names of the first teachers were not recorded until 1874 and 1875, at which time Miss Arlie Hennison and Miss Callie Buster were listed. Most of the ensuing teachers were graduates of San Jose Normal School, now renamed California State University-San Jose. Outstanding during the 1880's and 1890's were Mabel Richards, Ruth and Helen Stewart, Gertrude Trace and Katherine McKensie, most of whom received early schooling in Cambria before obtaining their teacher's certificates.

Miss Olmsted, who attended the school in the 1890's, recalls
the children were nice, timid, innocent country young-
sters, thoroughly behaved; with strict, civilized parents
of some culture who expected their children to obey
and who took strong measures at home if they didn't.
Swiss children who first came to the area in the mid-1870's took schooling very seriously. Any Swiss child who misbehaved at

school "was subjected to a bad time at home."

Herbert Olmsted, father of Miss Frances Olmsted, was clerk of the board of trustees for several years and aided in the accumulation of a good library which was contained in a large hardwood cabinet. Typical books were the complete works of Louisa May Alcott, Charles Lamb's books, Scott's Ivanhoe, and Scottish Chiefs.

In the beginning few children attended school regularly; sickness, farm work and bad weather were all deterring factors. In spite of the number of families with children who lived nearby, attendance was seldom more than 12 at a time until the Nick Storni family arrived in the late 1890's with six youngsters. Moses Phillips also arrived with four or five youngsters, which caused the daily average attendance to jump to 20.

Soon after the school was erected large portions of Santa Rosa Rancho were sold, providing good ranch lands for new families. Primarily, it was children of these families, mostly Swiss in the later years, who attended the school. Don Julian Estrada had several children of school age at the time the Olmstead School was built. These children associated with the other children of the valley but did not attend the school as the Don preferred a private tutor for them.

The Hesperian School District was also formed on May 4, 1868, from parts of the Santa Rosa and San Simeon School Districts which lay adjacent to the town, at this time called San Simeon but soon renamed Cambria. Like most of the other district schools, its earliest history is vague. Rufus Rigdon, G. W. Lull and 11 other men with families signed the original application. The first Hesperian School was constructed on property loaned by James D. Campbell and his son, J. D. Campbell, Jr. The school was one large room of dressed lumber with a front porch supported by four handsomely carved redwood pillars. The first record of a teacher is in 1874 when on September 26 a Mr. Williams became principal. His wife, trained in music, conducted private singing lessons to supplement her husband's meager income.

Succeeding Mr. Williams was F. E. Darke, who took over in 1877. He remained for 12 years, at the end of which time he was highly commended by the Supervisor of Public Schools for the excellent attendance record he was able to maintain. Enrollment during his tenure reached as high as 150 students though daily attendance was quite erratic and averaged between 40 and 50 students, much lower than the 150 enrollment figure.

Mr. Darke came to the Cambria area fresh from the Civil War, which he entered as a drummer boy. His first years were spent in teaching in schools on San Simeon Creek. After moving to town he built a large two-story house on Lee Street and used a portion of the downstairs for additional classroom space until an addition was made to the schoolhouse located on the bluff overlooking Cambria at the north end of Lee Street.

When the addition was made the redwood pillars were removed and the porch converted into an entrance hall between the two rooms. Miss Bertha Music of Cambria was assistant teacher during a portion of the years that Mr. Darke was principal. On occasion he was assisted by his wife who, when not busy helping her husband either at home or at school, also conducted music lessons. According to several of the older citizens of Cambria, it is said that Mrs. Darke was better qualified as a teacher than her husband, whom she helped primarily by coaching from behind the scenes.

In the meantime, other areas within the original San Simeon School District were demanding separate schools and further divisions. On August 10, 1868, James H. Gouch and 10 others presented a petition for the Mammouth Rock School District comprising the upper reaches of Santa Rosa Creek, which then caused a subdivision of the Santa Rosa District. This same district was divided once again on December 18, 1870, to form the Franklin School District. At the same time the San Simeon School District was divided to form the New Era School District, serving the upper reaches of San Simeon Creek.

One acre of land on the H. W. Martin ranch, now known as the Stepladder Ranch, was donated by Mr. Martin for erection of the New Era School. He had eight children and was anxious to have them educated. The building of the school, as others in the area, was financed and constructed by the surrounding families. The upper reaches of San Simeon Creek were well populated by homesteaders, including the Albert Warren, Manuel Porte, Joseph Porte, Frank Williams, Jacob B. Compher, B. F. Dotty, James Pierce, Joseph Stilts and Manuel families, who contributed a total of 40 children. Two of the earliest teachers were a Mr. Burell and a Mr. Burrows, who were boarded free of charge by the Martin family. Martin also gave the teachers work clearing his homestead at $50 an acre.

Mrs. George Peppard, a lone woman with several children, homesteaded between the headwaters of San Simeon and Santa Rosa Creeks on property which eventually became known as the Mora Ranch. Her daughter, Willeamenna, was a teacher of the early 1880's and, like so many of the early teachers, she soon married. Her husband was Tom Liggett, a young man the family had known from early childhood and, at the time of his marriage, a blacksmith at San Simeon and active in affairs of the bay. Later he worked as blacksmith for the Hearst ranch, retiring after 30 years of continuous employment.

On August 5, 1872, the Washington School District was formed and served the northern most portion of the original San Simeon School District, extending southward from the Monterey County line to Pinalito Creek. The schoolhouse was built approximately two miles north of Piedras Blancas light house.

On February 3, 1874, the Home School asked for its own district, further splitting the San Simeon District. The Home School District was designated as comprising all the area west of the New Era District between Piedra Blanca Rancho on the north and the Hesperian District on the south. The San Simeon School District was now restricted to the area about San Simeon Bay and the recently constructed school at the bay was officially known as San Simeon School.

Finally, the people of Harmony Valley on the southern part of Santa Rosa Rancho petitioned for their own school district on August 2, 1875. This marked the end of district splitting in the area.

None of the schools followed a strict school term. Each was conducted according to the farm seasons and needs. School convened primarily during late summer and lax winter months with an extended vacation at Christmas time. All children old enough to work were needed at home on the farms during the busy seasons, especially in the spring when grass was green and dairy cows were heavy with milk. Some years a child did well to receive four months of schooling. For a school to be open eight months in the year was considered maximum.

In 1890 Professor Merritt R. Trace arrived as principal of the Hesperian School in Cambria and after a short term he learned of the erratic school program. At first he was inclined to resign as he could not support his family on the income from such a limited number of teaching months. However, with some inquiry and backing of the Masons, he resolved to establish year-round high school classes. With permission of the Superintendent of Schools, he was granted the use of the school building during the vacation period, and by charging a small tuition, he was able to meet expenses. The high school opened with 21 students, mostly older children of farm and town families who were desirous of further education so they could attend university or normal school.

When regular grammar school classes commenced Benjamin H. Franklin donated the use of his building on the southeast corner of Lee and Main Streets for use as a high school. The building was surrounded by a high board fence with a yard barely large enough to provide room for a croquet court, the only recreation the students had while at school.

During the five years that Professor Trace taught in Cambria, he left a deep impression upon the town and the students under his tutelage. Likewise, the town and surrounding area left a lasting impression upon his children who, after finishing school, returned to San Luis Obispo County to make their homes. Gertrude, concluding San Jose Normal School, returned to teach in local schools; Lois returned from San Jose to marry Alex Webster, a young attorney of Paso Robles; and Verne married a San Miguel school teacher whom he met when his father was principal there for a short time. From San Miguel, Professor Trace transferred to San Jose where he was eventually honored by having a school named for him.

Albert Lincoln Jones, a member of Stanford University's first graduating class and a math major, replaced Professor Trace at the Hesperian School, taking over the high school instruction. He was assisted by Albert Taylor in the grammar school. Jones, however, stayed only until Christmas vacation when he left for a position as mathematics teacher in the Oakdale High School. After these rapid changes the high school continued intermittently until 1899 when it was temporarily discontinued to be reformed shortly after 1900.

In 1903 the Home School was moved. Some say it was moved as a complete unit, others contend that only a portion of the school was moved from its location on the south bank of San Simeon Creek to its present site, about one half mile down the creek and across to the north side. School continued here until 1944 when the Home School District was combined with the Cambria Elementary School District and the children transported by bus. The school building remained idle for 15 years. During this time it was sold to Will Warren who eventually deeded it to his son and daughter-in-law, Mr. and Mrs. Willis Warren of San Simeon Creek, who dedicated the building to Girl Scout use. After extensive repair and restoration, it was officially accepted by the Girl Scouts of Cambria March 12, 1961.

In 1906 a new building was designed and constructed on the site of the old Hesperian School in Cambria. A portion of the old building was moved a short distance west for auxiliary use as the new school was erected by C. D. Dean and Company of Los Angeles at a cost of $5000. It included three 33x26 foot class rooms, a reading room and library, two 8x26 foot hallways at right angles to each other, cloak rooms and storage space, all placed on a cement foundation.

Soon afterward a small lean-to with a brick foundation and wall part way up the sides was added at the rear to store yard equipment. These bricks, remaining at the site years after the school was moved, were of particular interest, being the product of a brick yard and kiln set up on San Simeon Creek by Elmer S. Rigdon, who planned an all brick building in Cambria using his own brick to avoid paying the excessive cost of brick and hauling from San Luis Obispo. The nearby mines used bricks extensively, which had been supplied for some time by Ah Louis of San Luis Obispo from his brick yard near Bishop's Peak.

Rigdon felt a local yard would benefit all but found setting up the kiln, testing and producing a slow process. Also, the bricks failed to meet required standards in time and Rigdon, a man of impatience as well as means, ended up buying brick from San Luis Obispo for his own building.

As a member of the school board, Rigdon was influential in persuading the board to use the inferior brick from his kiln for the small addition. These brick were unique and fascinating as they were made from the soil of the brick yard which was located on an old Indian encampment. The bricks were full of coarse chert chips and other debris, refuse of the Indians. After 60 years, and in spite of their sub-standard, coarse composition, the crude brick remained strong and intact though continuously exposed to the weather.

Adjacent to this school ground J. D. Campbell constructed his first large public water storage cistern. It was built in 1915 by Lawrence Shaug and C. Minoli from local rock and lined with cement. This cistern remained in excellent condition until 1972 when it was bulldozed away with surrounding hill soil to make way for a larger parking area on Main Street.

After completion of the new school building several high school subjects were taught to advanced students and in conjunction with the seventh and eighth grades. These advance students ranked scholastically with those of Santa Maria High School and San Luis Obispo Polytechnic School with whom they frequently competed, winning more often than they lost, at debating and sports of which basketball was the favorite.

The first school "year book" to be published in the county was that of the Hesperian School in 1907, called the "Red and Green." Familiar names of people still residing in the community were on the editorial staff of that first edition: Irma Music Jones, Katie Gamboni Jewett, Phoebe Maggetti Storni, and the late Hazel VanGorden Gamboni.

March 25, 1921, the Coast Joint Union High School was founded. This school provided a high school education for students of Cayucos Elementary School as well as the Cambria area. It received students from as far north as Pacific Valley School in Monterey County. Besides teaching fully accredited, standard high school courses, special agriculture classes were added with students participating in farm projects at their homes and on the school farm. At the present time, graduates from this high school find they are better prepared for college and university work than many students from bigger and supposedly better schools.

During the past few years new buildings have been supplanting the old to comply with modern building codes. Contractors demolishing the old buildings found they were unusually strong and experienced extreme difficulty in breaking them down. With the unforeseen change in building code requirements, necessitating demolition and rebuilding, Cambria citizens were unexpectedly forced into bonded indebtedness. During 100 years of providing outstanding education for its children, this area has had the only schools in the county which have consistently maintained a surplus in the treasury to care for normal growth and emergencies.

Not included in the above text is a notation found in a book by Joe Smeaton Chase, *California Coast Trails*. Mr. Chase mentions the existence of a school at Piedras Blancas sometime prior to 1913 which consisted of "a 10x12 foot tent with three small kitchen-type tables, two plank benches, a chair and desk, a nail keg and demijohn of water with a tin cup, a square yard of blackboard and a handful of books—fourth-hand." No mention has ever been made of a school at Piedras Blancas, either in local records or by residents over 90 years of age. If a school existed at Piedras Blancas at any time it was undoubtedly a private one temporarily in use at the lighthouse station. Other descriptions of the area by this author, however, do coincide with local fact.

Another school which county records have ignored is the Alta School which served residents of San Carpoforo Creek for a few years during the 1880's and 90's. Notable among its students were Emory and Lorin Thorndyke, sons of Captain L. V. Thorndyke, and Irma and Maud Rogers, their wives in later years.

The old Home School with board and batten siding and small-paned sash windows before it was moved in part to the north bank of San Simeon Creek. Mrs. Smith, teacher. About 1900.

Old Hesperian School. Picture taken beside new classroom addition. Bertha Music, teacher.

Deep mortar holes in base rock are common along the north coast area of San Luis Obispo County.

Basin and basket mortars, as well as bowl mortars in large cobbles, are often found in old Indian camp sites.

Indian blades of chert were found with tile and buttons.

Chapter 5

Indian Trails to Highways

Relocation and reconstruction of California State Highway 46 from Paso Robles west to the coast marks the beginning of a new era in the history of Cambria and San Luis Obispo County's north coast. It ends an era of semi-isolation not far removed from the first decades of Spanish occupation, when overland travel in California was by horse, mule or donkey because of the rough terrain and unimproved travel routes; when ox-drawn *carretas* were used for hauling heavy items a short distance on or between connecting ranchos where suitable roadbeds could be quickly constructed. Coastal trails followed the mountain ridges and canyon streams wherever possible.

The *carreta* was a handmade, clumsy, two-wheeled cart. Wheels were made from cross sections of large logs. The body was bound together with heavy thongs of rawhide. Oxen, in teams of two or four, wore heavy wooden yokes placed on the heads close behind the horns to which they were firmly tied. Harnessed in this manner, the oxen were unable to move their heads up or down or from side to side but plogged along slowly with heads tilted slightly upward. Some believe this method of harnessing the yoke puts an undue strain upon the beast. The pull was accomplished primarily by neck muscles, horns and the bones of the head rather than by shoulder muscles.

On occasion the *carretas* were used to carry the large Spanish families to special fiestas and celebrations if the distance was not too great or the route too difficult. Even then, accidents often happened, especially when attempts were made to cross the frequent, steep-sided gulches or ford streams, at which time the cart would be prone to turn over or break down and strand the whole party. For festive occasions the sides were enclosed with skins or material to ward off some of the dust. Further comfort was provided by covering the floor with dried grasses.

In 1850 Captain Dana managed to haul pine logs by such a cart from the banks of Santa Rosa Creek to his home in the southern part of San Luis Obispo County. This is believed to be the first attempt to use the coast horse trail as a roadway. One can imagine the extreme difficulty encountered by the oxen and heavily laden cart over the 40 miles of tortuous hill country containing numerous deep washes, gulches and boulder strewn streams. At this time most goods were transported overland by pack mule.

Indian, Spanish and American travelers on horseback or foot used several major routes in the county over which the right to pass was seldom disputed although the "track" lay across grant or homestead property. Four such routes radiated from Mission San Luis Obispo. On July 1, 1854, a little more than four years after the formation of the county, the Board of Supervisors received a petition from county citizens asking that these four routes be declared "public highways." The petition was granted and the routes described as

> 1 . . . being the most direct and practicable route usually traveled between San Luis Obispo and the county of Monterey, 2 . . . between San Luis Obispo township and the port of San Simeon, 3 . . . the port of San Luis Obispo, and 4 . . . the county of Santa Barbara.

This declaration of public right of way conveyed no property to the county. It simply provided free and undisputed passage over the land along the designated common routes which everyone knew. A general description of the four routes was recorded by William Borland, county surveyor, and they were officially advertised as public thoroughfares.

Realizing, in 1855, that there was a growing need for better county administration and road supervision, the supervisors laid a ground work during their August and November meetings whereby an expanded county road system could be developed. Separate voting districts were also formed. Three supervisory districts and four road districts were instituted in lieu of the single county district for both.

The north coast supervisorial division was designated as the *Coasta* District with precinct headquarters established at the Estrada adobe house, or Santa Rosa House as it was sometimes called. This district included all the land north of Morro Creek in line with its source and east from the source to the San Luis Obispo County line. Mariano Pacheco, Julian Estrada, and his brother-in-law, Valentine Gajiola, were named precinct inspectors and judges. The following year Gajiola was also elected Justice of the Peace for the area, which probably contained less than 150 people, excluding Indians.

The boundaries of the road districts were vaguely outlined by natural land divisions. The north coastal area was designated as District 1. It contained all of the north part of the county between the courthouse in San Luis Obispo and the port of San Simeon. It differed from the supervisory district by its eastern boundary, which was half way between the Coast Road and the Monterey Road, excluding Rancho Los Osos. The area to the north of San Simeon Bay was not included in any road district at this time though Don José de Jésus Pico, owner of Piedra Blanca Rancho which occupied this part of the county, was appointed first "overseer" of the Coasta Road District.

The office of County Surveyor was established with the formation of San Luis Obispo County in February, 1850, the surveyor to be elected to office for a term of two years. This position required very little practical knowledge of surveying. In the beginning services consisted of lineal measurements and a record of the position of the property in relation to adjoining neighbors. Even this rudimentary knowledge was used primarily within the bounds of San Luis Obispo. Francis Branch was the first surveyor, followed by Borland in 1852, and by David P. Mallagh in 1854. It was during Mallagh's term that the county road "survey" was first instituted.

The duties of the first district overseers were also vague. Their principal job was to ride over the road, more often referred to in county records as a "track," which drifted over the hills and through the gullies in "the most practicable" manner, and ascertain that it was free from such obstructions as locked gates or fences. It was their duty to report excessive wash due to run-off in the creeks which would necessitate a change in the crossing place. Once in a while it required supervision of workers, probably Indians, who would smooth down the bank after a heavy winter rain in order to provide access to a fording place.

On December 4, 1856, a Capitation Tax of $2 was levied against every able bodied man between the ages of 21 and 50 to provide salaries for the surveyor and district overseers.

Nothing was done in the north coast area to improve the route. People there depended almost entirely upon the schooners visiting San Simeon Bay and the beach landings for travel to outlying points, and for the transport of commodities and supplies. The Spanish Dons and others living in the north coastal area who had frequent business in San Luis Obispo, also maintained homes there. They commuted by means of fast horses, unhampered by baggage.

The fertile, well watered rolling hills and mountains of the north coast received early American settlers in large numbers before the rest of the county. A need for adequate roads into and about the area became a major issue with the new residents.

Early in 1859 a delegation of coastal residents proposed an improvement in road administration to the supervisors. At the supervisors' meeting of February 28, 1859, the Coast Road District Number 1 was divided into two districts. The division line, commencing at the mouth of Cayucos Creek, ran in a direct line eastward to the summit of the mountains where it intersected with the line of the new Santa Margarita District. The north division retained the name of Coasta District to conform with the supervisorial district name, while the southern part received the name of Morro District. Franklin Riley of San Simeon Creek was appointed overseer of the Coasta District, and a road tax of $2 (previously designated as a Capitation Tax) was again levied. A special county-wide road tax of five cents on assessed valuation of property was also levied at this time.

Beginning May 2, 1859, residents of the Coasta District

started petitioning the Supervisors for roads and road improvements, in what proved to be an almost never-ending bit of harassment, as they endeavored to obtain adequate road connections with the rest of the county. Outside of the town of San Luis Obispo, the north coast area had the largest population in the county and provided the largest share of county taxes. The petition submitted at this time asked that

> the track now traveled from San Luis Obispo to the
> Bay of San Simeon be declared a public highway.

The route connecting these two points had previously been declared public, but in the intervening time it had been relocated several times for various reasons. The petitioners now wished the existing route on record to insure right of way. The petitioners were also in hopes that the county officials would use some of the tax money to make improvements on it. They described the route as going northwesterly from San Luis Obispo to Morro Bay, then

> up the coast on the present traveled road, or as near as
> may be, to Santa Rosa Creek and across same, up the
> first ridge following the horse trail and wagon track to
> the landing of the Bay of San Simeon, allowing the
> overseer the discretion of varying the road a few rods
> on either side of the present track where the road can
> be improved by so doing,

No survey was required, the traveled route being the accepted road. The petition was granted and the road again declared to be a public highway. No work was done on the route, however.

At this time a large number of newcomers were settling in the high mountains adjacent to Santa Rosa Creek, with the result that considerable argument over land trespass in the area developed. Some of the citizens entered a petition requesting that the existing "track" from the Coast Road up the creek be made public. The petition was read and quickly granted. At the next session of the Board of Supervisors, February 9, 1860, another group of optimistic citizens presented a petition which elaborated upon the first one. It asked for a survey and establishment of a road from San Simeon Bay by way of Santa Rosa Creek to the "road leading to the settlement of Visalia" in the San Joaquin Valley. If a reason for this extensive survey was given to the Board, it was presented orally.

It can, however, be surmised that the people of the coastal area, with an eye to business, were planning on a traffic from the San Joaquin Valley wheat farms to San Simeon Bay. They reasoned that if a proper roadway to the coast were constructed the cost of marketing valley produce by ship from San Simeon would be greatly reduced.

Their argument in favor of the road must have been strong. The supervisors immediately approved the request and appointed M. E. Palmer, the newly-elected county surveyor, and Harrison Dart and F. F. Letcher of the north coast area as viewers to traverse the mountains and select a plausible route.

The men quickly set to work and selected what they thought to be a satisfactory route from the Bay to San Miguel Mission, beyond which point they considered the wagon road already in use to be quite good. Their report to the supervisors is of interest because of the simple means by which the route was laid out and recorded. It reads in part:

> Commencing on the tableland at the present landing (San Simeon Bay) we traveled until arriving at an isolated rock, then diverging from the road, on a direct course to the lower fork of Pico Creek, crossing the creek to the right, we raised the bank 150 yards from the ocean bank, then in a line with the coast to the mouth of Arroyo del Pinal. Then across the creek and to the present road following which, to the mouth of San Simeon Creek, then to the county road (declared in February 1859) through the pines to the crossing of Santa Rosa Creek, where, taking the road up the creek as laid out by Dart and Palmer, we (Palmer and Letcher) followed it to its terminus. Then through property of Hardy and Johnson, Van Valier and Buffum by blazes, then following the north branch by stakes, we ascended to the divide which we followed in the trail of persons engaged in hauling cedar from the summit of the coast range, then, following a small mountain stream to the summit of the mountains (a

distance of about 13 miles from the junction of the coast road). Thence, on the old Mission Cart road, deviating from it occasionally by blazes to the Rio de las Tablas . . .

Such was the way in which a new road was determined. No compass directions; no measurements in feet, rods, chains or other accepted survey methods; no information on the type of roadbed, grades or problems of construction. Also, bear in mind that no work had been done on the previous survey by Dart and Palmer. After the foregoing survey was presented to the Board the route was declared a public right of way. The county did nothing to clear it for use as a wagon road. The entire project went no further, probably due to lack of funds and an organized, able work crew. In part, such surveys establishing a public right of way satisfied the settlers as it gave them the undisputed right to use and improve existing trails if so inclined.

J. N. Lockwood was appointed road overseer, following Riley in 1860, then Harrison Dart in 1861. During the first half of 1862 all road work was suspended. Stephen A. Jacques took over the combined office of road overseer and Justice of the Peace in the coast township which was now designated as San Simeon Township. At this time the Coast Road District was further limited to that part of the county west of the summit of the coast range and south of Rafael Villa Creek (known today at Villa Creek). By 1863 the people along Santa Rosa Creek were playing such an active part in county affairs that the term "Santa Rosa" was often substituted for the official designation of San Simeon when referring to the district in county records.

On February 6, 1865, residents of the high mountain area near the eastern boundary line of the coastal area petitioned for public roads branching out to the east and northwest from their area. Following the discovery of cinnabar, and the development of several mines in 1863, numerous homesteads and mining claims were filed in this back country area, causing a heavy increase in traffic. These people asked that the "trail leading east from the Santa Rosa Road past the Josephine Mine *hacienda* and down San Francisco Canyon, past the adobe of J. Riley to the Paso Robles-Hot Springs Road" be declared public.

On the same day another petition requested a route from Mammouth Rock northwest to San Simeon Creek and down the creek to the coast, be made public.

The people living on the upper reaches of San Simeon Creek were already using these trails for travel to San Luis Obispo in lieu of the Coast Road, as they were shorter. Because of several rich mining claims in the area, feuds were developing over land trespass. There was an urgent need to clarify the right of way.

Though the petitioners presented a bond to cover the cost of viewing, the Board suddenly became cautious about declaring roads as public. In this case they appointed M. E. Palmer, John Patton, Jerry Johnson and Rufus Olmsted as viewers but set no time limit for the report. As a result, neither report nor action was forthcoming for several years.

In 1866 O. P. McFadden of Santa Rosa Creek was appointed overseer. The entire year was an unsettled one with many road changes taking place and, for the first time, a young survey engineer, R. R. Harris, was appointed to the office of County Surveyor instead of being elected from unknowledgeable candidates. P. A. Forrester, who preceded Harris, continued to assist him by serving on numerous viewing boards in the north part of the county, as did Carolan Mathers from the headwaters of San Simeon Creek. Neither of these men had the technical training of Harris and were assistants only when Harris was unable to head a viewing party.

Road petitions continued to pour in from the north. Viewing parties were sent out to check over the proposed roads. In most instances the roads were found to be necessary and were declared public. As before, nothing was done by the county to insure their improvement or upkeep. Width of right of way was now determined by fences placed along the roads by property owners. Where no fence existed the road had a tendency to wander from its designated track. This frequently happened during rainy weather or when ruts became excessively deep.

Between 1866 and 1868 petitions were received which requested road and supervisory district changes. Each change nullified previous decisions. None affected the road situation. County officials were unconcerned with the problems of the north coast residents and, widely scattered over rough terrain, they found little time and less money for a united effort among themselves to improve local conditions.

Up to this time there was a notable lack of road petitions from other parts of the county which, to some extent, provides further evidence that the major portion of the county's population resided in the northern section.

Morro Creek was first designated as the southern boundary of the San Simeon Supervisory District. After several relocations, as previously noted, it was adjusted to Toro Creek. In February, 1867, it was again moved south, this time to Chorro and San Luisito Creeks east of Morro Bay, following the main channel of the bay to the ocean. At the same time the supervisory district was divided into two road districts and voting precincts, with the division being made at the south boundary of Santa Rosa Rancho or Puerto Suelo, now Harmony, and extending to the ridge of the Santa Lucia Mountain range.

Consideration for ranchers was the prime concern in road viewing. Roads, where possible, followed property lines in order to avoid property splitting. Late in 1866 the practice of posting a notice of a proposed road route for 30 days prior to acceptance was instituted. Property owners affected by the route had time to file objections or claims for anticipated damage. After the grace period lapsed the road survey was approved, and work started when money and conditions permitted. Few complaints were ever made. Those that were seemed to have been taken care of easily.

The route through the pines from Santa Rosa Creek to San Simeon caused the most friction. It meandered considerably from a direct line to its destination in order to serve several ranches. Some land owners did not wish the road to pass so near their land, while others desired it closer. After two relocations, it was established as passing through Leffingwell property between their flour mill and saw mill, a route maintained until abandoned as a public road in favor of one passing westward along Santa Rosa Creek to the ocean where it connected with a branch road from San Simeon Bay to Cambria.

In 1868 the state enacted a road labor law. It replaced local road and capitation taxes. Every able bodied man was required to spend four days of each year working on roads in the vicinity of his home under the direction of the road overseer. This law was easier to enforce than a tax requiring the collection of money. Few people could afford the additional tax, whereas they could afford a few days' work. Anxious to benefit from this new work policy, citizens of the north coastal area increased their pleas for more road surveys and changes.

When the county supervisors agreed to relocate the road from San Simeon Bay to Santa Rosa Creek, so it would intersect as the citizens wished, they seem to have misunderstood the exact route desired for the survey they approved. As the route neared the town of Cambria (called San Simeon at that time) it did not intersect with Santa Rosa Creek road. Citizens were furious. Survey work was redone, but not until repeated petitions for readjustment had been filed with the Supervisors.

During this same year action was finally taken to approve the surveys of the Mammouth Rock-San Simeon Road and Josephine Mine-San Francisco Canyon Road. Work on them continued to be postponed for two and a half years.

November 9, 1868, Angus M. Hardie of Green Valley was appointed road superintendent of San Simeon Road District. This replaced the term "road overseer." November 10 the surveyed portion of Green Valley Road was declared public. This road had been used as a right of way over the mountains by Indians and Spanish for centuries. In the early days of the Spanish it was called the Cienaga Trail as large portions traversed marshy areas. This route extended from the coast road eastward along Encinalitas Creek, across the low-lying hills into Villa Creek and on to Cienaga Valley to intersect the Old Creek-Hot Springs trail from Cayucos.

The following anonymous letter sent to the newspaper by a citizen working off his four days of forced labor in 1868 is of special interest. Bear in mind that roads were constructed entirely by pick and shovel. The letter to the paper was addressed to the road overseer:

> The road runs into such enormous rock piles by the
> viewer's plans where there is a chance to do better with

much less labor. Also, provision should be made for running the road out of the reach of the surf at such places as the crossings at Cayucos, Old and Toro Creeks which, undoubtedly, are the worst places on the road from San Luis Obispo to Santa Rosa.

The writer also expressed his hope that the next supervisors . . . would have sense enough to appoint a good road viewer.

It seems that the road viewer was not particularly happy with his job for he answered the complaint by offering his job "gladly, to anyone who could do it better." He explained, however, that the route of the road was planned

to avoid inconvenience to farmers whose land would be divided by a straight route; to keep the road high enough above the creek bottom to afford drainage, and after complying with the two other things, the road was made as straight as possible whether there might be rock material in the way or not.

Testifying to the poor condition of the roads, an anonymous traveler reported to the San Luis Obispo *Tribune* in 1868 about the road to San Simeon, saying:

The road is as good as it ever was, once you get down to it. I am convinced that four days of work from every man between San Luis Obispo and San Simeon will be entirely inadequate to put the road in proper traveling condition.

With this one road needing all available labor to keep it near useable, it is small wonder other public roads were neglected.

The Santa Rosa-San Simeon area was enjoying a continually increasing prosperity. The people resented the poor road communication to other parts of the county which hampered full exploitation of this prosperity. New schemes and ideas for opening the area to overland travel were continually suggested. One plan was to construct a wagon road from the Bay of San Simeon 12 miles northward to San Carpoforo Creek, then northeast across the coast range to intersect the stage road near Ojitos ranch in Monterey County, a distance of about 30 miles. The estimated cost was $5000. Proposers of this plan claimed the Los

Angeles Stage Company would pay $1000 toward its construction, Monterey County was expected to contribute $2000 and the remaining $2000 "will be easily raised by people of San Simeon and Santa Rosa." The article extolls the benefits such a route would provide.

> Freedom from valley heat while traveling from Ojitos to San Luis Obispo, abundance of feed for stage horses, increased patronage by tenfold . . .

and,

> The Piedra Blanca Rancho, owned by Castro, Hearst and Pico, in a remote corner of the county, distant from all roads and comparatively out of the world, containing thousands of acres of the most productive and easily cultivated land in the state, would be open to settlement and afford homesteads (sic) for thousands of families.

For more than a century this same theme was echoed again and again. The scheme, whose ever it was, was never presented to the Board of Supervisors. In all probability it was quickly squelched by the land owners it would involve before it had the opportunity to gain momentum. The large property holdings, then as now, were *not* open for homestead or small farms, nor did the owners encourage travel north of San Simeon Bay.

By 1870 the general economic situation had changed. More cash was available and a new pattern in road management began to evolve. The compulsory road labor law was abolished. The Capitation Tax was re-established at $3 per man, to be used for the purpose of hiring regular labor crews. The appointment of district road overseers or superintendents was placed in the hands of the individual district supervisors. More of the petitions and complaints, which continued to pour in, were filed without action or laid over for future consideration.

Ah Louis arrived in San Luis Obispo in 1868. Shortly afterward he set up business supplying Chinese laborers on contract to various work projects in the county. These Chinese became the work crews on county roads after 1870. Five of them could be hired for the price of one local citizen, and feeding them was no great problem.

Land feuds increased. People living in remote areas with property a distance from a public right of way road often found themselves hemmed in when unfriendly neighbors refused them exit through their lands. Frequent unsuccessful petitions to the supervisors for regulations permitting limited access roads to these land-bound ranches forced many to abandon them for lack of exit. Property values were increasing rapidly, causing difficulty in relocating old roads and locating new ones. In 1870 the first small bridges were placed across the deeper creeks and gulches. In 1872 the county acquired its first deed to property on which a road was located. San Simeon Road District was divided again to become Road Districts 6, 7 and 8, with B. Short, J. M. Buffum and B. F. Mayfield as overseers.

At his suggestion, County Surveyor R. R. Harris prepared the first map of the county on a scale of one inch to the mile. It was to include all rancho boundaries, all subdivisions with names of owners and the acreage, all surveyed roads and all other roads "which could be located," and all surveyed government lands with names of the original owners. Also to be included were the proper location of the summit of the Santa Lucia Mountain Range, all townships, school districts, rivers, creeks, houses, "as far as practicable," and an exact delineation of the coast line. The extensive project was to be completed in six months. After two years and nine months it was presented to the supervisors in November of 1874, a masterpiece of survey and charting under trying circumstances. Harris had little help during his survey of wilderness and settled country. The map is on display in the recorder's office at the county court house.

Numerous petitions, surveys and declarations to the Board of Supervisors concerning construction of a road to the Hot Springs road at Paso Robles produced no results adequate enough to construct a wagon road across the mountains. In January of 1874 the editor of the *Tribune*, following a visit to Cambria, wrote:

> Our coast from San Luis Obispo to Piedra Blanca is
> peculiarly situated. To travel conveniently from any of
> its points to San Francisco, it is necessary to go south
> to San Luis Obispo and then take the stage road north.
> The only relief is in the Josephine Road, up Old Creek

and the road to the headwaters of Santa Rosa Creek, then to the Hot Springs Road—roads sometimes available, never eligible. It is not likely the stage route will ever be started over either unless much more labor is expended than has yet been attempted by the Board of Supervisors. Due to the rising town of Cambria and convenience to inhabitants of the north portion of the county, safe, commodious and easy roads should be constructed at public expense.

Still nothing was done. Before long, coast residents abandoned all hope of county help. Plans whereby a private road company might be established were considered. On March 21, 1874, a meeting was called by J. C. Baker and Merritt Utley to seriously discuss the feasibility of such road construction through a private enterprise. In May the *Tribune* reported:

It is only a question of a few months before there will be a road open to intersect the northern stage route, thus shortening the distance considerably. The road is awaiting legislative action.

This was a very optimistic outlook, though it was a foreshortened view of things to come. In March of 1875 citizens of Cambria incorporated to form the Cambria-Paso Robles Wagon Road Company with 800 shares of stock at $25 per share. Offices were at the northwest corner of Main and Bridge Streets with E. N. Conway, secretary, and J. C. Baker, G. W. Lull, W. T. Lockhart, William Leffingwell, Sr., and J. M. Mannon as directors. They hired H. C. Ward to survey a practical route over the mountains, then secured right-of-way deeds for the entire route.

When it became evident that they would have clear title to the route, the company approached the Board of Supervisors and asked for action. The Board, apparently impressed by the drive and accomplishment of the north coast citizens, appointed viewers to estimate the cost of construction. They called for bids on the road, a small portion at a time.

Satisfied with the sincerity of the Board, and with progress of construction, the Wagon Road Company deeded its interest in the road to the county in August of 1876. This action seemed to give impetus to the county government, which slowly but steadily secured deeds to north county roads, especially the coast road, but not before it was relocated several times.

In December of 1876 the approach to Cambria was re-routed from the Estrada adobe by way of Cambria Hill and a small ravine into town (north edge of Lodge Hill and Bridge Street). Previously the road crossed from the adobe into Santa Rosa Creek Valley over a saddle to the east of Cambria Hill, then it skirted the creek bank to a crossing several hundred feet downstream. The new route directly approached the same crossing. The Bridge Street crossing of Santa Rosa Creek was hazardous in rainy weather and citizens asked that the Cambria Hill road be continued down in line with Lee Street and a bridge placed over the creek to intersect with Lee. It was 1888 before the approach to Cambria was switched to the opposite side of the ravine and the Lee Street bridge built. Total cost was $3150.

The demand for more roads subsided. Those in existence continued to serve the community in varying degrees of repair and without further re-routing until 1924, when the coast road approach to Cambria was changed once more. This time it was moved to another ravine northeast of town to intersect Santa Rosa Creek road by means of a new bridge and the road oiled providing, for the first time, a dustless entrance to town.

Many of the old mountain roads were abandoned as ranchers sold or gave up their homestead holdings. Some of the public roads reverted to trails and private use, especially those linking the ranches of the back country. As business declined, after establishment of the railroad and decreased ocean shipping, Cambrians paid little attention to road improvement. With poorly maintained roads the area became isolated again. Few outsiders attempted the tortuous trip over narrow, dusty, or mud-laden roads. In 1937 a narrow, twisting road was completed along the coast between San Simeon and Carmel. This afforded some relief for those making trips by auto to points north of San Luis Obispo.

A fight for construction of this road began in 1917 when Elmer S. Rigdon, then in the Senate, introduced a bill for its construction under the Military Roads Act. Forty-eight miles of the southerly portion of this addition to the coast road system represented "pioneer construction through one of the wildest, most precipitous sections of the entire coast." It was 16 years (1921-1937) in the building at a cost of nine million dollars.

The entire coast highway in San Luis Obispo County was incorporated into the state highway system in 1939 as part of State Highway 1. The narrow coast road was finally oiled, as were roads leading inland along San Simeon and Santa Rosa Creeks, to create passable, safe routes throughout the year.

Though state owned, further road improvement along the coast remained at a standstill until the home of William Randolph Hearst near San Simeon was opened to the public by the state. Extensive advertising immediately drew, thousands of tourists to the area. Numerous complaints reached state offices concerning the road conditions. Plans were soon drawn for an improved state highway and completed as far as Cambria in 1963. The following year a Cambria by-pass was constructed, shuttling traffic northward toward the Hearst "Castle." Further improvement between the Cambria by-pass and San Simeon Bay in 1968-69 finally brought the San Luis Obispo-San Simeon route to a standard comparable to other major roads in the county, with the exception of State Highway 101.

The Santa Rosa-Paso Robles road, now known as Highway 46, when completed was dangerously narrow and steep, as well as impassable during the winter months. After this road became part of the state highway system, north coast citizens again started agitation for an adequate road which would connect directly with the Highway 101 stage route to the north. As in the past, Cambrians still had to travel to San Luis Obispo for connections with bus, train or air service.

In 1974 a new Highway 46 by-passing the Santa Rosa Creek road will terminate at Highway 1 through Green Valley, finally providing an adequate and safe road across the Santa Lucia range, as visualized by Cambrians just 100 years ago.

For more than a century north coast residents continuously voiced their unhappiness over inadequate roads. However, it was this imposed isolation which undoubtedly did more toward development of the pleasing, unique and independent character of the area than any other factor.

Chapter 6

One Hundred Years
of Mining

The discovery of cinnabar ore by a group of Mexicans in the Santa Lucia Mountains east of San Simeon in 1862 renewed the latent mining fever of local homesteaders who came to California during the gold rush of '49. News of the discovery soon spread to other parts of the state, causing a rush of prospecting and claim staking on every bit of ground that gave a show of cinnabar as the price of mercury was high due to the Civil War.

This early prospecting also disclosed the presence of coal, copper deposits, and claims to other fabulous minerals which petered out in the testing.

Local Indians, when first encountered, were using a paint made from ground cinnabar ore. However, early Spanish prospectors could not learn the secret of their source. Local legend relates that the first outcropping was finally found as the result of a lead given by one or more Indians still living in the area. The need for secrecy was no longer important, Indian body decoration having been given up through mission influence, but the Indians kept their secret from white men for nearly 100 years.

The first cinnabar discovery at the headwaters of Santa Rosa Creek, midway between San Simeon Bay and Paso Robles, became known as the Tartaglia and George Mine outcroppings. The Mexican discoverers were without funds and had little knowledge of ore processing, though samples indicated a "remarkable richness and prospects were for a valuable mine."

In the meantime, William Leffingwell, who settled on public domain between San Simeon Creek and the northwest boundary

70

of Rancho Santa Rosa in 1858, and as an enterprising business man established a saw mill in 1861, discovered an outcropping of coal on the beach south of San Simeon Creek during a low tide in 1863. He mined some of the coal for use in his blacksmithing forge and found it quite satisfactory. Others in the vicinity became interested. C. B. Rutherford, a wealthy resident of the county willing to gamble some of his money in a mining venture, looked over the site and tested the coal. He concluded it was worth mining and agreed to finance a company which Leffingwell and his immediate neighbors had started to form. Their first move was to file mining claims on their own, still insecure, homesteads and on property nearby.

The San Simeon Coal Mining Company formed by San Simeon Creek settlers Franklin Riley, C. W. Pinkham, E. A. Clark, Harrison Dart, Carolan Mathers, W. C. Rickard, Bolivar Jones and William Leffingwell, together with his sons, William, Jr., and Adam C., gave half interest in the enterprise to Rutherford as security for his investment. According to contract, Rutherford was to provide money for sinking necessary shafts, construction of a wharf, buildings, railroad, boats, and for the buying and installing of machinery and appliances. When actual marketing of coal began the company, first of its kind to be incorporated in San Luis Obispo County, was to pay its own expenses.

Claims started at the mouth of San Simeon Creek and extended southeast along the coast for 7,700 feet and inland for 2,640 feet. Each claim was 700 feet wide and taken up in accordance with the laws of the San Simeon Mining District.

The vein outcropping, which gave such promise of a successful venture, was two feet wide and mostly under water at high tide. After sinking a shaft to a depth of 100 feet, the vein was found to dwindle to a mere seam and the operation failed.

Soon after this venture an announcement was circulated that white coal had been found near San Simeon. Chunks of the new discovery were brought out of the mountains for demonstration. When ignited they burned fiercely but were not consumed. After the fire was gone the substance appeared much as it did before burning. This discovery, which caused some interest but no action, was made by a Mexican prospecting for cinnabar who did not disclose the location of his find. Further investigation of the material proved it to be petroleum saturated stone. With the real value of petroleum still unknown, the incident was forgotten and no further mention made of white coal until 1887 when the San Luis Obispo *Tribune* printed an unsigned letter to the editor from a man who claimed he operated the San Simeon coal mine in 1863. He wrote that while visiting familiar places near the headwaters of Santa Rosa Creek he met an old friend on a small *ranchita* who showed him a "white coal" mine near his home. The light colored rock, he said, appeared wet,

. . . but on being touched with a match, burst into flame and burned with a glowing heat. Upon examination I found a small spring of petroleum oozing from the cracks of a white sandstone, thus solving the mystery of the "white coal" . . .

Coal was also found on a peak north of Cambria which became known as Coal Mountain. It was never located in paying quantities and when tested the coal was pronounced as too soft for commercial purposes.

Several large, rich pieces of copper ore were found in the bed of Santa Rosa Creek near its source about the time cinnabar was first discovered. Though an intensive search was made, the source of this ore was never located.

Following discovery of the Tartaglia outcropping 40 Spanish, Mexican and Americans incorporated to form the Josephine Quicksilver Mining Company on January 4, 1864, under the laws of the Salinas Mining District. Among the partners well known in the San Simeon area were W. C. Rickard, Romauldo Pacheco, M. C. Parker, Charles B. Rutherford and P. A. Forrester. In spite of the advertised richness of the ore, barely enough work was done to cover assessment requirements until Baron and Company of San Francisco, hearing of the mine's potential, became interested and took over as owner in 1867. This company also owned and operated the New Almaden Mine, in Santa Clara County, which was originally discovered by the Spanish as a silver mine in 1824 and later as a quicksilver mine under Captain Castillero in 1845. During the first three years of operation at the Josephine, Baron and Company shipped

$280,000 worth of quicksilver through the port of San Simeon. This successful operation precipitated further intensive search for other outcroppings in the area. Many sites were located.

The fever with which men searched for cinnabar, and the fierceness with which they guarded their claims, were reminiscent of jealousies and battles in the gold fields of '49. New arrivals accidentally or wilfully trespassing on staked claims were in danger of gun fire or knifing. Many who staked early though short lived claims later homesteaded or in other ways added to the history of the area. Some names still in use or remembered for one reason or another are: James S. Coffee and Lewis Morss, who staked claims on land known as Godfrey's Sheep Ranch in 1869; Louis Pillard, whose claim lay due south of the Josephine, filed January 10, 1868; Corres Tibucio Lamida, whose claim joined Pillard; J. T. and E. L. Reed, George Proctor and D. W. Fuller, west of the north fork of San Simeon Creek.

Prospecting continued northward along the ridge of the Santa Lucia mountains. In 1870 outcroppings located between the headwaters of Arroyo de la Cruz and San Simeon Creek were claimed by W. E. Lopez, J. S. Oliver, Greenville Watson, Felipe Puente, B. F. Weimer, S. B. Bates and many others. These claims were all in the vicinity of Pine Mountain, eight miles north of the Josephine Mine and 11 miles from Cambria. This discovery did not create any undue excitement until Ozro Haskins, seeking a site on the mountain for a saw mill, discovered ore which was literally oozing with mercury. He brought samples to Cambria for testing. They were found to yield one ounce of quicksilver per pound. News of this discovery could not be withheld and, with little investigation, several of the wealthier men of the community immediately formed a company (a practice which occurred uncommonly often at this time) to raise funds for an operation. This claim had a well defined fissure vein. Because of this, and the unusually high mercury content of the ore, an immediate rush began for additional claims.

Need for a mining district in the area became urgent. The Pine Mountain Mining District was formed in 1871, and 150 claims within its bounds were recorded almost immediately, outcroppings averaging from two to eight per cent quicksilver.

Cambria, just four years old, began to boom. The port of San Simeon became a settlement catering to a lively shipping and mining trade. Those unsuccessful in locating a claim had no difficulty in securing work at a good wage. Others went into business for themselves: heavy draying, wood cutting for furnaces, blacksmithing and merchandising.

Eight separate claims were located on the initial lode at Pine Mountain. The first, discovered by Haskins, was bonded to Land and Brewster of San Francisco for $40,000, on which $3,000 was paid. Subsequently, it was bonded to Senator J. P. Jones of Nevada for $30,000 and, later, to other bonding companies. However, continuing mismanagement by incompetent superintendents eventually caused complete surrender of the bonds.

Owners of the Gibson and Phillips claim on the northwest end of the lode put $200,000 into machinery, furnaces and prospecting. They made this expenditure before the mine was thoroughly investigated. By the time the company was ready for operation the price of quicksilver took a sudden drop. This led to a suspension of work which, when prices rose again, they were unable to resume though the ore was rich. In March of 1874 a mining report on this claim reads:

"It is for sale for $70,000 and prospects are excellent."

This report, together with other advertising, led to immediate sale of the claim. It was purchased by the Ocean View Mining Company of San Francisco the same year. Other mines working successfully in the area were the Santa Maria, Buckeye and Jeff Davis, all of which were marketing ore by way of San Simeon.

In December of 1871 the Keystone Mine was discovered on patented land flanking the west side of Rocky Butte, just south of Pine Mountain. The owners worked this mine heavily for a short time after they completed installation of furnaces and condensers in 1874. It was the first mine to develop into a profitable undertaking in the Pine Mountain area, though it was worked on a small scale. All of its ore was considered very good. Crass and Company purchased the mine late in 1874 for $22,000 and placed it under the management of Jack Eva. In 1875 it produced 60 flasks of quicksilver. After a large amount of ore had been extracted from the mine it was discovered that the deposit was a slide from the main lode located on the summit of the mountain. Further development opened up the main lode with the result that this mine has continued profitable under intermittent operation and different owners to the present day.

Claims made in 1872 by three Cambria residents on land three-fourths of a mile north of Santa Rosa Creek and five miles from town made mining history. These claims were first known as the Sulphur Springs, Bristol and Morss. Bill Phillips and George Morss, riding after their cattle in the hills, discovered an outcropping when Bill's horse accidentally dislodged a piece of rock containing bright red streaks. Samples taken in for testing were found to have a high mercury content. The two men quickly staked a claim and were immediately followed by the others. The three claims were consolidated into one company on June 2, 1874, and incorporated in August under the name of Oceanic Quicksilver Mining Company. Several property owners adjacent to the discovery were induced to sell their land to the company, while others who evidenced an interest in the company traded their land for mining stock.

Among these initial stock holders were prominent men of Cambria and San Francisco, as well as several local ranchers. Included were James Sloan, P. A. Forrester, George VanGorden, Reuben Phillips, William and Jacob Morss, John W. and E. M. F. Morse and R. A. Cochran, who was influential in securing the interest of several San Francisco men who lent financial support by purchasing large amounts of stock. As a consequence, they were made the major directors. These men were Layfayette Maynard, A. E. Peachy, M. Zellerbach and T. F. Cornise. Mining started and was a profitable investment from the beginning.

In the meantime the Josephine Mine was experiencing reverses. In March of 1874 a general report on Cambria mines given by a correspondent to the San Luis Obispo *Tribune*, who claimed "strong familiarity with mining," had very little good to say about it. He emphasized the poorness of the ore which, he said, was averaging less than one per cent. Assessments against stock holders also indicated the mine was not making expenses. The mining company spent $100,000 in prospecting the value of the mine following the first three-year splurge. Many feet of exploratory tunnel cost $60 a foot to drive. In conclusion, the reporter said:

> At this time cinnabar is found where it does not naturally exist. It seems to be a reverse of almost anything known in the history of cinnabar deposits. The hill is telescoped into a honeycomb in which no extensive vein exists.

A. Dennis was superintendent with 20 men working under him. He, too, was reticent about the future of the mine. Baron and Company, however, was optimistic about the general area in spite of the losses. Their large loss at the Josephine Mine was balanced by the other more profitable mining ventures they had been conducting for 25 years. This company, continually looking for additional mines, had strong hope of purchasing the Oceanic and Todos Santos Mines. However, richness of the Oceanic ore was too promising an investment to stock holders and they refused to sell. On September 26, 1874, the *Tribune* reported:

> The Oceanic is going full blast. Shares are selling on the open market in San Francisco at $5 per share, which equals $25 per foot. Dr. Cochran is going ahead with the furnace and employing 70 men.

Mr. Jennings was named as chief engineer.

The price of quicksilver remained high until 1878 when a decided drop occurred and the mine shut down. By this time the corporation was having trouble in the form of two court judgments against it in excess of $110,000, which forced the company to sell the property and equipment to the Merchant's Exchange Bank of San Francisco in June for $50,000. The sale actually amounted to an attachment as the original owners continued to retain management of operations. The bank continued as owner for a number of years, during which time the mine operated with varying success and enthusiasm, according to the market price for quicksilver. Apparently discouraged by the turn of events, several of the original stock holders sold their shares though the company continued to show a profit under the new arrangement. In 1883 surface rights to the many acres of "company" land were sold to Battesta Gregonia Tognazzi. Elmer Rigdon, uncle of Elmer S. Rigdon of Cambria, leased the land for farming. At the same time he became mine superintendent.

Ah Louis, following completion of his labor contract with the Southern Pacific Railway Company on a line to San Luis Obispo, moved to the mine to oversee the approximately 200 Chinese laborers he was supplying as brick makers and miners in the tunnels. According to his son, young Louis, who was a small boy at the time, his father was working as a partner with a Mr. O'Leary who, he believed, was superintendent of all mining operations. Other Chinese acted as cooks and general laborers at the furnaces, etc. It is said that the first brick for the mine were made on the site by the Chinese laborers from mill dust, in a very old-fashioned furnace. Later, Chinese supplied the labor at Ah Louis' brick yard between Bishop's Peak and San Luis Mountain. This yard then supplied brick for mine furnaces.

By 1901 the mining company accumulated enough money to buy back the mineral rights from the bank. The years following this transaction were the mine's most profitable, and continued so until another industrial slump shortly before the outbreak of World War I. During this period George "Jack" Steiner was employed at the mine. He recalled that most of the miners at that time were, as he termed them, "Cousin Jacks" or Welchmen; only the cook was Chinese.

Tognazzi released the land to Guiseppi Curti in 1905, who was able to purchase it in 1907. When this sale was made the mining interests located above ground and on the property consisted of five cottages, a barn, shop, office, boarding house and two bunk houses, and the mill and furnaces besides the buildings over the mine shafts which housed machinery and equipment necessary to bring ore and miners to the surface. Included with the surface rights, aside from mine buildings, were a two-story farm house, a one and a half story house, hay barns, cattle barns, miscellaneous out buildings, creamery, farm implements and machinery.

During the 1872-74 mining boom, even those who could not actively participate in prospecting and mining operations enlivened the scene by recounting experiences of Gold Rush days. Several families living in and about Cambria had been employed at Sutter's Mill when gold was discovered there.

Jeffrey Phelan and his brother from Waterford, Ireland, came to California in 1846 and worked at the mill following their participation in the revolt against Mexico. Following the excitement of the gold rush, Jeffrey moved onto public domain near San Simeon Creek in 1857 as the first British-American settler in the county's north coast area.

Ira VanGorden, also an early settler along San Simeon Creek, was employed at the mill in 1846 and had his tales to tell, not only of the rush of '49 but of his experiences en route to California as a member of the Harlan Wagon Train. Recounting, however, was not left entirely to the men. A "little old lady," as a written account describes her, had her story, probably the most interesting of all and vouched for by Phelan, VanGorden and her husband, Peter L. Weimmer.

Mrs. Melinda Leah Lovall Weimmer was a rugged pioneering woman. Together with her husband, Peter, she had moved from her Ohio home to various places in the United States before coming to California. The Weimmer's last stop before settling at Sutter's Mill with 10 children had been the gold fields in Georgia. At Coloma they lived with Marshall and other mill employees. Mrs. Weimmer was cook and laundress of the camp, while her husband worked as a wheelwright. History books have recorded John Marshall as the discoverer of gold at the mill, but Mrs. Weimmer proclaimed to her friends at Cambria that this was "quite an untruth" as she was the original one to discover the gold. She continued her story by saying that Marshall found a piece of metal which he thought rather interesting but not to the extent that it raised his curiosity. He showed the piece to Mrs. Weimmer because he thought it a curiosity and nothing more. Mrs. Weimmer was very interested in the lump as it was so similar to the gold she had seen in Georgia. Due to her interest, Marshall presented her with the nugget, disbelieving her claim that it *was* gold.

She took the lump home and boiled it in lye soap, a test she had learned about in her travels. This further convinced her that the metal was gold. She again confronted Marshall, explaining the outcome of her test. He continued to ridicule the idea so she took it upon herself to send the lump to Sutter's Fort for a scientific test. When the nugget, with the report, was again in her hands she showed the paper to Marshall. It was when he saw this report in 1847 that he was finally convinced, "where-upon," she related, "he immediately took full credit for the discovery," never giving her a word of acknowledgment. Her closing comment about Marshall was that "He was a first class thief, having stolen all my thunder." Mrs. Weimmer still had the nugget while living at Cambria. According to Bancroft, Mr. Weimmer worked at Sutter's mill and was one of the men at Coloma when gold was discovered, probably being with Marshall on the morning he picked up his first sample. Mrs. Helen Hafley, granddaughter of Ira VanGorden, said. "My sister and I both remember our dad telling us about Weimmer being with his father at Coloma, and the story about putting the gold nugget in Mrs. Weimmer's homemade soap to see if it was real."

During the gold rush the Weimmers ran a boarding house. Later, at the instigation of their friend Ira VanGorden, they moved to San Simeon Creek early in 1870. Mr. Weimmer worked for VanGorden, participated in local prospecting and was occasionally employed by William Leffingwell. Eventually the Weimmers acquired property of their own near Cambria.

Shortly after the turn of the century H. J. Price and Henry W. Martin, of San Simeon Creek, discovered an outcropping of cinnabar on property north of the creek which was owned by Jeffrey Phelan. Unknown to Price and Martin, when Phelan bought the property for $5 an acre from the Cambria Bank (acquired by the bank through foreclosure) the mineral rights were obtained separately by Elmer S. Rigdon, president of the bank.

The two men believed their find was worth mining. When Rigdon visited at his home one day Martin, believing him to be a good friend, confided his find to him. Martin was highly elated when Rigdon offered to have the sample tested for him. Several months passed before he saw Rigdon again, only to learn that he had been doublecrossed. The supposed friend, on learning the value of the ore, had staked a claim in his own name, leaving the discovery team out of the picture.

Rigdon started exploitation of his claim, located eight miles northeast of Cambria, in 1903 under the name of Bank Mine.

Will Warren was one of Rigdon's first employees. Will lived near the headwaters of San Simeon Creek but stayed at the mine. He was 21 years old at this time. His first boss was a mulatto by the name of Dye, then Bill Murphy, followed by a Captain Henry, formerly of the New Almaden Mine. For a time both Will and his father, Albert, worked there. Will says he worked 33 months for Rigdon, receiving $2.50 per nine-hour shift. At one time he worked seven months and eight days without time off. Room and board cost $18 per month.

In 1906 Rigdon sold out to H. R. Gage and C. W. Carson, who renamed the operation Cambria Mine, doing business as Cambria Quicksilver Mining Company. This company soon received considerable attention due to the high mercury content of the ore. The surface yield was poor but the underground body, consisting of cinnabar on serpentine fragments, was rich. After one year, during which time preliminary tunnels and exploration were completed, a reduction plant was installed.

After the furnace was installed the mine continued in steady production for 18 months, averaging better than seven and a half pounds of mercury per ton with a production cost of $26.03 per 76 pound flask. Early in 1908 the ore gave out, the ore body having shifted at some time during earth faulting. Due to the need for further prospecting to locate the lode, and dropping prices, mining was temporarily abandoned.

With prices rising again in 1914 prospecting was resumed on a higher outcropping. Three profitable deposits were located, separated by eight and a half miles. By December of 1915, using Chinese labor on much of the work, about 1400 feet of new drifts were completed on two levels. Cross cuts equaling three and four hundred feet of raises and winzes were drilled by hand. This new operation lasted for one year, when the mine was again shut down. With tunneling completed, full operation of the mine prior to closing was handled by 34 men, 22 working below ground, four at the top and eight at the furnaces. After a lengthy period of inactivity, machinery and buildings fell into disrepair. With modern recovery methods, further activity at the mine was started in 1960. In 1963 the claim was purchased by Dr. F. J. O'Donnell of Stockton who, with Floyd Miller as mine superintendent, installed processing equipment which made feasible the recovery of quicksilver from the surface soil, previously considered worthless. Soil bulldozed into piles was fed to a crusher and Gould rotary ball mill. The powdered ore was then fed to a classifier where chemical reagents combined with the cinnabar to form an ore concentrate. Passing to flotation cells, the concentrate was retrieved in settling tanks, the resulting sludge cooked in furnaces for 12 hours, by the end of which time the vaporized mercury had been condensed and collected in flasks for shipment.

In 1914 Elmer S. Rigdon, temporarily in charge of limited operations at the Oceanic Mine, sold his interest there to Murray Innes, who took over in his place. Innes built a small concentration mill to handle ore from old mine fills and operated the mine until the early part of 1916 when he bonded the property to Dr. E. A. Clark (formerly of San Simeon Creek but then in New York). Clark's first interest in mining ventures about Cambria was the San Simeon Coal Mining Company in 1863-64.

When Clark took over management of the Oceanic the equipment consisted of a small Huntington mill and Deister table handling 15 tons of ore in 24 hours and handled by three men. Clark replaced the equipment with larger machinery able to handle 300 tons of ore a day. This time the mill was equipped with ball mills, classifiers and a slime table. After installation, the operation was again turned over to Innes (1917). In 1918 Innes dismantled the mills and treated ore direct from the mine in two 50-ton Scott furnaces. At this time the mine was quite active and provided work for a number of young men from Cambria, and a crew of Chinese. Maximum employment was between 60 and 70 men. Improved mining methods could now put out the ore with a fourth of the crew necessary during the first mining boom.

Candles were still used in the tunnels and miners worked in shifts around the clock. Will Warren, previously employed at the Bank Mine, was now working at the Oceanic, as well as Joaquin "Jack" Soto. Will, recounting his recollections of the Oceanic, said all ore was hauled by horse and wagon from the mine to furnaces located some distance down a steep, winding road cut into the sides of the mountain. Dangers were many at the mine and on the road. He vividly recalled a rather serious accident which occurred when John Proctor, riding a young colt down the grade, met Joseph Galbraith, grandfather of Agnes Soto of Cambria, who was driving a team and empty wagon upgrade to the mine. They met at the narrowest point on the road, referred to by the miners as "Cape Horn." The mountain rose sheer above and dropped sharply below. Instead of turning the colt around, Proctor tried to force it by the wagon. Both Proctor and colt tumbled over the precipice to the canyon below. Proctor's fall was broken by a maple tree 100 feet below, where he landed briefly before careening on many feet farther to the bottom. Proctor suffered an injury to his neck but otherwise was not seriously hurt. The horse, on the other hand, was killed. Will's father eventually became owner of the saddle worn by the colt.

About this time there was a mine cave-in which trapped 20 Chinese who were never recovered. After the incident none of the Chinese would work below ground. Those who stayed were employed as cooks and at the furnaces. Underground laborers, thereafter, were supplemented by Mexicans.

Jack Soto, founder of Cambria's Soto Market, relating one of the brash deeds of his youth, recalled the day several of the miners walked off the job because of a quarrel with the management resulting from a miner breaking a teacup over the head of the Chinese cook. Protesting the harsh words of the superintendent who, witnessed the affair, Soto grabbed his ever-handy guitar, started playing "Marching Through Georgia," and, followed by the rest of the men in the building, marched out of the boarding house. He kept on walking and suddenly realized the full impact of what they were doing—it amounted to striking, so they continued on to Cambria. All participating lost their jobs.

Several miles of interlacing tunnels extend to a considerable depth at the Oceanic. Some are as much as 3,000 feet beneath the surface. Water flooding these tunnels finally forced abandonment of the mine and full scale operation. Mr. Curti bought the mineral rights from the company. For many years nothing was done at the site of the mine. Occasionally, various forms of salvage were attempted as new lessees worked tailings and material under the furnaces where puddles of pure quicksilver were found. The Curti property and mineral rights were purchased by Harold Biaggini, owner of the Klau mine near Adelaida, in 1968, but little has been done since that time other than prospecting and calculations with an idea that the tunnels might be made usable again, at least in part.

Early mining records tell of many more operating mines in the area, each of which had varying degrees of success. A few still continue to operate intermittently when the price of quicksilver is high enough to warrant the expense of mining.

The Klau Mine was first owned by Felipe Villegas and known as the Santa Cruz. It was later known as the Sunderland Mine, then the Dubast. Adolph Klau's mining claims adjoining Dubast were eventually incorporated with it, as were others nearby. At this time the mine was renamed as the Klau Mine. It is the most productive mine in the area today. During its early history this mine depended on Cambria for its supplies, but lying closer to the Salinas Valley than to the coast, modern transportation has diverted its business and activities to the east side of the range.

During early mining days the most productive year was 1876 when 6,428 flasks of quicksilver were shipped from local mines for a total return of $282,832. From 1888 and 1894 mining came to a complete standstill. By 1918 the second mining peak had subsided. Many small mines were exhausted or abandoned as unprofitable. Renewed mining during World War I never affected the community as the first activity did. Though increased business aided established merchants and provided work for all able-bodied men, the fever for mining had passed.

Beginning in 1963, a third mining flurry began as quicksilver prices soared to new heights, eventually reaching more than $900 per flask. This high price encouraged mining at previously unprofitable mines and on abandoned claims. In a few years, prices again spiraled downward and mining activity receded accordingly, with only three mines mildly active in the past six years, these being the Keystone, Klau, Cambria, and sporadic activity in the vicinity of the Oceanic.

Huge buildings over the shafts of the Oceanic Mine. Taken about 1917. Outbuildings held blacksmithing forges, the office, crushers, etc.

Cambria Mine on San Simeon Creek as it appeared in 1964.

These old furnaces at Cambria Mine were used to vaporize quicksilver from ore during the World War I mining boom.

Ruins of Cambria Mine ore crushing plant during World War I, overgrown with trees and brush high on a hillside overlooking San Simeon Creek.

Beginning with the Leffingwell saw pit in 1863, logging and saw mill operations continued in the pines about the Cambria area until recent years.

Chapter 7

The Early Chinese

The first record of Chinese immigrants to California is February 2, 1848, when Charles V. Gillespie, a resident of China for several years, landed on California soil with two Chinese men and one woman from the brig *Eagle*. The men went to the gold fields, the woman staying with the Gillespie family as a servant.

On March 6, 1848, Gillespie approached the Thomas O. Larkin shipping firm in Monterey with a proposal for bringing over additional Chinese, as laborers. During 1849, 54 Chinese immigrated and 707 reached California shores in 1850. Each year saw increasing numbers of Chinese immigrating to California to work in the gold fields, on roads and railroads, or wherever cheap labor was needed. Immigration reached a peak in 1876 when there were 116,000 new arrivals. In 1882, legislation against the continuing influx of Chinese resulted in the enactment of the Exclusion Law.

Chinese are known to have reached the California coast as long as 3000 years ago by way of the Black Stream or Japan Current which, for many hundreds of its transpacific miles, propels drifting vessels eastward at the astonishing speed of 75 to 100 miles per day.

After discovery by the English and Spanish, disabled, drifting junks were infrequently sighted on inshore waters of the California coast and noted in ships' logs. In 1774 Juan Bautista de Anza encountered a "strange" craft in the coastal waters and, in 1814, a Captain Adams reported seeing a rudderless craft fitting the description of a Chinese junk adrift near shore. From time to time Chinese artifacts are unearthed in archaeological diggings not related to historic times. Probably the oldest known find attributed to these involuntary immigrants were several Chinese coins and an ivory fan 3000 years old.

No one knows when the first Chinese came to San Luis Obispo County's north coast. They were living along the ocean cliffs prior to the founding of Cambria and many stories about them have been wrapped in an air of mystery and legend. Chinese were established as fishermen in Monterey as early as 1854. Some of these may have drifted down the coast to the shores of San Luis Obispo County.

During the 1870's Chinese were used as miners and laborers in various quicksilver mines of the area. However, these Chinese were immigrants brought into the area by Ah Louis of San Luis Obispo for employment on various work projects, especially for work on the Southern Pacific Railroad as it was, continued into the county. The earliest Chinese of the north coast area, however, came quietly and unobtrusively to settle on lonely, isolated spots along the shore where they took up farming as the principal source of income, supplemented in the beginning by dried abalone which was shipped to San Francisco by schooner for trans-shipment to China. These Chinese squatted at regular intervals from the Monterey County line to the mouth of Villa Creek near springs on the cliffs and steep hillsides overlooking the wave washed rocks where the produce of their farms grew. Their crop was seaweed. The "weed" was actually farmed; one particular variety was induced to grow abundantly on the rocks while other varieties were suppressed.

Day or night, whenever the tide was low, the men and women, isolated from their neighbors by long stretches of rugged coast line, worked at their trade. No machinery was used and there were no shortcuts. Weed farming required painstaking, hard, and often dangerous hand labor.

Sea lettuce or Ulva, one of the few seaweeds which is bright green, was the cultivated plant. Modern commercial references listing numerous practical uses for various sea algae, as most ocean plants are called, omit this group of greens. Kelp and other brown and red algae are dwelt upon at considerable length. However, no reference is ever made to the process which the Chinese used, and which can technically be designated as farming. Literary reference deals only with harvesting of seaweed after time and nature have produced a crop.

Sea lettuce grows as a large, broad, luscious-looking, green, wavy-edged leaf a foot or more in length. It requires specific conditions in order to flourish abundantly. Only certain types of rock are suitable for the algaeal root-like holdfast. It also requires very fresh, clean tidal water of limited temperature range.

The Chinese seaweed farmers found the rocky coastal area of San Luis Obispo County ideal for their trade. The Ulva already grew here but competed with many other forms of algae. In order to encourage luxurious and fast growth, the Chinese made sure the rocks preferred by the Ulva were plentiful and strategically placed to receive full benefit of wave action and sun. The selected rocks were thoroughly cleaned by scorching or burning, originally accomplished by smouldering pine shavings in a wire basket held against them. In later years a blow torch was used, eliminating the job of scraping the dead algae away. The Ulva was encouraged to "root" and other algae discouraged.

Eventually Cambria became the social center for these Chinese who, for the most part, were smart business men and well liked by the community. Their numerous children attended local schools and often ranked among the top students scholastically. The Chinese developed their own small community within the town, which became known as the Chinese Center. It was located on Bridge Street to the south of Center Street, extending along the north bank of Santa Rosa Creek. It consisted of a Buddhist Temple, a Joss House, bunk house and a few small buildings used as dwellings in which various Chinese lived from time to time.

The older residents of Cambria recall with pleasure their childhood associations with the Chinese who frequented this Center. Mrs. Phoebe (Maggetti) Storni lived, as a child, directly across from the Chinese on Center Street, as did Mrs. Hazel (VanGorden) Gamboni. The Center was a big attraction to them and they frequently visited it, unknown to their parents, to satisfy childish curiosity.

Chinee Mary ranked high in their memories. She was a resident at the Center for a number of years in the late 1890's and early 1900's. People who knew her describe her as a small, aging woman who looked after the welfare of the various young, unmarried men, often still in their teens, who came to reside there from time to time. She did their laundry and in many ways acted as a mother to them.

Lee Bow was remembered as an elderly Chinaman noted for inveterate gambling. He is still referred to as a typical permanent resident of the Center. According to the late George Steiner, born in Cambria in 1879, Lee Bow originally had his home at San Simeon Bay where he raised a family while he farmed the coast to the south of the bay as far as Pico Creek. As members of his family matured and left the area, Lee Bow spent more and more time at the Center until he finally became an aged, semi-permanent resident, his family all living in San Francisco. Because of his gambling the town residents were particularly aware of him. However, the children remembered him bcause of the special attention he bestowed on them in the form of Chinese candy. He was always very courteous to neighbors of the Center, remembering them with gifts of roast pig and other things on Chinese New Year. It is said the pig meat was so highly seasoned with Chinese herbs and incense, however, that recipients were barely able to eat it.

Mrs. Storni recalled the experience they all had with tamales Mrs. Yrculano Soto made to sell each week. Young Louis Maggetti, Mrs. Storni's brother, would peddle the tamales in order to earn some spending money. He set forth with a bucketful at a time. His first stop was always at the Center where he would sell the complete bucketful at once. This weekly purchase of tamales by the Chinese was purely courtesy. They never ate the tamales but promptly brought them over to the VanGorden family (living next door to the Maggettis).

Each Chinese New Year was celebrated by a gathering of the entire coastal Chinese population at the Center for several days of feasting and merrymaking. Usually 50-60 remained for the entire duration of festivities. Pigs were purchased from the ranchers and roasted, together with chickens still retaining their heads. The Joss House was used as the general meeting place, and the food was spread on a long table in front of the building to be eaten as individuals became hungry. Rice wine was plentiful, and gambling continued day and night. The loser at each game was required to take a drink. When a man lost so often that he was both broke and drunk, he retired to "sleep it off" while another man took his place.

It was common practice for the Chinese, when gathering the seaweed, to also gather and dry abalone. When the seaweed was shipped they would secrete the abalone in the bales, an unlawful practice which netted them considerable additional revenue if they were not caught.

Joaquin "Jack" Soto, born in 1886, recounted his experience with a Chinaman by the name of Ah Fey, who was arrested for taking illegal abalone in 1918. Ah Fey was given the alternative of a jail sentence or a fine of $50. The Chinaman did not have the $50 and so deplored the thought of jail that, out of compassion, Joaquin loaned him the money against the strong advice of the game warden. At this time Joaquin Soto was operating his own meat market and grocery store in Cambria. Most of the Chinese traded with him, charging their accounts, and usually paying once every six months. A week after Joaquin loaned the money, Ah Fey returned and paid off his debt. About this same time all the other Chinese along the coast who owed him money came in and paid their bills. They also deposited money in advance against future charges to show their appreciation of his trust and friendliness.

Today seaweed farming by local Chinese is a thing of the past except for one lone man who carries on as he has done for more than 60 years. His grown children left many years ago to live in the San Francisco area where they earn good livings at trades less dangerous and more lucrative than that of their father. How Wong, born in San Francisco in 1894, has been farming the ocean shore since he was 15 years old, living in a lonely house situated on the cliffs at China Point, four miles northwest of Cayucos. Thin, small boned, his fragile figure belying his strength and determination, Wong continues to ply his trade, now helped by a young wife from Hong Kong.

He raised and educated six children whom he seldom sees, not because the children have deserted their father but because he prefers to continue his life where he is, away from bad air and the noisy commotion of city life. How Wong, however, maintains close contact with world news and business markets through radio and newspaper, as well as by correspondence and occasional trips to Cayucos or Cambria for supplies. His present wife, many years younger then he, replaces his first wife who died a number of years ago. Though the present Mrs. Wong speaks little English, she is a willing helper and a gracious hostess to infrequent guests.

In his younger years, How Wong walked the distance of coast line included in his farming activities. Today he saves his strength whenever possible by driving along a narrow road hugging the mountains as they plunge seaward to precipitous cliffs. He gathers the sea lettuce into bamboo baskets carried at the ends of a long shoulder pole. Some places are so steep and rough he cannot use the big baskets and poles but must resort to sacks, more easily handled as he scrambles over slippery, wave swept rocks. After gathering the Ulva, it must be transported to his drying yard for curing. This is accomplished by arranging the leaves in a shallow square frame which measures them into "neats." The frame is then removed and the neat allowed to "set" until the leaves cling together well enough to permit turning of the neat without disturbing its shape. If the sun shines brightly the squares, with frequent turning, will dry within a week. Dampness and rain hinder the drying process and often cause rot or bleach, a sign of poor curing. Proper drying turns the leaves a rich, deep brown. The cured squares are tied into bales of 40 pounds each and stored in a dark shed until shipping time. The cured product is eventually shipped to San Francisco and Hong Kong to use in manufacturing special Chinese medicine.

Mrs. Storni spoke highly of sea lettuce as a food which her family and others of Cambria enjoyed by toasting in the oven until crisp, then eating as a condiment, soup additive or ingredient with other combined foods. The fresh leaves were sometimes added to salads. Others of the community recall that the weed was used extensively as a food supplement in early days when drought caused a scarcity of other foods.

Previous to Communism in China, and the subsequent curtailment of trade, there was a large market in that country for the Ulva. Stoppage of trade and consequent shipment of the product to China was the chief reason for nearly complete discontinuance of "weed" farming along the coast of San Luis Obispo County. Few records appear which indicate the quantity of seaweed shipped from this area. A notation made in records of 1869 indicate $3000 worth of Chinese products were shipped from San Simeon Bay that year. Another reference in 1880 states that 104 bales of seaweed were shipped over the George Hearst wharf. Undoubtedly some was shipped from Cayucos and, after the railroad was brought to San Luis Obispo, a great deal of it was shipped by rail. However, earliest shipments were probably made at beach landings, as were shipments of hide and tallow, long before any export records were kept.

China Point and adjoining China Cove are said to be named because Chinese were smuggled ashore there. Whether true or not, How Wong was preceded by his uncle at China Point, taking over his squatter's right as the old man grew too old to ply the trade, indicating Chinese residence at the Point for more than 100 years.

The late George Lum was the only other Chinese to continue seaweed farming along the coast in recent years. His home overlooks the ocean on cliffs of the Sibley Ranch (Rancho Marino) just south of Lodge Hill, Cambria. George, with his family, lived there approximately 35 years. His five children attended Cambria schools, graduating with honors. They helped with the seaweed farming until through school, when they all left for positions in San Francisco. One continued to return periodically and assist his father as time and his job permitted. Unlike Wong, Lum was a frequent visitor in San Francisco between favorable tides. He retired in the late 1960's to spend the remainder of his life there, which ended in May, 1973.

The other Chinese disappeared from the coast, one by one, leaving memories and an occasional homesite where odd bits of pottery, Chinese dishes and bottles may be found in century-old rubbish heaps.

Long Hop Wo raised eight children who attended the Washington School when it was located two miles north of Piedras Blancas lighthouse. His son, Harding, was an outstanding artist, according to local classmates. The Tong wars affected these men. Long Hop once spent a full week with John Heng in a Hearst Ranch hayloft located in San Carpoforo Canyon as they hid from members of a warring Tong bent on killing them. Another Chinaman whose name has been forgotten lived alone a short distance south of the lighthouse. He was not as fortunate as Long Hop and John Heng. As the story is told, he disappeared one night. All that was left as evidence was his spilled blood and tracks where a body appeared to have been dragged. The local constable checked off the murder as a Tong incident and no further investigation was conducted.

Another story tells about a Chinaman by the name of Lung who lived near the mouth of Villa Creek. Neighboring ranchers claim two people driving a Hudson sedan were seen to arrive at his home, apparently as visitors. One was a Chinese, the other a white man. No one observed the men and car leave. Later Lung was found shot to death. His death apparently followed a gesture of hospitality as evidence indicated he fed his guests, admitting them to his home as friends. The killers were never apprehended and the murder, again, was attributed to Tong war.

Big Jim lived on the ocean cliffs of the Arando Storni ranch where he raised a family, naming the girls born there after the Storni girls as a token of his friendship wth the Storni family. Big Jim's Chinese name is vaguely recalled as Ah Kee Wong. When China fell into the hands of Communists, Big Jim and his family moved to San Francisco.

The late George Steiner, a never-ending source of information concerning events in Cambria and vicinity, lived at San Simeon from 1887 to 1897. He spent many happy hours with some of the Chinese families in the area, sharing their meals and observing their Oriental way of life. Recalling his experiences, he spoke of the enjoyment of the pipe by old men when opium pills heated in the porcelain and brass bowls of their pipes sent them off into pleasant dreams following a puff or two. The smell of the heated opium nauseated Steiner to the extent he could not stay in a room where it was being used. Mrs. Gamboni said she could also remember the Chinese of the Center smoked frequently and she presumed it was opium as they had small rooms for the purpose into which they retired.

Steiner, as a child, was particularly impressed with the exceptional beauty of the Chinese teapots which snuggled in padded, basket-encased cosies. The use of sleeping mats placed on the floor was common practice and remained as a vivid memory.

Will Warren, whose memory of the Chinese goes back to the late 1880's, was particularly impressed by a Chinaman called Old Sam who lived at the Center in a shack overhanging the creek bank where he operated a laundry. Some of the older boys of Cambria often teased Old Sam by shaking his shack. This disturbance upset the old man, probably causing him to believe the fragile building might tumble from its poor foundation or collapse. In any event, it always brought him outdoors with haste and queue flying. One day, following such a shaking, he spied Will and surmised that he was one of the culprits. Much younger than the boys given to such pranks, Will was totally ignorant of the episode when he saw an angry Old Sam coming after him with a large, sharp butcher knife. The sight of the old man running toward him scared Will. He ran to the John McCain saloon on Center and Bridge Streets where he hid beneath the bar for several hours before the barkeep persuaded him all was clear so he could go home.

When Old Sam left town Chinee Mary filled his place. When she left due to old age and illness, the rest of the Chinese at the Center gradually disappeared. Center residents, for the most part, were never a stable group but came for a day, week or month, then left to return to their own abodes along the ocean. Several of these part time residents "vacationed" at the Center between work periods. The youngest ones were single men who farmed the coast to the west of Cambria. They dried their seaweed along the cliffs but spent their nights at the Center until they were ready to establish their own home and family.

Others who made the Center home for any length of time made a living by gambling. Law officers often raided one of the houses used extensively for this purpose. At the least indication of an unfamiliar noise, those gambling within would scatter. The back door of the building opened into the tree and bush shrouded Santa Rosa Creek. Most of the occupants were able to slip through this door, free of the law. Many men of the town besides the Chinese participated in the gambling games held there.

When the automobile became a popular means of transportation the Chinese spent more and more of their "vacation" time in San Francisco, diminishing the need for a Chinese community center. After the last of the Chinese left the Center, about 1916, members of the Warren family purchased the property. The older and less stable buildings were torn down. Others were moved to new locations. The temple and Joss House, built of redwood, were moved a short distance to front on Center Street. They were joined to the old B. H. Franklin building, once used as Cambria's first high school, then moved to form a home which was occupied by various members of the Warren family until 1970. At one time the building housed the Cambria Telephone Company owned and operated by Will Warren. The temple forms the living room of the house and still retains the altar shelf for the Buddha, flanked by the paraphernalia closets. The Joss House, joined to the temple, forms the kitchen. Bits of tile, broken glass and pottery, and an occasional coin still come to light when the soil is cultivated for garden use.

Chinese who came to the area for work in the mines remained aloof from the seaweed farmers. When their local employment was ended they moved elsewhere. Forty Chinese landed at San Simeon on June 22, 1874, from the steamship *Senator* for work in the Santa Cruz Quicksilver Mine. The same year, the Sunderland Mine employed 32, and approximately 200 were employed at the Oceanic Mine during the 1890's.

Home of How Wong, Chinese seaweed gatherer, for 60 years.

Chinese seaweed farmer, How Wong, still operating on the California Coast. He gathers his sea lettuce into bamboo baskets balanced on poles across his shoulders. If the sun shines brightly the neats of seaweed, with frequent turning, will dry within a week.

Opposite: Above. Roast pig for New Year's feast, taken at Chinese Center in Cambria. Note little queque started by young lad at right. (Paul Squibb) Below. Chinese medicine, ink and wine bottles found in old rubbish heaps.

Chapter 8

Dairy Farming

A milk cow was as essential to every early pioneer family of the Cambria area as was the horse. But, prior to the terrible drought of 1863-64, these people had not thought of the milk cow as a major source of income. They depended on large herds of long-horned Spanish and American cattle or sheep which roamed the land practically unattended except at branding or slaughter time. When these herds all died in one harsh winter season, leaving people with the choice of waiting two or three years while they rebuilt their cattle herds, or investing at once in a few head of good dairy stock for the production of butter and rearing of hogs, many of them chose the latter.

By spring of 1865 the ranchers were fully convinced of the real value of the dairy cow as a substantial source of income. Those surviving the losses of the drought immediately started improving and increasing their stock, and by the close of the year almost every rancher owned 20 to 25 head of good dairy cows. Many had also started farming wheat and other grains for additional income.

By 1869 dairying on the San Luis Obispo County north coast was of top importance to the shipping trade, with steamers picking up farm produce and discharging freight at San Simeon Bay at regular intervals each week. Records of the major shipping firm, Goodall, Nelson and Perkins, show $30,000 worth of butter and nearly 2,500 head of hogs left the port for San Francisco on their ships between January 1 and July 1 of that year. By this time marketable cheese was being produced in small quantities.

While most of the hogs were shipped by steamer, many of the people living far south of San Simeon found it more profitable to drive their swine to the San Luis Obispo market, taking a full week to make the 35 mile trip.

Other ships, besides those of the above-mentioned firm, also put into San Simeon in the course of a month or stopped at Leffingwell Landing to pick up additional produce after discharging lumber and other goods.

By the end of 1869 the dairy industry had attracted the attention of the partnership of Messrs. Ivans and Everett who, by November, had established a cheese factory at a site on the lower part of Santa Rosa Rancho, later known as Harmony. It was considered a major addition to the area, and county road maps were careful to note its location. The first years of this cheesemaking establishment were stormy ones. Messrs. Bower and Black became owners in 1871, operating under the company name of Excelsior Cheese Factory. According to the records they were producing cheese at "the astonishing rate of 1,200 pounds a day from a total of 9,000 pounds of milk." These figures were taken during the "green months" when milk production was at its peak. After June production fell off rapidly as the green feed diminished. Supplemental feeding for year-round production was not practiced at that time.

Cheese sold wholesale at 17 and 18 cents a pound, and the company is said to have established a high reputation for its products, which were competing on the west coast with similar cheeses imported from New York (a famous cheese center) and environs. The local factory consisted of a 40 by 50 foot building two stories high, and was fitted with "the most modern equipment New York could supply."

The largest of the early dairy farms was that of Morgan Brians who dairied in Sonoma County before coming to San Luis Obispo County. When he heard of the ideal dairy conditions on the Cambria coast, with its abundant wild feed which grew after the drought, he moved his family into Green Valley, just north of Harmony, and soon had a herd of 165 milking cows devoted exclusively to the production of butter.

Many hogs were grown in conjunction with the local dairy

business which, in 1870, attracted Messrs. Chapin and Company. This partnership secured a ranch on Santa Rosa Creek where a pork curing establishment was opened. Their bacon, lard and sausages were advertised as of "the best quality" and were in demand in the San Francisco market as well as locally.

A need for additional skilled craftsmen brought new residents to the town of Cambria. They included tinsmiths, blacksmiths, carpenters, cabinet makers and wagon makes. Laborers found steady employment on farms, and several teamsters were occupied exclusively in the hauling of dairy products to the steamers and to San Luis Obispo. The mining boom which also hit the community at this time gave further impetus to the dairy industry. An increased demand for its products aided in the firm establishment of the industry, which later insured Cambria's economic welfare regardless of the mining status.

Swiss farmers, who eventually became the backbone of the local dairy business, first gained their reputation as excellent dairymen in Marin and Sonoma Counties where large herds supplied milk and milk products to San Francisco and the Sacramento Valley. The excellent progress of the dairy industry, through efforts of the early settlers in the county, was good news to the north-state Swiss. Choice lands in that area were at a premium and prohibited further expansion. With more Swiss people migrating to California, friends and relatives started directing them to this central coast area with its rolling hills full of native grasses, ample water and cool, even climate.

These stable, hard working Swiss families lost no time establishing themselves. Many began work as milkers on already producing farms, others leased land and started their own dairies. A few were able to buy property immediately but the majority were relatively poor and had to work long and hard in order to accumulate enough money to purchase suitable land.

Melodic yodeling of the young men echoed about the valleys as they called to neighboring Swiss when bringing in the cows, especially in the afternoon and evening. Unlike the rough miners who were flocking to Cambria, the Swiss seldom frequented the saloons or squandered their hard-earned pay. They quickly gained a reputation for sobriety though were not above taking a social drink when they came to town once a week for relaxation and a round of visiting, or joined in the community activities.

Actual purchase of land by the Swiss came slowly. The early settlers owned most of the desirable areas. Many of the settlers grew restless, however, and in a few years they moved away or changed to other business enterprises, thus providing an opening for the Swiss. In order to become land owners, the new arrivals often lent money to each other and they were very careful not to bid against each other when land was sold at auction. When possible, they also sent money to Switzerland to aid others who wished to settle in California. These Swiss made permanent homes with plans for their future generations. For more than 100 years they have continued as the backbone and steadying influence of the community.

The most influential and best known of the early Swiss families were the Fiscalinis. The first to arrive was Joseph, who came directly from Switzerland in 1876. He was unable to understand or speak English, but was willing to work hard in his newly-adopted country. He was befriended by a fellow countryman, George Tognazzi, who had been here long enough to master the English language relatively well. Tognazzi secured a milking job for Joseph at the large Morgan Brians dairy. The life of the young milker was similar to nearly all the other Swiss. Cows were milked in an open corral which, in winter, was a sea of mud. On cold winter days the mud froze hard and when it rained, according to some, as much water as milk found its way into the pails. Each man had 25 to 30 head of cows to milk twice a day. Between the morning and afternoon milkings there was other farm labor to perform as well. When one milker became ill, others had to divide his string between them. When but two or three men were employed on a farm this meant each one often milked 50 or more cows until the ill hand was on the job again. In order to save every penny they could, these young men often deprived themselves of winter wraps and endured the frost, wind and rain in thin shirts and jeans without underclothing, relying upon their hardy breeding to remain healthy.

By enduring such hardships, Joseph Fiscalini saved enough money in two years to venture into the dairy business on his own. Another Swiss, John Filipponi, who also wished to be independent, joined Joseph as a partner. They leased the George Hearst properties in Green Valley together with 60 head of cows. At the end of their first year they had each accumulated a profit of $1,000. Joseph immediately bought some land and a few cows of his own. John, unfortunately, was killed in a tractor accident and his wife sold her interest to her brother-in-law, Attilio Filipponi.

Joseph continued to increase his private holdings and was soon able to be independent of his partner. Other close relatives of the Fiscalinis soon came to the area. They all prospered. Before long, parents and children numbered 45. Relating the history of the family, Mrs. Peter Fiscalini said, there was "a regular population explosion." Though many of the third generation children have moved away seeking diversified interests, the family is still prominent in the community, and remaining members have widened their ranching interests to include cattle raising and general farming.

Many other Swiss leased small farms from Juan Castro and George Hearst on Piedra Blanca Rancho holdings. As lease fees increased they resettled on their own ranches along the coast, in Santa Rosa, Green and Harmony Valleys. Prominent among them were the Gamboni, Maggetti, Bassi, Ricioli, Bianchi, Storni, Bianchini, Negranti, Molinari, Ioppini, Berri, Caporgni and Bassetti families.

During the summer months and until green feed was available following early fall rains, milk production practically ceased. The cheese factory closed completely or operated on a very limited basis. In 1872 the factory is noted as "operated" by a Mr. Polly. Silas Williams of New York arrived at that time and was employed by Polly as an experienced cheese maker. At the close of the 1873 season Williams obtained employment with Grant and Lull in Cambria, but in January of 1874, with Mr. Purdy as his partner, he was able to buy the factory, which opened under the name of Messrs. Williams, Purdy and Company. They advertised themselves as "making cheese on the plan of the famous cheese makers of New York," their "modis operendi" being a profit sharing co-operative.

Milk was weighed in as it came from each patron. The cheese was made, hauled and shipped to market with an accounting made to the dairymen on the net receipts. Two and a half per cent of the net was deducted for labor and profit to the company, the rest went to each farmer according to the percentage of milk he supplied. The dairymen found this method of operating much more remunerative than methods then being used in other parts of the country.

In September of 1874 the cheese factory closed and Mr. Purdy found employment with Grant, Lull and Company. Williams married Emmer Olmsted of Green Valley and sought various types of employment, finally leasing the Miles Marks ranch where he farmed. He moved to Walla Walla, Washington, for a change of climate and for better health, but after two and a half years of ill health there returned to Cambria to become the town's first milkman. In 1884 he moved beyond the Mammouth Rock School where he farmed and cared for the school for 13 years, retiring to Vallejo in 1897. Of his and Emmer's 10 children the oldest daughter, Juliet, taught at Washington School.

In 1875 the cheese factory was advertised in the *Tribune* as "under forced sale to settle an estate." Assets were listed as being a large factory building, a dwelling house, outhouses, implements, new steam engine and several acres of land. No record of further ownership or operation at the "factory" is in evidence for the next several years though it is known to have operated intermittently though unsatisfactorily for several years.

During the 1880's and 1890's dairymen depended primarily on butter sales. Cream was usually churned by horse power. Large churns were used with big paddles attached to a center turning post. A horse hitched to a beam extending from this post walked continuously in a circle until the churning was completed. Various alternatives to the walking horse were tried. George Dickie, having an inventive mind, tried to rig a goat-powered treadmill to his churn, but never quite succeeded in the operation. Some used water power, and the most progressive experimented with noisy gasoline engines. After the butter was churned it was placed on a large wooden table with a built-in paddle. Here it was worked until completely free of whey and water, then it was packed in large wooden "butter boxes" for shipment. In order to have fresh butter at home throughout the summer and early fall months, the Swiss made what they called "cooked butter." Fresh butter was put on the stove and slowly heated until it was a golden yellow. While cooking all scum was removed. The heat was carefully controlled during this sterilizing process. After the remaining impurities settled to the bottom, the golden butter was ladled into molds and stored in a cool place. Old farm families claim it never turned rancid during use.

The several men engaged in draying dairy products to San Luis Obispo, Cayucos and the steamers at San Simeon three times a week did not have the easiest of jobs, according to many stories related by them. Local roads were of the worst kind, especially during the winter months when hauling was the heaviest. Four and six horse teams were required to pull the burdened wagons, often over narrow, steep and winding roads deep in mud or dust. Few bridges existed. Those that did were often washed out in time of flood. Fording the numerous creeks and streams became a major problem. On the days of heaviest rainfall, the drivers and their rigs were usually stranded until the swollen, raging streams subsided. In dry weather, poorly or hastily constructed bridges would collapse with the weight of the ladened wagons passing over them.

In 1894 two co-operative creamery companies were organized, and incorporated in 1895. The Home Creamery, located on VanGorden property on San Simeon Creek road, was incorporated on February 5 with Gilbert VanGorden, Antonio Luchessa, Benjamin F. Martin, Ira R. Whittaker and Amos Smithers as directors. This creamery manufactured cheese and butter. and served the dairymen of the Cambria-San Simeon area as far north as San Carpoforo Creek.

The Cambria Creamery incorporated February 19 with directors representing both Cambria and Cayucos interests. Those elected to serve were B. Tognazzi, R. A. Minor, Phillip Hartzell, Paul Silacci and John Taylor. This creamery had 38 subscribers, primarily from the Santa Rosa Creek area and south to Cayucos. It was located on Santa Rosa Creek at what is now the junction of Main Street and the Santa Rosa Creek road.

The creameries did a fair business for about 10 years until both burned to the ground within a few months of each other. Many dairymen belonging to these co-operatives felt they lost money or made relatively poor profits and they were not sorry when the plants burned. According to C. L. Mitchell, butter inspector for the United States Department of Agriculture, Dairy Division, 1907 to 1909, these co-ops failed because they had poor plant methods which produced inferior butter and, as a result, received the lowest market prices for their products.

Until the introduction of the centrifugal cream separator, cream was separated by hand skimming after it had set in flat, open pans for 24 hours. The even, cool climate of the area was especially good for butter making as the milk stayed sweet during the rising period, and the cream gathered no bad odors. Occasionally a wood stove was fired to aid in keeping an even temperature on the colder days. In contrast to this local advantage, Leonelda Fiscalini, daughter of one of the early Fiscalini families, noted that a relative in the dairy business near Vallejo had to give up butter processing early in the season because hot weather soured the cream, giving the butter a bad taste.

Cream separators were introduced locally soon after 1900. John Taylor of Green Valley purchased the first one, a Simplex, from a salesman by the name of Glass, but only after a long sales talk and much discussion among the dairy farmers. Joseph Fiscalini was approached first but was skeptical about the "contraption." He told Glass that if he sold one to John Taylor, he would also buy one; so—Joseph became the second dairyman in the area to own a separator. These first models were hand operated, hard to turn, and often gave considerable trouble. Gas engines were soon employed, however, which speeded up the operation and made the work much easier.

George Dickie gave up his dairy to start a draying business. For several years Manuel Williams, George Bright and George Dickie took care of most of the hauling business, milk products and lumber constituting their principal loads. In 1912 Nick Storni and his cousin, A. V. Rammonetti, bought a four ton, solid-tired Kissel truck and secured a franchise to haul from San Simeon to Cayucos. Nick related that it wasn't long until Bright and Williams were practically out of business. In the meantime, George Dickie had abandoned the draying business and established himself as a hardware merchant and car dealer.

With the truck, delivery time was cut tremendously and three trips a day could be made between the extremes of their route. A round trip to San Luis Obispo, 35 miles away, took but eight hours. This quick trip was utilized for hauling hogs to market, whereas they had previously been driven on foot, a long and tedious journey. Storni and Rammonetti also hauled gasoline from the San Simeon dock to the Dickie store for use in the "new fangled cars invading the community." During seasons of scant rainfall, they hauled in quantities of hay to keep the dairy stock going, a practice heretofore virtually impossible as well as economically impractical.

During the peak dairy season Storni and Rammonetti picked up and delivered 150 cans of cream a day besides hauling flasks of quicksilver from the mines, especially the Oceanic, at $4 per ton, and lumber to the mine on a per foot basis. Even at this date, Storni says it was not all roses hauling with a truck for the roads were still extremely bad. The road beds were not uniformly solid and mud holes existed in which they would bog down. It usually meant unloading the truck of 100 or more cans of cream and other heavy items before the truck could be freed from the hole. The truck was equipped with solid rubber tires which frequently popped from the rims, necessitating their being sent to Los Angeles for repairs, causing considerable delay in their hauling business. A complete set of new tires cost $600.

Sharp competition for the milk and cream developed as four receiving stations and creameries opened to serve the area north of Cayucos in 1910. The Los Angeles Creamery maintained a depot at the George Dickie store, Swift Creamery had a station on Main Street near the Soto Market, with Ed Sutter as manager. Golden State Company, operating under the name of California Creamery and Butter Company, owned a processing plant in Cambria and Morris Salmina was running the Harmony Valley Creamery under the name of Diamond Creamery.

The large corrugated tin building in downtown Cambria, now utilized by various business firms, was first erected in 1912 according to the late George Steiner who helped in its construction. It became the home of the California Creamery. After the building was completed, Steiner became manager for the five years of operation. About two tons of butter were processed each day during the peak season. It was molded into pounds which were cut into cubes, wrapped and shipped by steamer to the retail trade in San Francisco until 1915. After 1915 it was shipped by railroad from San Luis Obispo.

Very little cheese was made as a good cheese maker could not be found. Casein, however, was a major by-product and was sold as a base for water soluble paints. Nick Storni often hauled the casein as far as Cayucos, the end of his regular run, where it was transferred to another truck and hauled into San Luis Obispo. On one trip he picked up a hobo who rode in the rear of the truck with the casein. According to Storni the hobo ate casein all the way to Cayucos, with what results he was never able to determine.

After the Golden State Company closed its Cambria creamery in 1917 Filipponi and Maggoria took over the building and started a cheese factory. They had very poor luck with their curing and went broke by the end of the year. Morris G. Salmina, who was operating a small cheese factory at Cayucos, came to Harmony in 1907 on the invitation of his brother, Paul, owner of a small dairy in Harmony Valley. Salmina established a small cheese making plant and, because the product was so good, he immediately had excellent support from neighboring ranchers.

In 1908 the Nelsons, who owned the property on which the early cheese factory was located, offered to loan the property to Salmina as a better site with more room for installation of equipment and operation. The offer was a gesture which the Nelsons thought would, if accepted, be of considerable benefit to all the ranchers of the area. After some hesitation Salmina accepted the offer with the advice and help of his friend, C. L. Mitchell of San Francisco, previously mentioned. He sought to further improve the quality of his product and to persuade the ranchers to form another co-operative. Operation of two cheese plants, for he still maintained the one at Cayucos, and increased popularity brought more work than he could manage as a private owner.

The dairymen were skeptical of another co-op arrangement as they remembered, all too keenly, the losses they had recently suffered as subscribers to the Home and Cambria Creameries. Through the combined efforts of Mitchell and Salmina they were finally convinced of the advantages a good co-op would bring. In the meantime, Mitchell joined the newly-formed Challenge Creamery and Butter Association in 1910 as their first manager, a position he held until his retirement in 1947. In this new capacity he was able to offer further help to Salmina in the form of advantageous marketing suggestions.

Arrangements for forming the Harmony Valley Creamery Association were completed in 1913 with 22 charter members: Peter and Dante Donati; John, Ulisse and Attilio Filipponi; Peter Bassetti; Vicente, Allessio and Americo Bassi; James and Martin Barlogio; Victor Ricioli; Silvio Maggioli; Galetti brothers; Constantino, Calenti and Peter Brugheli; John D. Fiscalini; Lino Molinari; Constantino Lesnini and Paul Salmina. Morris Salmina continued as manager. In 1915 the association became a subscribing member to the Challenge Creamery and Butter Association with an assured market of all dairy produce members could provide.

In 1921 Carl Hansen of Cambria became the chief cheese and butter maker at the Harmony plant, as well as general superintendent. He learned the trade in Europe and was considered one of the best butter men in this part of the country. Prior to his employment at Harmony, Hansen worked in the Hanford area for a subsidiary of a large Los Angeles creamery, being awarded a gold medal for his proficiency as a butter maker.

Electricity was installed in 1922, and in 1924 the plant was expanded to include the California Polytechnic College operation. In 1930 the processing plant now serving dairymen all through the county was relocated in San Luis Obispo on Broad Street, a more central and economic location for its members. The plant at Harmony Valley was retained as a depot for the collection of milk from the north coast area, from which it was shipped to San Luis Obispo. A small co-op store was maintained at the Harmony plant where dairymen could buy clothing, dairy equipment, canned goods and products manufactured by the creamery. A garage was also maintained in conjunction with the creamery to service trucks and other association equipment, and was occasionally patronized by association members.

Membership reached a peak of 400 subscribers in 1936. In 1964, with the trend from small dairying establishments to large concerns with several hundred milking cows, milk production remained the same but membership dropped to 53. During the last years of plant operation at Harmony 10 men were employed within the plant. Two mechanics, two truck drivers, Hansen and a bookkeeper completed the roster. Cream was processed from dairies located at San Carpoforo Creek in the north to Lompoc in the south. During the green feed months of spring, 10,000 to 12,000 pounds of butter were shipped each day, as well as 3,000 pounds of cheese. In the late summer production dropped off sharply, the heavy part of the season lasting about five months. Mild cheddar, usually made in large molds, was the major cheese produced. A small amount of sharp cheddar was made, but in a family size of three pounds.

The association continued under its affiliation with the Challenge Association until 1956, when the Harmony Valley Creamery Association again became independent, selling most of its output to Foremost Dairies. Cheese and butter making was discontinued in 1958 and the operation switched to handling bulk milk for pasteurization.

As supplemental feeding methods brought year-round milk production, other sections of the county engaged in profitable dairy farming. The Cambria area, less suited to large scale dairy farming due to lack of sufficient permanent pasture fields, began a trend away from the dairy business to resume, once again, the less strenuous job of raising top quality beef cattle.

Swiss Independence Day celebration. Bridge and Main Streets, September, 1911. Albert Music driving team. (Courtesy Mrs. Irma Music Jones)

Rodeo and horsemanship, Phelan Grove, 1910. Sponsored by the Native Sons of the Golden West. (Paul Squibb collection)

Lull, Guthrie and Company store and Western Union and Telegraph office. Butter boxes piled to left. Samuel Guthrie, Wm. Minor, Jim Ford and Mr. Sawyer with his two sons are standing in front. (Paul Squibb collection)

Native Sons of the Golden West, about 1910. Left to right, back row: Judge Gay, Warren Smithers, Elmer S. Rigdon, Fred Cantua, Milton Mayfield, Wm. J. Leffingwell, Will Morss. Bottom row: Ross Soto, Wm. Phillips, E. C. "Boots" Blake, Rafael Hora, J. D. Campbell, Jr., Dr. Percival and Joe Cantua. (Paul Squibb collection)

Part III Early History

Chapter 9

The Portolá Expedition and the Indians

A history of the north coast of San Luis Obispo County is not complete without reviewing events of the 100 years prior to the founding of Cambria. This period began with the Portolá expedition in 1769. As elsewhere in California, the expedition discovered Indians whose existence today is marked only by their indelible imprint upon the land they inhabited. Few farms exist which do not contain evidence of ancient camps or Indian mortar holes. Many homes are built upon soil blackened by Indian use.

These coastal or *Playa* Indians, according to the diaries of expedition members, were gentle, kind and generous. Aside from these qualities they were considered inferior, being of poor physique and lacking the cultural aspects of those encountered further south. As missions were founded they were discovered to have close language affinities to the Indians of the Salinas Valley who were dubbed Salinans by the mission fathers. The coastal Indians were then designated as the *Playa* Salinan to distinguish them from the valley Salinan who differed in dialect and culture patterns.

The first encounter with the *Playa* Indians by the Portolá expedition within the area touched upon by this book was at the mouth of Villa Creek where a small lagoon existed. The Indian camp bordered the creek and lagoon on the rolling hills to the northwest. Fresh water was obtained from a spring issuing from the hillside behind the camp.

Describing the country, Portolá wrote:

On the 9th of September we halted at a lagoon where
a stream came down from the hills. On this day we
(had) encountered six running streams.

Father Juan Crespi, the more inspired writer accompanying
the expedition, says:

We traveled four hours making, at most, three leagues
and crossed eight rivulets which run from the moun-
tains to the sea. We halted at the last in a moderately
wide valley into which enters an estuary, fed by an
arroyo. The hills which surround this valley reach to
the sea on the west and prevent our passage to the
north and northwest.

The league as determined by the missionaries was calculated
according to the speed with which the pack mules could travel
in a given length of time, not by carefully measured distances.

After an overnight halt at this lagoon which the party named
El Estero de Santa Serafina, the expedition, traveling northward
from San Diego in search of Monte Rey Bay, turned inland
from the trek along the seashore as it veered sharply westward
into precipitous mountain cliffs. This decision was taken after
council with returning scouts sent out the evening before. The
route taken by the expedition was always influenced by natural
land formations which channeled them along a predetermined
compass bearing, and by the ease with which a passage could
be made for the 100 heavily burdened pack mules and 67
men. Each day's travel was limited from three to five hours,
thus giving the scouts ample daylight to reconnoiter for the
following day's travel.

From *El Estero de Santa Serafina* the trek continued up the
valley to the north-northwest and, according to Crespi

. . . traveled for a good two and a half hours (Cos-
tanso says 3 leagues). We then left it (the valley), as
we saw that it turned to the north where we discov-
ered a mountainous region covered with pines and a
canyon of great depth whose sides were thickly filled
with trees.

Pursuing our route (NNW) we encountered a large
creek by whose banks we made our halt for the night,

high above the *cañada* (overlooking Santa Rosa Creek).
There came to visit us some 70 *gentiles* of a *ranchería*
which was not far distant from us and they presented
us with bowls of *pinole*, for which we returned beads.
They brought and offered to us a bear cub, which they
had bred up; but we refused it. From this circumstance
soldiers took occasion to name the place *Del Osito*. I
called it *San Benvenuto*.

Portolá, curt and to the point, says:

We marched for two hours through a canyon and have
halted in an arroyo surrounded with hills of pine.

According to these accounts and those of other expedition
diarists it is believed that camp was made overlooking the
present site of Coast Union High School on Santa Rosa Creek.

Following this encampment the party again turned westward
toward the ocean. Engineer Miguel Costanso says:

We went down to the coast which bore to the north-
west, one and a half leagues by good trail, with springs
at every step.

Crespi continues by saying:

We descended to the shore and followed it on a good
trail northwesterly along the cliffs for one and a half
leagues.

Traversing this same approximate distance today, the day's
journey could only have ended at the banks of Pico Creek. They
named the stream *El Cantil* because of the steep bluff of the
creek. The day's journey was slow as the way abounded with
rivulets and creeks whose washed channels "gave much trouble,
as a great deal of labor had to be expended in creating a pas-
sage for the beasts of burden." The seashore was followed be-
cause the higher lands were "extremely broken and rough."

From Pico Creek the route continued more northerly, away
from the uneven and broken shore. September 12, seeing San
Simeon from a distance, they referred to it as a point of land.
Continuing on some distance from the sea, Crespi says:

We then went off to the north northwest crossing sev-
eral valleys and arroyos, three hours. Covered two
leagues and crossed eight watering places. We stopped

on a hill at the edge of a steep valley, which has suffi-
cient water in a deep pool.

Costanso also makes specific mention of the pool of water, and
they all refer to the Indians that came to their camp from a
rancheria not far away, presenting them with gifts of food. They
named the stream *San Vicente*. Today this stream is known as
Arroyo de la Cruz and a large pool of water some distance up
the stream easily identifies it as the expedition's resting place.

On the 13th Portolá says they traveled "three hours over hills
and stopped at the foot of a very large range." Costanso refers
to the resting place as being "at the foot of the sierra where it
reaches the sea." Here they were again approached by Indians
with gifts of food. The party camped for two days while scouts
explored the mountains ahead in search of a passage that would
lead them toward their destination. They had now reached San
Carpoforo Creek. At this point the Indian trail veered inland
and was of no help to them as a guide to Monte Rey Bay. They
named the stream, or actually two streams, for they were en-
camped at the confluence of a small mountain stream and a
large one, *Los Arroyos de Santa Hunuleana*. At this point the
expedition proceeded out of the area with which we are pres-
ently concerned.

The several expedition diaries contain frequent comments
regarding the numerous flowing streams encountered along the
northward route in September; streams with water enough to
make crossing difficult. Also noted was abundance of pine and
marsh area, indicating either an unprecedented rainy season or
a damper climate than known today. On the return journey in
December many more Indians were encountered southward
from San Carpoforo Creek than on the journey in September.

Recent study of Indian camp sites throughout the area in-
dicate these *Playa* Indians maintained seasonal camp sites, mi-
grating inland a few miles during the latter part of summer and
autumn when they utilized ripening acorns, wild berries, seeds
and forest animals for food. As winter advanced they migrated
to banks of streams near the seashore or spring sites along the
bluffs overlooking the ocean where low daylight tides laid bare
the rocks and sandy beaches abundant with easily gathered

sea life. With nets made from roots of marsh plants they snared migratory water fowl wintering on and about the adjacent marshy ponds and stream estuaries. As spring appeared some family groups scattered a short distance up streams and the populace devoted increasing attention to a diet of green plants, roots and young rodents.

So, as Portolá passed northward in the late summer it is noted he met more Indians at the points touched furthest from the sea than during the trek along the shore. On the return in winter, he found Indians encamped on seashore and estuary bluffs.

The casual and friendly nature the Indians displayed toward the Spaniards has been accepted as an indication they were not ignorant of the existence of other radically different people. During the 250 years prior to Portolá's appearance records indicate both Chinese and Spanish ships infrequently touched on California shores, some came involuntarily, disabled and wafted ashore by wind and the Japan current and undoubtedly with survivors, others by deliberate voyage. Among the better known voyagers were Sir Francis Drake, who landed for several weeks just north of San Francisco Bay to make extensive repairs to his ship in 1579 and who may have touched shore at other areas along the more southern portions of the coast; Sebastian Cermeno, whose ship was wrecked and stranded on the California coast in 1595; Juan Cabrillo, who is reputed to have landed men for water and supplies at both El Moro and the Bay of Sardines or San Simeon Bay in 1542; and Vizcaino, who made a coastal exploration and noted the Indians of the Santa Barbara area in 1602. Fortunately these early, friendly contacts, carried in story and legend, produced no fear or alarm when Portolá and his men appeared.

After the expedition returned to San Diego others soon determined, through additional exploration, that travel to Monte Rey Bay and San Francisco was easier and swifter through the inner coastal valleys; the missions were established to accord.

The founding fathers of the missions concentrated first upon converting the Indians in the immediate vicinity of the mission sites. Communication with Indians along the north coast of San

Luis Obispo County area was slight following the founding of Mission San Antonio de Padua in 1771, and San Luis Obispo de Tolusa in 1772 until neophytes could be trained and used to recruit new groups for teaching. By the time Mission San Antonio sent her recruits to the coast over steep and rugged Indian trails traversing the Santa Lucia mountain range, the coastal Indians were swiftly succumbing to disease spread by expedition soldiers. The few who survived were quickly gathered into the folds of the mission compound.

Seafood from the coast was also sought to supplement the early mission diet. Indian runners were sent to the coast daily to gather shell fish during favorable seasons. The land, marked by several tall, gleaming, white bird-inhabited rocks at the water's edge, was granted to the mission as grazing land and designated Rancho de Piedra Blanca, Ranch of the White Rock.

As Mission San Miguel de Archangel, established in 1779, sought timber suitable for beams in the mission structure, tall cedar and hardy pine were found growing several miles distant on the coastal slope of the mountain range several miles west of the mission. Indians were dispatched to clear and construct a cart trail adequate to haul logs from the headwaters of Santa Rosa Creek. Trees, ample water and good pasture from the mission westward induced the padres to ask for land grants encompassing the area. Their request was acknowledged and Rancho San Simeon and Rancho Santa Rosa became part of the vast mission San Miguel holdings which extended eastward to Cholame. The crude cart trail was extended to the ocean and to the bay of San Simeon. By the time Mission San Miguel was ready to recruit Indians from the coastal area, few remained. Mission records would indicate that no *Playa* Salinan continued to live outside mission compounds after 1800.

It is only from scanty notations in these early mission records, and archaeological discoveries that we are able to piece together a vague picture of the people once populating the coastal lands between Cayucos and the Santa Lucias where they descend to meet the sea. Indications are that they had few artistic qualities as might be manifested in clothing and implement decoration or design. Their durable tools were crudely made, their prime skill lying in the fashioning of basketry and nets. Accumulation of household articles was prohibited by their migratory pattern. Scant clothing and housing of brush or lean-to shelters gave them poor protection from the elements. The neighboring Chumash Indians to the south, and the Salinan and Yokut Indians eastward, spoke belittlingly of them and associated with them only on trade missions, the principal items of exchange being abalone shell, fresh seafood and flints. Their habits, both in their native habitat and at the missions, were considered slovenly and dirty though the few who survived to reside at the missions are spoken of as intelligent.

Their peaceful nature indicated a strong bond between husband and wife and abounding love for the children who were never punished, the parents exercising extreme patience and commiseration toward their family members. Despite a general slovenliness and dirty appearance, they were noted for exceptional cleanliness about their food. Shamans had an excellent knowledge of medicinal herbs which was often adapted for use by the padres. Social life was simple and limited. Gambling was an obsession as they were observed to often stake everything on a single game of chance. They enjoyed their music and dance, which was less expressive and lacked the color of other tribes.

Ceremonies for the dead and burial seem to have included either cremation or full inhumation with very few or no grave goods. Affection for the dead was fully expressed by ritual wailing and mourning. Government, such as existed among them, was patrilineal. Of their original religious beliefs or tendency, little is known with certainty. Families were bound to each other by inter-relationship strongly dominated by common customs, rituals and legends.

Mission notations indicate the padres' fervent desire to teach and impress the Catholic religion upon the Indian to the complete exclusion of his own cultural background, whatever it might have been. These padres had no ingrained interest in their pre-mission history or ethnology and the Indians soon realized that any information about themselves sought by the padres was desired only for the purpose of ridicule; and they learned to tell them nothing or appease them with false stories.

The *Playa* Indians remaining in the missions after the year 1800, without familial and tribal ties and rituals, continued to degenerate to become completely dependent on the white man. The younger generation inter-married with Indians from other areas, completing the loss of their *Playano* identity.

A canonical decree from Spain in 1813 made it mandatory for the padres to record pre-mission facts concerning the Indians. The few notations concerning the *Playano* come from these records, too late to reap the rich harvest of stories and legends they could have given had the missions fathers been interested in them as human individuals from their first encounter.

Well worn Indian trails existed along the coast and through the many valleys which were used for intra and inter-tribal communication. Trails still exist over which trade goods were transported on a travois or stretcher-like device, two arms of which were fastened to a shoulder or a head harness while the other two dragged on the ground behind.

Trails led north northeast from San Carpoforo Valley to the San Antonio River area, others crossed the mountain range after passing through San Simeon and Santa Rosa Creek valleys to intersect with mountain ridge trails running north and southward, and still others descended eastward to connect with the tribes of the Central California valleys. A notable trail proceeded through Harmony Valley to intersect the Spanish named *Cienega Trail*, still marked on county maps, leading through the Cienega (marsh) Valley. The coastal trail was well marked when Portolá arrived. The route was often adhered to, deviation taken only when necessary for an easier passage for the beasts of burden or for a more direct bearing toward his destination.

Redistribution of mixed groups of trusted Indians to the coastal outposts was practiced by the padres of San Miguel Mission who needed their labor for maintaining herds and tilling the land. When ranchos Piedra Blanca, San Simeon and Santa Rosa were reopened for grant, it was this mixture of Indians relocated on the lands which fell under domination of the Dons.

Chapter 10

The Development of Coast Trade

The first missions in cental California were founded immediately after the Portolá expedition of 1769. All equipment and supplies, by law, had to come from Mexico or Spain in Spanish vessels or pack mules over long and hazardous trails.

The problem of securing the simplest tools and supplies was a major one for the founding fathers. The initial supplies of seed and small tools were brought direct from Mexico by pack trains. Orders were sent to Spain for more supplies by way of Mexico and the returning muleteers or accompanying soldiers. Spanish ships were slow and unreliable. When they did arrive, their cargos for the central California missions were discharged at Monterey Bay or San Francisco Bay, the cargos distributed and carried by pack mule or on the backs of Indians or, if livestock, driven over the Indian trails to their destination.

Following delivery of the most essential items which included seed grain, breeding stock, tools and a few items for religious instruction and worship, the Spanish government expected the missions to establish themselves and to become self sufficient without further help. It is no wonder the padres felt additional early support was needed. Many promises of help were made by the Church in both Mexico and Spain. However, such promises as the padres received did not materialize.

From the beginning, commercial contact with foreign vessels, which followed on the heels of the Spanish colonization, was strictly forbidden. Spain insisted that all trade must be reserved exclusively for her own ships. In spite of this manditory decree,

Spain failed to send trading ships with supplies to satisfy the basic needs of either the colonists or the missions, though rich trade was awaiting them in the form of otter skins, a trade already being exploited by Russians who were commercializing along the American north Pacific coasts.

In urgent need of additional supplies, if they were to continue their task of converting the Indians to the Catholic faith, the padres encouraged the hunting of sea otter by the Indians and lost no time in contacting foreign ships whose men landed frequently along the beaches, themselves hunting and taking these plentiful animals. The captains were not only glad to trade for the skins but welcomed fresh produce from mission gardens.

In spite of the limited variety of products along the coast at the close of the eighteenth century, strong interest was now evidenced in California trade by enterprising British concerns. These concerns had already developed an extensive and profitable business with South America. Eastern firms engaged in a lucrative trade with the Orient showed similar interest.

Under the rigid management of the padres several of the missions were able to build up a quantity of surplus products by 1800. In an effort to enforce her shipping laws and prevent further illegal trade by these rich missions, Spain fortified the major California ports with garrisons and strategically placed cannon. Due to the scarcity of soldiers and her own neglect in sending adequate supplies, the lesser ports and vast stretches of coast line could not be protected against foreign contact nor the coastal waters adequately patroled.

At first the major shipping companies were inclined to proceed cautiously. They had large vessels often laden with costly goods from China and their interests along the north Pacific coast were secondary to the China trade. To enter a major California port for ship's supplies or repair entailed risk of seizure by the Spanish because of illegal cargo taken enroute along the coast. Few captains tried entry except in extreme emergency. However, the independent, smaller vessels which often made repairs on cove beaches had no such restrictions and regarded the Spanish government with contempt. Captains of these ships took delight in playing hide and seek with authorities as they sought trade wherever inhabitants could be contacted. These small ships were easily handled near shore and in small coves, the principal danger being the chance they might suffer some serious damage and find it necessary to seek a legitimate port for help. These ships often remained away from their home port for two years.

Few of the coves and sandy beach landings had common names at this early date. Sea captains, entering the ship's activities in their logs, seldom made reference to specific landings. In the log of the Schooner *Lelia Byrd* the captain recorded, during the year 1804-05, "We entered the lesser ports of California . . .", obviously referring to the unguarded landings where he carried on his smuggling. About this same time Captain William Shaler wrote concerning Morro Bay, which he called Bernard's Bay:

> A very commodious anchorage . . . well sheltered against prevailing winds . . . also protected from southerly gales by a reef and the holding ground is good . . . The bay is unknown to the Spaniards.

By 1813 both English and American ships had developed a flourishing business. The schooners *Flora* and *Eagle* out of Lima, Peru, sailing for British concerns, were also picking up hides, tallow, grain, wine and otter skins in exchange for manufactured goods, primarily cloth. Larger vessels had adopted a ruse which worked fairly well for some time. As a limited amount of trade was permitted these vessels in legitimate ports they would pick up commodities bearing the minimum export duties. Receiving clearance papers they set sail southward, apparently headed for their home port, only to be met off-shore through previous arrangement by boats or smaller ships loaded with contraband. When they left the California coast they were well loaded with hides and other products. With clearance papers from the northern port they would sail into more southern ports for additional supplies of water and food, exhibit the previously obtained papers, and proceed without additional inspection.

Soon after 1800 Mission San Antonio de Padua and Mission San Miguel secured official possession of large parcels of coastal lands west of their mission locations which were respectively on the San Antonio and Salinas Rivers. The missions wanted these coastal lands, not only for their rich and productive nature, a fact they emphasized in their request for the property, but also because of the advantages these particular lands offered for a profitable, surreptitious coast trade. Ideally located as they were many miles from any official port, these lands contained numerous sandy beaches which were perfect for landing and embarking cargo. Thus San Simeon Bay, as well as nearby areas, was used frequently to the advantage of these missions, particularly Mission San Miguel.

The Spanish governor of California, well aware of the complete disregard for Spanish trade laws by both ships and inhabitants of the territory, was helpless in his attempts to control the trade. He fully understood the reasons behind its success and, in all probability, was actually in sympathy with the colonists who were so grossly neglected by their native country.

Following the revolt of Mexico against Spanish domination, Governor Sola was enthusiastic when, in 1822, William Petty Hartnell and Hugh McCulloch, partners of the shipping firm by that name operating out of Liverpool, England, and Lima, Peru, approached him and the Prefect, Payeras, with a proposal for a formal government agreement permitting trade contracts with the missions for hides and tallow. Sola expressed it as "an opportunity for which we have been waiting." He felt that such an agreement would aid in controlling the extensive smuggling carried on by the mission fathers, as well as help enrich the coffers of the treasury of California. Hartnell and McCulloch also felt they were gaining a strong advantage over other trading vessels by having this exclusive and binding contract with the wealthy missions, acceptance of which would obligate all contracting parties to a three-year term beginning January 1, 1823. The finalized agreement stipulated that ships were to pick up goods from all legitimate ports from San Francisco to San Diego. Hides for the English market and tallow for the South American market were the principal objects of trade. Of secondary interest were soap, horse hair, horn, brined beef, *manteca* (lard), *aguardiente* (brandy) and wheat. A price scale for each item was arranged, hides being valued at one peso each and an *arroba* or 25 pounds of tallow at two pesos.

San Antonio de Padua Mission, located well inland and with its coastal lands still undeveloped, agreed to the general terms of the contract, but San Miguel Mission refused to enter into any such formal agreement, saying they preferred to supply such produce as they might have on hand when the boats arrived. Obviously, they already had well established contacts with the illegal coasting vessels which picked up the produce of the mission on the shores of the ranchos on which it was raised. Nevertheless, San Miguel was instructed to take its produce to the "harbor near San Luis Obispo," which is now called Port San Luis. This port was neither convenient to the mission on the Salinas River nor to its coastal ranchos.

San Antonio Mission was requested to transport its products to Santa Cruz above Monterey, this being the closest point north along the coast which could be easily reached from the interior valley. Other points, while closer as determined by a straight line, were difficult to reach due to the high, rugged mountains without passes. Other missions, less able to make their own contacts, were happy to sign the contract, supplying as many as 1000 hides a year, as well as specified quantities of other items.

Three ships were to visit the coast each year. To save the expense of sending large vessels of 200 tons burden up and down the coast to pick up hides and produce, the company compromised, sending the *Young Tartar,* a small 50-ton schooner, to the coast for fast trips from depot to depot. When filled, it unloaded into larger vessels kept at anchor in Monterey Bay, San Pedro and San Diego. Other early company ships participating in the Pacific trade included the *John Begg, Bahia Packet, Neptune, Hebe, Pizarro, Esther, Junis, Speedy, Eliza and Inca.*

Prior to shipment, hides were lowered over ocean bluffs to the beaches where they were soaked in sea water, scraped and pegged to dry. When dry they were folded once with the hair side out, and stacked ready for delivery to the awaited schooner. On board ship they were heavily salted and stored with the aid of jackscrews to compress them. A brig of 160 tons was capable of storing 14,000 hides while a three-masted schooner of 360 tons could hold 40,000 hides.

A large percentage of the merchandise purchased by the early missions and by the Spanish Dons, who received Spanish grants as early as 1820, came from China as the ships of the China trade plied back and forth between California and the Orient. This profitable Pacific interchange eliminated frequent dangerous, costly and time consuming trips around Cape Horn.

Silks, dishes, furniture and chests were among the most popular items from China which were sold to the Dons. The beautiful "Spanish chests" so highly prized by the Doñas originated in China. They were covered with California hides which were tooled and dyed in the Orient before being placed over the aromatic camphorwood from which the chests were made.

Trade items carried specifically for the missions included costly articles for the religious services and furnishings for the mission: holy images, gold and silver thread for embroidery of frontals, capes, altar cloths and hangings, gold and silver lace, musical instruments such as horns, violins and flutes, books, sacred games, gun powder, carpets, window glass, general merchandise of cotton and linen cloth, thread, needles and buttons, knives, culinary utensils of copper and iron, wearing apparel of all types, agricultural implements, and food products which included rice, coffee, sugar and chocolate.

The contract negotiated by McCullock and Hartnell soon caused other Anglo-American traders and those from Peru to make greater efforts for coastal trade with and without agreements with the California governor. Among these competitors was Captain George Newell of the schooner *Mentor*, who wrote in his ship's log on July 30, 1824:

> We arrived from the north at San Luis after running
> into every berth along the shore.

While mentioning no names he clearly indicated the use of the small coves and landings in obtaining his cargo; coves and landings which were illegal "drops." The firm of Bryant and Sturgis with their vessel *Sachem*, by offers of cash and higher prices, was able to buy up every hide they could find at the drops along the beaches and cliffs and in the bays and harbors.

Captain David Spence, when writing the chronicles of his sailing days, said he "did a great deal of coastal smuggling between 1834 and 1842." And F. W. Beechy, writing in 1831, emphasized the value of California mission horses for trade, there being a good demand for them in Hawaii where the schooners stopped for fresh supplies before proceeding on to the Orient with their cargo of hides and otter skins. Other items listed by Beechy as being in demand by the missions at that time included salt, carts and deal boards—a fine quality of lumber, usually fir or pine.

Following secularization of the missions by Mexico, trade laws became less rigid and a brisk trade with the colorful sailing vessels at unscheduled drops continued to flourish along the coast as large land grants were given to Spanish gentlemen who also established cattle on previously unused land.

With increased American immigration into the newly formed state (1850), regular and frequent runs into San Simeon Bay were soon established. Beginning about 1850 a very crude cart road was developed over the horse trail from San Luis Obispo to San Simeon Bay which connected the various Mexican and Spanish grants along the coast and, during favorable weather, permitted limited hauling of produce to the centralized, protected deep water landing of San Simeon Bay. Because the ox cart trail was impassable much of the year, several of the most convenient drops and landings on the sandy beaches continued in use for another 20 years.

Mariano Estrada, father of the Estrada brothers who settled in San Luis Obispo County, offers an example of the extravagance of these early Dons in adorning themselves and their families. It is recorded that Mariano paid the equivalent of $600 for a tortoise shell comb for his wife. It was purchased in the 1820's from an American sea captain by the name of Henry Fitch. Three other Dons also purchased similar combs at the time, and for the same price.

Other forms of extravagance were shown in their clothes. It was the habit of most of the Dons to wear shoes of deer skin embroidered with gold and silver, and breeches of velvet or satin cloth reaching to the knees. These were bordered with gold braid and silver buttons. The breeches were open part way on the sides to show full under drawers of white linen. A vest of velvet or silk was worn, and over it was a short jacket of blue, black or green cloth embroidered in gold or silver thread. A gay sash of red satin and a wide sombrero heavily embroidered and with a cord of gold or silver encircling the crown, completed the costume.

The women wore silk and satin dresses, gold necklaces, and earrings set with pearls. The chemise had short embroidered sleeves and was richly trimmed in lace. A full, gathered muslin skirt flounced with scarlet and secured at the waist with a silk sash, shoes of velvet and blue satin, and a cotton scarf over the hair completed their costume. Some also wore costly shawls.

This same extravagance continued with the succeeding generation. Don Julian Estrada, owner of Rancho Santa Rosa after secularization of Mission San Miguel, obtained his lavishly adorned saddles and other finery, as well as rancho furnishings, by schooner, just as the padres had done before him. Occasionally he had many of his long horned cattle driven over the trails to San Francisco markets as during the gold rush fresh beef there was extremely high. To supply this demand Don Julian found it expedient to dispose of some of his cattle this way. Primarily, however, he dealt in hides shipped by way of the schooners plying the coast for trade. The arrival date was announced in advance by a courier who rode forth from a previous port of call. Apprised of the impending arrival, rancho produce was lowered over the cliffs to the beach and a lookout stationed nearby who watched for sign of the approaching schooner.

In 1854 Captain John Wilson received half interest in the portion of Rancho Piedra Blanca surrounding San Simeon Bay. He may have thought the bay would soon develop into a major port of call because of the protected deepwater anchorage available there. However, transportation from nearby areas was more difficult than using established areas along the cliffs. So few people lived near the bay a scheduled schooner call was impractical. For many years after Don José de Jésus Pico received this rancho only two of his sons lived on it besides the necessary Indian and Mexican *vaqueros* who did the work. They lived scattered about the vast holdings and traded with the schooners only when hides were ready to ship from various sites along the 14-mile ocean frontage. Prearranged shipments into and out of

San Simeon Bay, as elsewhere, required no storage facilities. Local contact with areas beyond the ranchos was by foot or horseback over mountain trails, eliminating any major effort to transport sufficient produce to warrant a regular port of call.

By 1860, however, trade in and out of San Simeon Bay was comparatively brisk due to the large number of Americans who, in three years' time, had settled on land behind the ranchos in the Santa Lucia mountains. Some also located on land recently included in public domain lands between Santa Rosa and San Simeon Ranchos. Still others working as laborers on the ranchos increased the population. With the advent of more people the horse trails soon widened to accommodate carts and wagons for the hauling of supplies and produce.

William Leffingwell, Sr., who arrived in 1858, settled on coastal land between the aforementioned ranchos. An enterprising business man, he sought to add to his own income by the establishment of a beach landing on his own property which would accommodate the many people pouring into the San Simeon Creek area. This became known as Leffingwell Landing, located at the intersection of the coast trail and wagon road from San Luis Obispo to San Simeon Bay and the trail which came from the east and down San Simeon Creek. The beach, here, was considered ideal for the discharge of produce or merchandise. The people who lived in the back country appreciated the saving in distance of about eight miles (round trip) and the crossing of several creeks that the new landing afforded.

Fine timber, including fir and redwood, for the building of homes was floated to the landing from ships anchored some distance off shore. Commodities which could be packed in barrels and tins were floated ashore in nets. Other things were brought ashore by row boat. Passengers embarking from this point waded out to the row boats for transport to the larger vessel. A similar procedure was practiced at San Simeon Bay, the difference being that the schooner could anchor in sheltered water. During high or rough seas passengers could not be loaded or discharged at Leffingwell Landing. Those passing from ship to shore at San Simeon frequently resorted to the use of the bos'n chair in rough weather, landing on overhanging cliffs.

Piedras Blancas, the name given to the white rocks used as roosts by numerous sea birds, situated eight miles north of San Simeon Bay, was one of the first "recognized" (official) landings in the north coast area in the early 1850's, according to county records. It was located on the lee side of the point jutting toward the rocks. The water was deep and in good weather small coasting vessels were able to put in close to shore to discharge freight at a small dock constructed for the convenience of residents at the nearby Pacheco adobe, and ranchers who later purchased or leased land from Juan Castro, administrator of the Pacheco properties (properties inherited by Mariano Pacheco from his stepfather, Captain Wilson).

Many early sea captains seemed to develop a sixth sense, sailing in and out of unmarked harbors and landings at night or in fog with surprising safety and confidence. Prior to installation of the lighthouse at Piedras Blancas Point the weekly *Tribune* of the time states that Captain Alexander of the steamship *San Luis* brought supplies to the small pier there "in fog so thick it might have been cut into quarter sections."

For several years prior to any wharf construction the steamer *Active*, under the guidance of Captain Bogart, made regular though infrequent trips into San Simeon Bay until county permission for construction of the first commercial wharf in the county was granted to Captain Joseph Clark, owner of the whaling station at San Simeon Point, and George Hearst in 1868. The first wharf rates in the county were set up by the Board of Supervisors for this pier on August 15 of the same year. Prediction for the success of the enterprise was good as shipping in and out of the bay was increasing rapidly due to mining activities in the vicinity, and it was apparent that the San Simeon beach landing was

> dangerous to human life and expensive and trouble-
> some for unloading of merchandise because of the
> strong swell coming in and rolling against the shore.

When work on the pier was finally started in 1869 Grant, Lull and Company of Cambria was admitted as a full partner. The site chosen for construction was some distance seaward from the flensing wharf, already constructed and used exclusively for processing whales, near the extremity of the point. This site was chosen primarily for the convenience of sailing ships which were the main ships still frequenting the coast. Here they could put up to the pier in calm weather and pick up a good breeze when ready to leave. Cost of construction was estimated at approximately $3,000. The warehouse was built by Grant, Lull and Company and the operation of the wharf was under their supervision, at least part of the time.

Wharfage fees were collected on all animals and produce shipped out of the harbor by means of the boat landing for six months prior to construction of the pier. Likewise, all merchandise coming into the harbor was taxed. Some of the rates charged at that time were: General merchandise, including storage for one month when necessary, $1 per ton; wool, $1.50 per ton; 50 cents per horse, mule or ass; 25 cents for each head of cattle; 10 cents per head of hogs, calves and sheep except where the number exceeded 49, then the price dropped to 6¼ cents per head. Two horse vehicles cost $1, four horse, $2 each.

In 1870, shortly after construction of the pier in San Simeon Bay, P. A. Forrester and F. F. Letcher of Cambria purchased a small piece of land one and a half miles north of the town from William and Warren C. Rickard at the mouth of what is now known as Leffingwell Creek. They applied for a wharf franchise and beach privileges on a 10-year basis and established a landing for the discharge of lumber and freight. This location was especially convenient for residents of Cambria. This new landing seems to have taken the place of the old Leffingwell Landing to the north.

Previously the Rickards had applied for a wharf franchise at this site but did nothing about construction after receiving it. The sales and transactions dealing with the Rickard properties are, at most, hazy due to various attachments, sheriff's sales, etc. In any event, Forrester and Letcher did not make use of the wharf franchise other than to collect wharfage on beach landings and Leffingwell ended up with the property and with the franchise originally offered to the Rickards. However, while the Rickard brothers had the property they built the first store on the coast and handled some merchandise. Later Leffingwell erected a small warehouse in conjunction with the store, using both for storage only. In 1964 foundation remnants and other debris were located at the site of the old store on the south bluff of Leffingwell Creek overlooking the cove.

In 1874 William Leffingwell, Sr., and J. C. Baker purchased the land and the Rickard franchise. These men started construction of a pier which was variously called Leffingwell Pier and Leffingwell Wharf, together with the old appellation, Leffingwell Landing. Oxen, still much in use, aided in handling piling and timbers during construction of the pier. On November 7, 1874, the weekly *Tribune* reported:

> The wharf being constructed within one and a half miles of Cambria . . . has not yet been completed but boats can lay alongside in safety. The pier is to be extended another 200 feet in a few months. Mining companies are already shipping all freight over this pier.

The pier measured 300 feet in length and had a storehouse 60 by 20 feet at the head. At low tide a ship was still safe in 13 feet of water. The first coaster came along side the pier in August of 1874 at which time the community had

> a big celebration and speeches, after which the crowd went trout fishing up San Simeon Creek and caught 15 strings of fish.

Lumber ships bringing in redwood and fir were considerably bigger and less easily maneuvered than the coasters. They anchored off-shore and floated the lumber into the beach, as was done prior to the construction of the pier. An addition was soon made and on February 20, 1875, the *Tribune* noted:

> The pier is now 400 feet long and on January 26, during a heavy northwester the steamship *Twin Sisters* moored alongside, discharged 120,000 feet of lumber and loaded 2,500 sacks of barley, potatoes and wheat in three days. If the pier extended another 100 feet the regular steamers could make landings.

Meantime, use of the new pier at San Simeon was proving as hazardous as the beach landing had been due to the heavy rolling swells about the point. Ships refused to use the facility for fear of battering themselves to pieces and continued to discharge cargo in the previous manner. The *Tribune* noted in 1875 that, again, "lighters are required in loading and discharging cargo." In 1877 Leffingwell reapplied for the wharf franchise at Leffingwell Creek, this time under the name of himself and his two sons, William, Jr., and Adam C., as partners.

According to the late Deville Bovee, who lived at the headwaters to San Simeon Creek, the warehouse stood at the south side of the cove and the wharfinger lived in a house on the north bluff. A flat to the south was also used for lumber storage. During the latter years the pier was in use, none of the lumber ships pulled to the pier but moored to an anchored log 600 feet off shore and floated the lumber into the beach. Pickets and posts were loaded at Gorda and transported to the landing for local use, as were the fine grades of lumber shipped from more northern ports.

This landing and wharf continued in business until 1894 when, according to Clayton L. Morss, the schooner *Electra*, after discharging a load of lumber, was blown on the rocks while trying to pull free and sail away. The ship was a total loss, as was most of the cargo on board. Morss, in relating his experiences about the wharf, said that, as far as he could remember, a barrel of sugar and a dog were all that were rescued from the ship other than the seamen. He doubted if little else was saved. By 1900 no landing or pier remained though the Leffingwells frequently erected a tent at the site and had picnics there.

Construction of a new, relocated pier at San Simeon Bay by George Hearst in 1878, and improvement of roads from Cambria and San Simeon Creek, gradually drew most of the shipping to that point. When the Leffingwell Pier was abandoned it was primarily due to lack of business caused by the unprotected position of the structure and the dangerous rocks on either side.

Hearst built his pier at the site of his San Simeon subdivision (see Chapter 13) which, in 1878, was a thriving community. The construction cost $20,000 and was far more elaborate than the dangerous affair built nine years earlier. The new pier, 20 feet wide, extended 750 feet from shore, widening to 50 feet for another 250 feet seaward. A set of steel tracks and wheeled platforms on the pier transported merchandise to and from a

48 by 100 foot warehouse on shore at the head of the pier.

By the time Hearst built his pier many of the coastal sailing ships had been replaced by steam. The location of the pier deep in the bay and to the lee of sheltering cliffs offered safe docking for steamers whose only concern was the high swell, moderated in-shore by deep water at the end of the pier. Primarily, the worst swells occurred in winter during the southwest winds.

Other fruitless attempts were made to construct commercial wharves in the vicinity of Cambria shortly after 1900. One, known as the Cambria County Wharf at the mouth of Santa Rosa Creek, was nearing completion in 1908 when a storm demolished the structure. The wharf was never rebuilt and the county was several years in paying for the $21,240 loss. Another small wharf called Russell Wharf was started but there is no record of its having been completed or put into use. These last feeble efforts to capture sea trade near the town of Cambria were doomed by changing times, even before they were started.

The gasoline truck and convenience of the Southern Pacific Railroad at San Luis Obispo decreased shipping and quickly took away the county's dependence on ocean transport. It completely changed the economy of the San Luis Obispo north coast which, until this time, due to its easy access to steamer for the shipment of mine and farm products, was able to maintain a position and reputation in the county second only to San Luis Obispo, both from the standpoint of population and tax value. Without the regular scheduled arrival of steamers, which stopped altogether in 1915, Cambria and the surrounding area were forced into a role of isolation due to inadequate, poorly maintained overland roads that discouraged visitation and investment, especially after the close of World War I. One of the last ships to make San Simeon a port of call was the steamship *Aurelia* which unloaded lumber there in 1916.

Abalone drying at San Simeon, about 1904, under operation of Lorin V. Thorndyke, Jr. (Courtesy Ralph Morgan, editor of *The Cambrian*)

I. Yamamoto established his own yard at the mouth of Leffiingwell Creek. (Paul Squibb collection)

Cambria County wharf was nearing completion in 1907 when a storm demolished the structure.

Site of original Leffingwell Landing where timber and cargo were floated ashore for early pioneers living along San Simeon Creek.

Chapter 11

Rancho de la Piedra Blanca

Of the three large Mexican grants affecting the history of Cambria, Rancho de la Piedra Blanca, or Ranch of the White Rock, is undoubtedly considered by most historians to be romantically the most interesting and enduring. Certainly the famous names of the Pico family, Captain John D. Wilson, the Pachecos, the Castros and the Hearsts which are linked with this rancho will continue to appear in the history books of California for many years to come.

Set forth here are some of the lesser known facts relative to these families and the rancho, many of which were eventually conducive to the founding and growth of Cambria.

The fertile abundance and "salubrious climate" of the region and its generous aboriginal inhabitants were briefly described in the diaries of various members of the Portolá expedition as they passed northward along the coast in search of the "port de Monte Rey" in 1769, so named on the map of 1840-42 drafted by cartographer Eugene Duflot de Mofras. Ample food for man and beast, numerous running streams, an abundance of fire wood, all made the area immediately south of San Carpoforo Creek a prize coveted by Junipero Serra and the founding fathers shortly after the establishment of Mission San Antonio de Padua, situated to the northeast of San Antonio River, in 1771.

A cluster of tall, white, glistening rocks occupied by countless sea birds stood off the shore of this fair land. So prominent were these rocks that they could be seen for many miles at sea and easily spotted from the high ridge of the coastal range. It was only natural to refer to the area as the land of the white rock and to make it the title of the land when it was officially annexed to the mission.

Freezing, often sparse, winters at the mission soon prompted the padres to dispatch Indian runners to the coastal property for the collection of sea foods to supplement their early meager diets. Finally, a continuous intercourse with the coast provided a daily supply of fresh fish and small game. The aboriginal Indians were quickly gathered into the folds of the mission, and Indian life on the coast, as the Portolá expedition first saw it, soon disappeared.

Selected spots along the bluffs were used for preparing large quantities of shell fish for easy transport over the rough mountain trails to the mission. Shells were removed from clams and mussels which gathered into large heaps in a few years. The raw flesh was placed in baskets carried across the shoulders or, if the load was large, on poles which were dragged behind the runners. Steep mountain trails made going difficult. Small rest camps were established along the way beside small springs where quick meals were prepared and short rests taken before continuing rapidly on the way. The narrow passes, rugged mountain terrain and scarcity of pasture between the mission and the coast were not conducive to the construction of a cart road or the driving of mission cattle to the coast fields. Probably, for this reason, the mission never established as close a contact with the land as it had once thought of doing. Besides, pasture for the horses, cattle and sheep was soon found to be sufficiently abundant in the valleys about the mission.

The decay of San Antonio Mission and its feeble grasp upon the wild, now uninhabited coast land began with the enactment of the Secularization Laws in 1833, which put into process the gradual removal of land and power from all the California missions. Don José de Jésus Pico was appointed administrator of Mission San Antonio in 1838. As the lands were released for redistribution, Pico was in an ideal position to place a first bid for the rancho on the coast. He immediately appealed to Governor Juan B. Alvarado. His request was granted January 18, 1840, as a reward for the part he played in the overthrow of Spanish rule. He was awarded all of the land south of San Carpoforo Creek to the Arroyo del Morena, and east from the ocean at high tide to the summit of the Santa Lucia mountains, an area later described as containing 48,805 acres, or nearly 136 square miles.

Pico, born in Monterey in 1807, was a cousin of Pio Pico who served as temporary governor of Alta California in 1845, and the son of José Dolores Pico, a Mexican soldier who came to California in 1790 as the son of Santiago Pico of Sinaloa, Mexico. Don José de Jésus Pico grew up in the Spanish-Mexican surroundings of Monterey, early seat of California government. He became thoroughly familiar with the uncertain politics of the time, as well as with the aristocracy and military leaders. From 1827 to 1831 he served as a regular soldier in the Monterey Company, taking part in the Solis revolts of 1828-29. As scion of a family which had grown in favor in California politics as well as in wealth, Don José was able to finance a substitute for his place in the service while he temporarily retired to Rancho Bolsa de San Cayetaño, a Spanish grant acquired by his father in 1819 as pay for his military service to the Spanish government.

In 1836 Don José again returned to active duty, taking part in Alvarado's revolution. His appointment to the administratorship at San Antonio was his reward for earlier military services. While still in residence at the Mission, but shortly after receipt of Rancho Piedra Blanca, Pico was visited by the young French cartographer and historian, Eugene Duflot de Mofras, who was compiling a map of western North America, primarily the Pacific coastal area. While staying at San Antonio Mission he secured accurate information about San Simeon Bay and the coast of Piedra Blanca Rancho from Pico, undoubtedly making a personal trip to the properties. During his sojourn at the mission, and probably because of continued inquiries for more information which seemed irrelevant to Pico, together with his typical French personality, Pico deemed him insane and slapped him into the mission prison where he treated him cruelly. He also made many disparaging remarks about the man. Fortunately, others about the mission were not of Pico's opinion and were able, surreptitiously, to release him.

The publication of the de Mofras map in 1844, together with his volume of historical notes, was a credit to the young man, fully attesting to his sanity and ability. On his map, de Mofras noted that the Bay of San Simeon was used as a regular anchorage. He also noted the San Miguel Mission outpost to the south of the bay on San Simeon Creek. This is the first known map to record these features.

Following the completion of his administratorship at San Antonio Mission, Pico was appointed to take over duties of administration at San Miguel Mission in 1841. Don José, now married to Doña Gabriella Villa, established a home in San Luis Obispo for his wife and children, known as Casa Grande. He also stocked Rancho Piedra Blanca with long horned Spanish cattle and set trusted Indians to watch his property. In order to retain his grant, Mexican law required him to establish a home on the property, plant an orchard and stock it with animals. All of these things were soon accomplished. His adobe home was constructed in a well sheltered spot a short distance from the ocean, on the bank of a creek three miles south of San Simeon Bay. Following the erection of his rancho home, this creek became known as Pico's Creek—later, Pico Creek.

The Don spent little time on the rancho. It was considered remote as no land between it and Mission San Miguel was occupied nor were other rancho grants to the south occupied by their new owners. Relocated mission Indians and a few Mexican *vaqueros* were the only inhabitants of these north coastal lands. Periodically, an Indian runner was dispatched to convey messages to Pico concerning welfare of his cattle and rancho. Don Pico made a special effort to visit his rancho twice a year when cattle were branded or slaughtered to personally supervise and count his stock or tally the hides as they were prepared for trade with the schooners that picked them up at various convenient "drops" along the 14 miles of coast bordering his rancho.

In 1844 Pico finished his duties at San Miguel. He rejoined the military by taking part in the movement against the Mexican governor, José Manuel Micheltorena, emerging as Captain of the Defensors. After this he settled with his family at San Luis Obispo and was appointed to the office of Juiz de Paz (Justice

of the Peace), an office he held but a few short months. Because
of his recent military action, he was arrested and condemned
by the Mexican government, but due to his good name and fam-
ily influence he was paroled. Realizing his precarious political
position, he now endeavored to concentrate his attention on non-
military affairs. He took his first real interest in Rancho Piedra
Blanca, retiring there for a short time with his family and sev-
eral close friends and companions (one or more acting as his
agents and informants) in order to escape a particularly lawless
period existing at San Luis Obispo when the Mexicans and In-
dians rebelled against the continually changing political super-
vision, which negated church teachings and regulations. During
this time the rancho was prosperous and Pico developed a fine
regard for the Indians entrusted with its care. In spite of his
apparent resolution to remain aloof to militaristic movements
and unrest, his life as a military man dominated and he broke
parole to support Flores in the Natividad Campaign.

General J. C. Fremont, often considered an arrogant, ego-
tistical and dominating man, was sweeping through the country
confiscating horses and supplies as he went. He had little or no
regard for the damage he was causing owners, or the economy
of the area in spite of the fact that most of the people were en-
tirely in favor of American troops taking over Alta California
from Mexican rule. These ravages directly affected Rancho
Piedra Blanca, depriving it of all the best riding horses, at least
some of which the Don needed in order to communicate with
San Luis Obispo. Adding insult to injury, Fremont also caught
and shot one of the Don's most trusted Indian servants, whom
he falsely accused of being a spy, the man actually being on a
routine trip to Pico bearing a message regarding rancho affairs.

While completely in favor of the movement to free California
Pico was, nevertheless, highly incensed by the many unwarrant-
ed actions and sharply criticized Fremont with the result that
Fremont ordered his arrest on grounds that he had "broken his
parole" and was "highly antagonistic to the cause." Pico was
immediately sentenced to death at San Luis Obispo. The sen-
tence angered local residents. With the support of Doña Ramona
Carrillo de Pacheco de Wilson, wife of Captain John D. Wilson,

and Pico's own wife, Doña Gabriella, and their numerous children, pleas were made before Fremont for Pico's freedom. The General was forced to release him with full pardon in order to avoid making a martyr of him. This release won Fremont the political support of the major families in the San Luis Obispo area. Later, Fremont and Pico worked together and became devoted friends and continued so during ensuing months.

As a member of a prominent Mexican-Spanish family of Monterey, Pico was a close friend of Romualdo Pacheco, sub-lieutenant of Engineers, and his family. After the death of Pacheco, his wife, Doña Ramona, married Captain John D. Wilson, also well known to Pico through his military participation against Micheltorena in 1845. The Wilsons and Picos continued as devoted friends, a fact well demonstrated by the preceding incident. This friendship was again proven in 1854 when Pico sold a large portion of Rancho Piedra Blanca to Captain Wilson for the token sum of $1,500. This sale involved the half interest in 1,000 acres surrounding San Simeon Bay, and full right to all the rancho lying north of Arroyo de la Laguna, the first stream extending down from the hills to the ocean, north of the bay.

When California became independent of Mexican rule, Pico turned his attention to local politics and government. He was influential in the formation of the county within the free state prior to its acceptance into the Union in 1850, and was elected the couny's first assessor. By this time, like other Dons, he was maintaining his home on his rancho while commuting frequently to San Luis Obispo by saddle horse in order to fulfill his duties as a county official. At the following election he was named state assemblyman from the area. Moving out of the county to attend to his new office, he leased half of his San Luis Obispo home, known as Casa Grande, to the county for its offices. He asked $100 for every six months of use. For the next 20 years this home continued to be county headquarters.

Once more, Pico spent little time on his rancho. Financial problems and indebtedness, as he endeavored to comply with United States laws regarding taxes and grant ownership, were causing him considerable distress. In order to save part of his rancho as security for his children, he deeded various portions to them. By 1860, afraid that he would have to sell portions of their holdings to meet mounting expenses, he petitioned for guardianship and the right to sell their properties if necessary. He received guardianship on April 13 of that year but continued to hold off creditors until the drought of 1863-64 when he lost his entire herd of Spanish cattle as well as most of his horses. This completed his ruin.

Still wishing to preserve the securities of his children, he accepted an offer from George Hearst for his own half interest in the 1,000 acres about the bay, as well as other portions of the rancho which were still in his name. Included in the sale, besides the bay property, was that portion of the rancho below his home and between his home and the bay. Hearst had apparently visualized ownership of the rancho for some time, especially that portion lying about the bay for, written into the sales contract, were plans for subdivision of acreage bordering the beach. The proposed subdivision included the property on which the homes of Pico's sons, Zenobio and Benigno, were located. To protect these homes Pico requested that, following subdivision, the two lots be deeded back to him.

No subdivision could be made, however, until Hearst had full ownership of the property, the other half of which was still owned by the heirs of Captain Wilson, who died in 1861, and by Captain Joseph Clark, owner of 12 acres on San Simeon Point and the whaling station. In the beginning these facts did not seem to worry Hearst. He seemed confident that acquisition of the Wilson property, now in the hands of people of Spanish blood, would be a simple matter.

On Wilson's death, his Piedra Blanca property was left to his grown children and step-children. These were Romualdo and Mariano Pacheco, his wife's children by her first marriage; Juana, now married to Juan Castro; Maria Ynacia, wife of Domingo Pujol, a young Spanish lawyer; Ramona, wife of Frederick Hilliard, and John D., a student in England. Mariano Pacheco and his wife, Francisca, received the north portion of the rancho. This was 17,360 acres where they built a large adobe home on Oak Knoll Creek near the ocean. Half interest in the bay property was held jointly by Wilson's own children. Hearst failed to take into consideration the brilliance of the young lawyer, Pujol, or the business acumen of Castro, both trying to protect the interests of the Wilson and Pacheco families.

Mariano Pacheco, the older of the two Pacheco brothers, after an education in Honolulu, attempted to keep pace with Romualdo, a robust, active young man who, early in life, had spent several years at sea with his stepfather and later had taken up politics as the government of the county and state emerged. On the other hand, Mariano was far from robust. After serving one term as county supervisor, beginning in 1852, he went to work as a clerk for William H. Davis Company of San Francisco. On receiving his inheritance he moved to the rancho in hopes of improving his health. The shock of the drought was apparently more than he could bear for he died immediately thereafter at the age of 36. He left his wife and six young children, all under the age of 15. His brother, Romualdo, was named executor of the will but, busy in politics, he declined in favor of his half-sister's husband, Juan Castro, who had recently lost his wife. Due to Juana Castro's death, Juan also became part owner in the bay property. He was very much interested in administering Mariano's estate.

It was at this time that Hearst began his campaign to secure the bay property. He was met with immediate and strong resistance by both Castro and the lawyer, Pujol. Pujol was already having trouble with Hearst over Rancho Santa Rosa, most of which he had purchased from Julian Estrada, unknown to Hearst, in 1862. Unwilling to lose his portion of the bay property, which he foresaw would eventually all be sold to Hearst, he concluded an arrangement with the other heirs, receiving clear title to 100 acres adjoining the Pacheco property for $2,000. This left 900 acres about the bay half owned by Hearst.

Two years after Mariano's death, Juan Castro married his widow. With her consent and that of her oldest son, Castro petitioned for guardianship of the children. He was now able to bend all his efforts to recoup losses the Castro-Pacheco portion of the rancho suffered by the recent drought.

Numerous people were seeking lands for dairying. Castro did not have sufficient money to restock the property nor was he, a

Mexican-Spanish aristocrat, willing to become a common farmer. He decided to lease parcels of land to these immigrants. He had the fertile areas surveyed into sizable farms. In some instances he put up fencing and built or paid for the building of small homes, especially in the vicinity of San Carpoforo Creek and Arroyo de la Cruz. Beginning in 1869 and continuing until his guardianship expired, he rented these lands except for the share which belonged solely to his wife. These acres he sold to pay the expense of survey, taxes and back debts. Those who leased from Castro were the Judson, Carrillo, Stanton, Wittenberg, Regita, Lopez, Dickenson, Ellisalde, Hildebrand, Hahn, Burnett, Norcross and Godfrey families, and Francisco Pacheco.

During 1869, Hearst finally succeeded in completing negotiations with the rest of the Wilson family, making himself full owner of the property about the bay except for the 12 acres owned by Captain Clark and the two lots on which Pico's sons resided. He now went ahead with the subdivision and leased lots for business purposes. Due to a mining boom and a thriving dairy industry several people were anxious to establish business enterprises at the bay.

Juan Castro was not friendly with Hearst and when forced to sell rancho property belonging to his wife, he refused to deal with Hearst in any way. Instead, he sold to reliable people seeking ranch property for a home. Among those who purchased land were Thomas J. Evans, Peter Gillis, William Moss and Franklin Phillips. As a convenience to the people now living on the rancho north of San Simeon, Juan Castro applied for a federal post office and was granted one August 25, 1870. Located in his adobe home as the Piedra Blanca Post Office, records indicate it was discontinued September 1, 1871, barely a year after its inception. No reason for abandonment was given.

Following his second sale of rancho lands to Hearst, Don Pico rapidly lost all interest in the area. In continuous need of money, he was eventually forced to sell the balance of his holdings which included his adobe home. Hearst always stood ready to buy the land, and it was not long before he acquired all of the southern portion of the original grant with previously mentioned exceptions. He not only purchased the few remaining acres belonging to Pico, but persuaded Pico's children, now of age, to sell the parcels their father had never touched.

When Pico abandoned his interest in the rancho, he appointed his son, Zenobio, as his attorney-in-fact to dispose of the bay lots as he wished. Apparently deaf to Hearst's demands, and probably influenced by Domingo Pujol, Zenobio sold the property to David P. Mallagh of San Luis Obispo who, having no personal use for it, permitted the Pico brothers to remain in residence for several more years.

Hearst, not using the adobe buildings of the Pico home, allowed them to fall into ruin. He continued to pressure for possession of the northern acres but was unable to make any headway until 1878, when the last of Mariano Pacheco's six children reached its majority. At this time Castro's responsibilities as administrator and guardian ended. In spite of Castro's efforts to interest these young people in ranch affairs, the seemingly large sums of money which Hearst offered soon persuaded them to sell. Now, without a home of their own on the rancho, Juan and Francisca Castro moved to San Luis Obispo where Juan already owned part of a prospering livery stable business.

Hearst continued to lease the dairy lands, and maintained a dairy of his own. In addition to land rentals he leased dairy cows, taking young heifer calves at weaning as payment.

Thomas James Evans, who bought his property from Castro in 1869, was born in Wales November 13, 1836. He came to America with his parents at the age of 10. The family settled in Waushesha, Wisconsin, but, in 1850, young Tom left home for California. He traveled by way of the Gulf of Mexico and the Isthmus, which he crossed on foot. Then sailing north, he landed at San Francisco. For several years he employed himself by driving stage and freight wagons over the sierras of eastern California; then, during a visit to the coast and Cambria in 1869, he was persuaded to invest in the Piedra Blanca Rancho property. This same year he returned to Wisconsin and married his brother John's sister-in-law, Mary Jarmon.

Tom and his wife returned to the newly acquired ranch, arriving from San Francisco by steamer at San Simeon Bay where they landed by means of a breeches bouy. Here they were met by Tom's friend and neighbor, Peter Gillis, whose property adjoined the Evans holdings to the south.

Six sons and two daughters were born to the Evans. The daughters married into the VanGorden family of San Simeon Creek and the boys, who obtained land to the north and east of the rancho, married into the J. D. Campbell, Dennis, Kraal, Clemence and Janssen families of the Cambria area. Descendents of these families still live about Cambria and San Luis Obispo County. Locally they include the Riciolis and Gillespies.

Several of Mary Jarmon's sisters came to visit her from Wisconsin and remained to marry locally. Sister Elizabeth Jarmon married Captain Lorin V. Thorndyke, keeper of Piedras Blancas lighthouse, and after her death another sister, Margaret, became his wife. Martha Jarmon married Benjamin Muma, who was active in San Simeon affairs for many years.

Tom Evans and his wife lived at their ranch for 50 years, during which time they also purchased 320 acres from Peter Gillis. This portion, however, they eventually sold to Leopold Frankl, a merchant at San Simeon after 1872. After Tom and his wife left the ranch, others of the family continued to live there. For more than 90 years the family waged a fight against the endless schemes and devious methods employed by George Hearst, and later by W. R. Hearst, who were determined to own the Evans property. It continued to remain in Evans hands until 1970, the only break in the 14-mile stretch of coastline owned by Hearst interests in northern San Luis Obispo County. At this time Hearst Corporation agents managed a negotiation with the late Mrs. Helen G. Evans and her son, Jim.

Peter Gillis and his wife, Nancy, purchased 1,414 acres from Castro in October of 1867. The Piedras Blancas lighthouse was constructed on this property in 1874-75, at which time Peter assisted in the building, working as a teamster. Gillis continued in residence on the ranch until his death in 1892. His property was left jointly to his six grown children and their heirs, who were all living in other parts of the county and state. Unable to come to any common agreement, they sold the property in portions to various parties who, either operating as speculators or in the direct interest of Hearst, immediately sold to him.

Little is known concerning the activities of either Franklin Phillips or William Moss. Both men continued to own the properties purchased from Castro for 14 years. Both sold to Hearst in 1882. In 1888 Leopold Frankl, too busy with his store and other affairs at San Simeon to operate his ranch, sold to Hearst. After the death of Captain Clark in 1894, Phoebe Hearst, following the policy set by her late husband, bought the whaling station from Hipolite Marshall, nephew and heir to Clark.

In spite of an almost constant effort to obtain possession of the two lots at San Simeon, they have remained outside the Hearst empire as has a small piece of beach property north of the lighthouse. Once part of the Evans property and now owned by Valois, it is primarily used for a motel and small restaurant.

During the many years George Hearst owned the Rancho he was variously liked and disliked by people of the area. He treated his employees well. But those who felt the pressure of his avaricious desire for land had little good to say about him, especially as he made continuing efforts to purchase and control other large land grants along the San Luis Obispo coast.

A tight hold was maintained on all activities at San Simeon Bay. Due to the precarious whims of George and later, his son, William Randolph, the community, though it flourished for a while, was never permitted to expand and develop into the extensive port it might have become.

Curtailment of lease holdings was brought about by a rental squeeze as fees were raised each year until the once successful dairymen were forced to abandon their homes, unable to pay the exorbitant charges. The dissolution of the prosperous business establishments at the bay was accomplished in the same way until the only people able to live independently within the boundaries of the rancho were those few who held title to the isolated islands of land Hearst was unable to buy.

At the death of Phoebe Hearst her son, William Randolph, took over management of rancho properties. Like his father, he devoted operations to his exclusive personal interest. He erected elaborate appearing Spanish style homes at San Simeon for his favorite employees. Bunk houses, horse barns and other out buildings at rancho headquarters some distance from the bay, were also patterned after the Spanish. His own quarters, however, were designed in fabulous elegance and have become famous as "Hearst Castle" overlooking his vast holdings from the crest of the "Enchanted Hill."

Preservation of historic sites on the rancho was thoroughly discouraged and often deliberately destroyed. The result was that Indian encampments were often bulldozed apart for rare and unusual relics without regard for cultural aspects; adobe buildings were allowed to disintegrate, often encouraged by the removal of protecting tiles, and eventually flattened; homes of the Chinese seaweed gatherers, established as squatters in the nineteenth century, were also bulldozed over the ocean cliffs.

Following the death of William Randolph Hearst in 1951, rancho lands were incorporated with other Hearst holdings. Piedra Blanca Rancho was put under management of the Sunical Land and Development Company, a subdivision of the corporation, with offices in San Francisco. The gift of Hearst Castle to the State of California as a historical monument in 1956 was considered a wise move by the corporation as the elaborate buildings, representing a huge tax burden, were deemed of little personal use to the various heirs. The gift, together with a previous gift to the county in 1953 of bay property known as the Phoebe Hearst Memorial at the junction of Highway One and the loop through San Simeon, has done more, economically, for the area than any other program ever instituted on Hearst-held properties since 1865.

When the Castle was opened to the public by the State Division of Beaches and Parks it focused attention, once again, upon the isolated and beautiful north coast area. Many thousands of curious tourists have been attracted to the splendors on display at the Castle of the world famous newspaper "king" whose life history, together with that of his father, is familiar to all visitors.

Schooner Electra was wrecked on the rocks adjoining Leffingwell pier in 1894. (Paul Squibb collection)

View of Piedras Blancas W. ¾ N. (Compass) 4 miles

Artist's conception of Piedras Blancas Rocks as seen by mariners standing four miles off shore in 1868. Illustration from 1869 *Coast Pilot*. (Courtesy Bancroft Library)

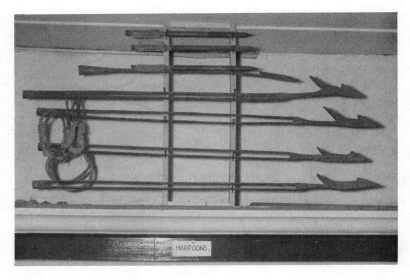

Harpoons and bomb lances as used by Captain Joseph Clark at the whaling station, San Simeon.

Bow gun for firing the bomb lance. On display at Sebastian's Store, San Simeon. Relic of whaling days in and at the bay.

Chapter 12

Whaling Station at San Simeon Bay

Late in 1863 a young Portuguese man who called himself Joseph Clark secured permission from Don José Pico and the heirs of Captain John Wilson to establish a coast whaling station on the inshore side of San Simeon Point which protects the bay of San Simeon from the prevailing northwesterly winds.

According to early whaling records, Clark was first known at San Diego by the name of Machado. In his early twenties he left San Diego and joined a crew of whalemen at a Monterey whaling station where he became known as Joseph Clark. Before long he was considered one of the best whalers there.

At 25, quite aware of his own talents, he left the Monterey area, already crowded with four separate whaling operations, to start his own station. He purchased 12 acres of land at San Simeon Point and began construction of his station in a design similar to those at Monterey.

In 1864, his first year of operation, he made a substantial profit, as in the immediate succeeding years, so he was able to obtain clear title to the property and equipment by July, 1867.

Deep sea whaling, a well organized industry of the north Pacific and Atlantic oceans, as well as coastal whaling, dates to prehistoric time. As a modern commercial enterprise, deep water whaling reached its peak in 1850 with 680 sailing ships (all but 40 operating in Pacific waters) pursuing the leviathan. Commercial whaling stations along the Pacific shore did not come into existence until this peak period when they were established to capture the gray whale of inshore waters, being encouraged, no doubt, by the admission of California into the Union. The first coastal station was located at Monterey by Captain Davenport in 1851. There is some indication that a small operation may have been in existence there as early as 1846 though no official records are in existence concerning it.

In 1859 the *California State Register* says, concerning shore whaling stations, that several had

already (been) established for four years at Monterey . . . their cruising ground being the Bay of Monterey and a short distance into the ocean. Operations are carried on by means of boats during the season which usually lasts 9 months, from March to November.

Shortly after Clark established his station, fishery records note that 11 stations were operating along the coast and employing about 60 whalers. These stations were situated at Half Moon Bay, Pigeon Point, Carmel, Monterey, San Simeon, Port San Luis, Goleta, Point Conception, San Diego and Point Abanda. The demand for whale oil was steadily increasing due to new uses in ointments and candle making.

Clark's station contained three large rendering vats bricked in side by side and holding 200 gallons each with stock-holds below; a flensing wharf built almost flush with the water at high tide and about 50 feet below the cliffs on which the vats were located; a capstan called a "crab," and a winch on an incline well above the wharf in line with the vats. In addition, there was a small cluster of buildings 300 yards from the extremity of the point, one or two of which were whitewashed while the rest were unpainted. One was the house in which Clark lived. The others were a combination bunk and boarding house, storage sheds and utility buildings.

Fresh water was obtained from a well a mile and a half northwest of the station near the sea. It was transported back to the station in large casks rigged with revolving handles on each end to which ropes were attached, enabling the whalers to roll them by pulling on the ropes held over their shoulders.

During the whaling season the station was manned by whalemen who worked in crews of six and seven. A daylight to dusk lookout was kept for the whales. Two 30-foot boats, each one

manned by a crew, were in constant readiness, awaiting the cry,
"Whale, ho!" There was also a supplementary watch at Piedras
Blancas Point where a crow's nest provided an excellent obser-
vation station for whales coming down from the north enroute
to the breeding grounds of Baja California. Two boats were
kept at this lookout, close to shore in readiness with at least
one man aboard all the time to prevent battering on the rocks.

On sighting a whale at Piedras Blancas Point a flag was
dipped to signal the San Simeon Point lookout. Boats then left
both points in pursuit of the quarry. One boat made the initial
charge as a second stood ready to help in case of trouble. One
man of the crew operated a 20-foot long steering paddle at the
stern, another manned the bow gun ready for instant action,
while the remaining four rowed or manipulated sail until the
first strike when each man had special duties to perform ac-
cording to varying circumstances.

A completely silent approach usually enabled the crew to
come within easy harpooning distance of the animal which, until
alarmed, proceeded leisurely on its way. A harpoon was shot
from the muzzle loaded bow gun, thus attaching the boat to the
whale with a 500-foot line fastened to a sliding ring in the har-
poon shaft. The line was played out to the proper length as the
startled, wounded animal sounded or swam away in a frenzy.

Prior to shooting, the barb of the harpoon was lightly held in
position parallel to the shank by means of a small wooden peg.
On entering the whale the peg broke, permitting the barb to
fall into a right angle position, making it impossible to pull out.

After harpooning, the whale often pulled the whalers some
distance from the shooting area. On rare occasions it would be
as much as 20 miles before the men were able to gain control by
pulling on the line to make him surface. At the same time they
would bring their boat nearer to the whale in order to deal the
death blow with a bomb lance. Their main concern at this time
was to be within shooting range the instant he surfaced for
air. The bow gun was again used to fire the bomb lance
into his side at a point called the "death point," just behind the
front fin. The explosion of the bomb lance, after a three second
delay, was expected to kill the whale at once. If the shot failed

to kill, the whalers were exposed to the rage of the infuriated beast which often attempted to destroy the small boats. Considerable trouble was always encountered before it succumbed to further attacks by harpoons and smaller bombs.

Harpoons with detachable wooden handles were manually thrown in the early days of whaling, but the gun operated harpoon was in common use by the late 1870's. Smaller shoulder guns, similar in appearance to the bazooka, were used to fire harpoons and lances of smaller caliber after the initial attack. These also carried lines which aided in maneuvering the animal to port after the kill. The bomb lance was about 20 inches long by two inches in diameter, carrying a heavy charge of powder. The smaller bombs were two inches shorter and about one inch in diameter. Both kinds were stabilized by three rubber fins which remained folded in the butt of the lance until released by firing. The firing charge set off a cap in the butt which, in turn, set off a delayed fuse to the bomb charge.

Once a whale was captured and towed to the station, 20 to 30 whalers were all activity as they turned to the work of stripping (known as flensing) off the blubber at the flensing wharf. The whale was first prepared by cutters who made a deep hole in the body just back of the head with sharp, long-handled cutting spades. By chopping with these spades from the deck of the wharf they also cut deep grooves a foot to either side of the hole. Then a whaleman climbed onto the whale and inserted a large iron hook into the hole. The hook was attached by cable to the winch and capstan above. To aid the whaleman retain his footing on the carcass, deep notches were cut in the surface for foot holds. Once the hook was well fastened, the workmen returned to the wharf. Whalers operating the winch began hoisting ropes while blubber cutters, wielding the spades, continued to cut at the whale, freeing the blubber in a two-foot wide strip six to 10 inches thick as it was torn from the carcass by the pull of the hoisting lines. As the reddish blubber peeled off the carcass turned over and over in the water. When the blubber reached the top of the cliff other men cut the strip into small pieces. Using long handled, pronged forks, the pieces were lowered into already hot try-pots.

The boiling oil was dipped from the pots into wooden barrels by means of ladles with 10 foot handles. Each ladle held approximately one gallon. Because of the intense heat of the oil it was never put directly into an empty barrel but poured into barrels partially filled with cool oil. Once filled and sealed, the barrels were dropped into the harbor and towed, in the early days, to waiting schooners anchored in the bay. Later, when steamers called at the port, they were towed to the Hearst Pier where they were picked up by nets and hoisted aboard ship.

After the blubber was removed, the carcass was towed into one of the deep caves located beneath the inner cliffs of the point. Here it was beached and other portions of the whale saved. The liver was barreled separately and shipped whole to San Francisco where oil was extracted and used for medicinal purposes. The baleen through which the whale strained its food was also saved as it was used in the manufacture of corset stays. Certain bones were also saved. The rest of the carcass was left to wave action and disposal by sea birds. Many of the bones eventually settled to the bottom of the bay and, during heavy storms, can still be found cast upon surrounding beaches.

Wood as well as water was scarce at the point. Fires under the vats were started with salvaged drift wood. As the oil was rendered the "fritters" or cracklings were removed from the vats and used to keep the fires burning. They created clouds of thick, black smoke. According to Captain Clark's notes, an average gray whale which seldom exceeds 45 feet in length, could be expected to yield 35 barrels of oil. His record catch in any one season was 23 animals. One season only three whales were taken. During the first years the station was in operation he averaged 17 whales per season. In 1869 the records of produce shipped out of San Simeon Bay by steamer indicate that for a six-month period the whale oil was valued at $8,000. Later, records kept for the George Hearst Pier for the year ending September 30, 1880, indicate 299 barrels of oil were shipped. These isolated accounts, however, in no way give a picture of the profits of the station.

The late George Steiner, who was raised at San Simeon, spent several of his younger years about the whaling station and often accompanied the whalers "just for the ride." Though he was too small to be of any real service, he tried to do his share by pulling on the ropes when the proper time came. He recalled with pleasure some of the swift rides the whales gave the crew. At times, he said, danger made it expedient to cut the lines to a harpooned whale. Often these same whales would be sighted in about a week, floating dead upon the sea. Then they were called "stinkers," said Steiner. "And they really were stinkers—good and ripe." When sighted, these whales were always brought in and processed.

In another account, a *Tribune* reporter said, "A whale hunt is exciting and dangerous sport which, once enjoyed, is never coveted again by the amateur whale hunter." A personal account by Captain Clark of an attempt to capture a huge Right Whale off San Simeon in April of 1880 gives some idea of the dangers involved in the hazardous profession:

The whale was sighted in the afternoon, five or six miles off shore. Two boats were sent in pursuit. On coming up to the whale he was immediately attacked with a harpoon and bomb lance. An exciting contest began which lasted until the whale made a savage and determined attack upon one of the boats and broke it in two amidships with his flukes. The boat's crew, left struggling in the water, but being good swimmers, were able to reach the other boat and save their lives. The second boat, now loaded (with 14 men) was unable to pursue the contest and the whale disappeared. However, during the brief encounter with the whale, 25 bomb lances had been fired into his sides as well as several harpoons.

Captain Clark went on to say he was much dismayed by the loss of the whale, for he estimated that the bombs alone cost him $100, besides the loss of harpoons, lines, boat and fittings.

Right Whales, the game of the larger whaling ships, were not often seen near the coast of California, only nine having appeared in sight off San Simeon in 17 years. Clark also estimated that, should this whale have been brought to the pier, he would have realized approximately $4,000 by figuring the yield at around 150 barrels of oil at 37½ cents per gallon and 1,600 pounds of bone at $1.80 per pound. This bone reference probably means baleen as other notes indicate whale bone, as such, was seldom saved.

During the processing of a whale the harbor swarmed with millions of sardines attracted to the carcass. These fish were so numerous inshore that Steiner claimed one could virtually walk across the harbor from Hearst Pier to the whaling station on a solid mass of them. Not only were the fish in abundance but the air was filled with birds attracted to them. At these times, it was one of young Steiner's keen delights to attach a string to two pieces of blubber, toss it in the air, and watch the struggle as two sea gulls simultaneously grabbed the tidbits. He said cardboard worked just as well when the birds were highly excited.

Fires beneath the rendering vats were allowed to subside between whales as there would often be a waiting period of several weeks. Whalers were on a 12-hour standby, awaiting the "Whale, ho!" from lookouts, and many games of checkers and cards were played. Some whalers were excellent whittlers who utilized the beautiful white sugar pine of the kerosene crates from Piedras Blancas lighthouse to carve fancy square picture frames of intricate, notched and layered patterns. They also carved large tops from eucalyptus wood which they presented to some of the young school lads who, in turn, had many hours of fun from the beautiful toys.

The whalers continued to live apart from the town of San Simeon after it was established. They had their own living quarters provided for them by Clark, their permanent homes being at Monterey where they lived during the summer. Only Captain Clark resided at the station throughout the entire year.

Once the rendering vats were fired and the blubber hot, the housewives of San Simeon made regular trips to them for frying doughnuts in large quantities. Steiner remembered the Portuguese whalers testing the temperature of the rendering blubber by spitting a stream of tobacco juice into it. This, however, did not seem to affect the excellent quality of the doughnuts the housewives produced, nor mar the delicious flavor of foot-long smelt fried in the boiling oil which were eaten, bones and all.

During the years between 1880 and 1890 young Steiner and his father, Charles Alfred Steiner, often borrowed the "Butter Box," a little six-foot, square-ended skiff belonging to the whaling station, for fishing in the harbor. One day while fishing for large mackeral with sardine-baited hooks, unusually heavy strikes were felt on the lines. Rebaiting with a wire leader, George and his father started hauling in King Salmon, of which they caught 28 that afternoon. The largest weighed 68 pounds. To Steiner's knowledge, it was the only record of King Salmon being caught in the harbor. Occasionally whale meat, of excellent flavor but very tough, was eaten by local people who usually preferred the venison and plentiful domestic meats carried by the Ed Asevaz meat market at San Simeon. Whale cracklings about a half inch thick were very tasty but had the quality of rubber and were hard to chew, according to Steiner.

Captain Clark died November 11, 1891, at the age of 56. Steiner remembered him as a stocky, strong old man, gray haired, round faced and clean shaven in contrast to his men, who nearly all wore beards. He was well liked by all who knew him. After his death his cousin, Hipolite Marshall of Adelaida, inherited the property together with the whaling business, in which he had no particular interest.

The continually decreasing number of whales being taken by shore stations at this time caused many of them to close. Hipolite finally accepted on offer from Phoebe Hearst who, following the death of her husband, George Hearst in 1891, wished to buy it. The transaction was concluded in 1894, marking the end of the whaling industry in San Simeon Bay. Various fishermen occupied the site after it was abandoned as a whaling station. One family that has been remembered was that of Johnny Sousa, who had 10 children. He caught large quantities of fish and shipped them to San Francisco by steamer.

Several relics of the whaling days at San Simeon remain as reminders of this historical past. In 1964 a few remnants of the old buildings still dotted the point and pilings of the old flensing wharf still jutted from the water. The rendering vats, though scattered, remain in good condition. In 1924 Hearst ranch employees moved one of them to the back country for use as a mixing pot for disinfectant during the hoof and mouth disease epidemic which was widespread among the cattle. This vat is now on display at the loading area of the State-owned Hearst "Castle." A second vat was put to use as a part time watering trough; the third is said to be partially or wholly buried in the sands and debris of the bay near the site of whaling operations.

Pete Sebastian, owner of the historic Sebastian Store at San Simeon, has a display of whaling implements which were in use at the station when it was abandoned in 1894; these include bow guns, harpoons and lances. Today, only one whaling station continues to operate on the Pacific coast. It is located at Richmond in San Francisco Bay. Whales are taken offshore and in the bay as they migrate north and south.

In early winter the gray whales migrate south as lone individuals to the western coast of Baja California where they give birth to pups conceived the previous year, and again mate. The female nurse their young until the following spring, then return north as large family groups. During these migrations they travel close along the shore, preferring shallow water in their quest for food. They frequently search the surf and delta areas of a stream outlet.

Under modern processing methods every part of the whale is utilized, with large quantities reaching the pet food market. Concern over the rapid destruction of whales in recent years, due primarily to fast and efficient whaling methods, has now caused some self-imposed regulation on whaling by some countries, which extend over the entire globe. Several attempts have been started for an international form of regulation but, as yet, nothing has been finalized though whales are noted to be rapidly decreasing in number with each succeeding year.

Residents and visitors to the San Simeon-Cambria coastline often catch glimpses of the gray whale as it migrates north or south. Large, black bodies surface and submerge to resurface again and emit a cloud of spray. As they swim close to shore they are easily seen with the naked eye; and in spring, as the families move northward, they gambol and play with each other, their giant bodies glistening in the sun as they clear the water in fantastic leaps.

Chapter 13

San Simeon

The first known reference to the Bay of San Simeon, by that name, is in the records of San Miguel Mission for 1830, though this geographical feature was outside the holdings of that mission, being included in the coastal properties belonging to Mission San Antonio de Padua. However, the bay, as an anchorage and landing, is known to have been used by sailing ships and by San Miguel Mission for the purpose of smuggling, probably as early as 1800. This bay is also said to be the same Bay of Sardines mentioned by Juan Cabrillo where he is reputed to have anchored and landed. However, the bay was not chartered and, like Morro Bay to the south, remained unknown to subsequent Spanish galleons patroling the coast.

Apparently due to a desire for secrecy, the name or specific reference to this bay was not written into records until its location became common knowledge. Spanish ships were not adapted to inshore sailing. As a consequence, exploration of the small coves and inlets along the California coast was neglected by the Spanish government. Large stretches of the coastline remained officially unexplored though familiar to the small sailing ships of the American and British sailing captains.

By 1840 the bay was a well known anchorage used by ships seeking shelter in time of storm, and for trade, now practiced openly under more lenient Mexican laws. Eugene Duflot de Mofras, a French map maker who visited the coast in 1840-42, made special note of the harbor as an anchorage when he charted it, for the first time, on his map of the Pacific coast.

Between the time of mission secularization and the issuance of Mexican grants, trade and shipping at the bay were slight, increasing again as rancho products were readied on the large holdings of Don José de Jésus Pico. Trading vessels called at the anchorage not more than three or four times during a year.

In 1854 Don Pico, who spent little time on his rancho, sold half of his interest in 1,000 acres surrounding the bay to his close friend, Captain John Wilson. Though there is nothing to indicate that Captain Wilson contemplated any improvements at the bay, there is reason to believe he entertained the idea that at a future date it would prove to be a sound investment.

In 1857 and 1858, the arrival of American settlers into the general area increased the need for frequent schooner visits. A wide variety of supplies was in demand and as production increased more produce was readied for market. By 1860 ships were frequenting the bay at least twice a month. As yet, no facilities existed for the protection of goods landed on the sandy beach, nor did anyone live nearby. Farmers and ranchers simply brought their produce by *carreta* or wagon on arrival of the schooner and carried home such items as they had ordered on a previous visit.

With the continued arrival of new settlers, including Chinese seaweed farmers, and the increased production of farm commodities, these sailing ships made still more frequent visits to the harbor. When possible, cargo was packed in water tight containers and lowered overboard in large nets or roped together, then towed ashore. Special items readily damaged by seawater were rowed ashore in the lighters.

After the whaling station opened in 1864 a few fishermen and their families settled on the point near the whaling station as squatters. They caught fish attracted by processing of whales. Other than for the station with its small cluster of buildings and occupants, the entire area surrounding the bay was uninhabited except for two sons of Don Pico. They established themselves near the beach landing in 1862 or 1863, but devoted their activities to rancho affairs. The Pico adobe home, seldom occupied by its owner, was located three miles south of the bay, well apart from any activity taking place there.

In 1865 George Hearst, taking advantage of Don Pico's indebtedness after the extreme drought of the previous year, obtained possession of Pico's half interest in the 1,000 acres surrounding the bay. Hearst's plans for development of the area included subdivision of several acres adjacent to the beach used for a landing. Included in the area were the two homes of Zenobio and Benigno Pico. Fortunately, when selling his interest in the bay property, Pico excluded the part on which these homes were built, requesting that the lots on which the homes fell would remain in his name. Neither of the brothers appear to have been married at this time. From events which followed later, it is believed the homes were poorly built wooden affairs with out buildings intended for temporary use.

For three years following his purchase, Hearst endeavored to secure clear title to the other half interest which, following the death of Captain Wilson, belonged to Wilson's several heirs. At last, in 1868, realizing his hopes would finally be fulfilled, Hearst instituted further plans for bay development.

His first and prime desire was the control of shipping in and out of the bay by a property-use charge in the form of wharfage. While waiting for clearance of his title to the land he teamed with Captain Clark of the whaling station and appealed to the Board of Supervisors for a wharf franchise, the first such appeal in the county. They immediately made plans for its construction near the end of San Simeon Point, south of the whaling station. The franchise was granted March 23, 1868, and the first county regulated wharfage rates established on August 15. Beginning January 1, 1869, with Mr. W. Pitney in charge, charges were levied by Hearst on all goods transported to and from the beach landing over his property.

In order to circumvent these wharfage fees, which people considered high and uncalled for at a beach landing, wagons and *carretas* descended to the beach sand from property still owned by Pico and proceeded to the landing over tide-washed beach, then left by the same method. In spite of this expedience there were those who found the route along the beach impossible and dangerous and were forced to cross Hearst owned property to reach the landing.

For the first six months of 1869, prior to the construction of the pier, the value of shipments out of the harbor and passing over Hearst property, according to records kept by Pitney, totaled $30,000 for butter, $8,000 for wool, $3,000 in Chinese products, $8,000 in eggs, $5,000 for hides, $250 for cheese and $100 for terrapins.

Wharfage rates as set by the county permitted collection of $1 per ton, including storage for one month, on general merchandise; $1 per ton for wool; 25 cents per thousand shingles; $1 per thousand posts; 50 cents a head for horses, mules and asses; 25 cents per head for cattle; 10 cents per head for sheep, calves and hogs in lots of 50 or less, and 6½ cents per head over 50; $1 for all two-horse vehicles and $2 for four-horse vehicles. Apparently all other unnamed items were classed as general merchandise, though a year later wharfage rates set for the People's Wharf at Port San Luis specified hides, vegetables and grains separately.

The *Coast Pilot* of 1869, in describing anchorages along the coast, cites that up to the time of its publication there was no wharf at San Simeon Bay, "all landings being made on the small sandy beach cove." Vessels sailing from the south, after first taking a bearing on a three-mile stretch of timber bordering the shore, must make short tacks close in shore "or they entirely miss the entrance to the bay." To make the bay from the north, "a lookout is kept after sighting Piedras Blancas." Finally, with Grant, Lull and Company of Cambria as a third partner, the pier was completed in the latter part of 1869. No other mention is made of Captain Clark in association with operation of the pier. Presumably he soon took advantage of a clause in the original agreement by selling out his interest to Hearst.

After the pier, costing $3,000, was completed, Grant, Lull and Company took over management and erected a warehouse for the protection of goods, adding a small store either late in 1871 or early in 1872.

Sailing vessels soon found it impractical to heave-to beside the pier because of heavy rolling swells which swept around the point. These swells caused considerable damage to the ships tied at the pier and made transfer of commodities dangerous.

The schooners, therefore, continued to anchor away from the pier and transfer cargo to and from it by floating, by lighter or by breeches bouy, as the occasion demanded.

To further insure his complete control of shipping at San Simeon, Hearst started proceedings, in 1870, to secure title to the tidelands of the bay itself. Through his lawyer, McD. R. Venable of San Luis Obispo, he applied for and received a grant of 100 acres of tidal property in the bay under the recently enacted "Tidelands Act." This transaction, completed in 1871, permitted him to control the transport of goods along the sandy beach to and from land which was outside of his control.

In the meantime, subdivision of property fronting the beach was concluded. Zenobio Pico, acting as attorney-in-fact for his father, sold the two subdivision lots on which he and his brother were living to David P. Mallagh of San Luis Obispo in 1870. The purpose of the sale is unknown but it seems to have been done to prevent acquisition of the property by Hearst, who would have dispossessed the two men. Mallagh, however, permitted them to continue in residence, and in 1872 Benigno converted his place into a saloon and billiard parlor with some lodging facilities for the benefit of various passengers and members of the ships' crews.

His establishment was also patronized, though to a lesser degree, by some of the whalers and a few of the Mexican-Spanish ranch hands. To add further to his income he bought a good wagon and a four-horse team which he used to haul and deliver freight from the beach landing and pier to neighboring ranchers leasing dairy land from his friend, Juan Castro. Castro was administrator of Mariano Pacheco's estate which was part of Rancho Piedra Blanca acquired through Captain Wilson, as explained elsewhere.

In 1873 Leopold Frankl arrived at San Simeon and, seeing the need for a good store in addition to the saloon and billiard parlor, rented a portion of the Mallagh property from Benigno Pico where he promptly opened a little store, selling general merchandise.

No water existed at San Simeon so Hearst, as part of the development plan, had water piped from mountain springs to his subdivision. This has continued as the sole water supply to the area. The convenience of the cove landing as compared to the point location was obvious and Hearst, taking advantage of continuing increase in shipping, augmented at this time by a mining boom in the hills east of the rancho, leased several of his lots to business people at the astonishingly low rates of $2 a year.

A livery stable was started. Benigno applied for and received a postmastership, opening the San Simeon post office on December 29. The following year he sold his business to Peter Ferrari, who also took over the post office though Benigno's name remained on the records as postmaster.

Reduced business caused by the success of the Frankl store and the continuance of beach landings forced Grant, Lull and Company to abandon their store and warehouse in 1875. Steamers, which were replacing the sailing ships, were able to anchor well within the bay, making discharge of cargo comparatively simple. Increased shipping now required the steamers to call three and four times a week.

Ferrari, doing an excellent business, joined into a partnership with a Mr. Righetti in 1876 and, because of the increased number of passengers arriving weekly, they expanded by building a hotel with a dining room to accommodate them. They also built a barn, and according to the records, "improved the saloon." As near as can be determined, this improvement appears to have been a relocation. It was probably combined with the hotel as it was common at the time for the hotel dining room, saloon and other side activities to be located on the first floor while room accommodations were placed above. The hotel was built on the lot adjoining the old saloon and Frankl store. This left the lot on which the store was located available for Frankl's exclusive use. The Pico brothers had moved from the area by this time and were no longer interested in the property. Frankl immediately purchased the lot from Mallagh for $75. When the saloon was relocated the San Simeon post office was closed as of April 5, 1876. By 1878 Frankl was in need of more store space. He bought the abandoned store building on the point and moved it by ox team to his lot where he joined it to his other building and did extensive remodeling. After settling in the newly arranged quarters he applied for a reopening of the post office and was granted postmastership on August 9, 1878. Until this time Frankl's store was the only one in San Simeon.

During this same year Hearst secured another wharf franchise for the erection of a new pier which he started as a major move to improve port facilities. This pier, located deep in the bay and sheltered by the cliffs extending along the northwestern side, reached southward from the sandy beach for 1,000 feet into deep water permitting ships drawing up to 20 feet to anchor in safety at low tide.

Six rows of piling were driven, providing a solid support. The fenders of the pier were of Oregon Pine with side plates 12 inches thick. A special gangway 21 feet wide extended from the pier to the shore where a large warehouse was built. A narrow gauge railway was laid the length of the pier and extended into the warehouse to facilitate handling of the freight. Cost of construction was estimated to be approximately $20,000. Leopold Frankl was placed in charge of the new pier as wharfinger. He then hired his nephew, Adolph Frankl, to assist him in the store and at the wharf.

The next year Frankl again enlarged his store and stock, and continued to operate an increasing business, hiring various young men of the settlement to help him. About this time his store was also designated as the official polling place of the area.

On several of the unoccupied lots Hearst constructed small homes for his top ranch hands, as well as some to rent to people employed in work at the port.

By the time the Steiner family moved to San Simeon from Cambria, the subdivision had grown into a compact community with two general merchandise stores (the second one owned by Mr. Lippman), two hotels (the Ferrari-Righetti now owned by Frankl, and the other owned by William Gillespie and known as the Bay View), Peterson's blacksmith shop, the Ed Asevaz butcher shop, at least two saloons, a livery stable and stage depot, and a school. Frankl's store, the two hotels and the big warehouse were at the western end of town, while the other business places were at the eastern end near Arroyo del Puerto de San Simeon. Between these two sections and to the north were scattered 14 houses. All store entrances were high above ground. Several steps led up to a broad platform across the front, an arrangement convenient for drays and wagons handling freight.

When not employed by Frankl or other people about the bay, young George Steiner worked for Tom Liggett, who later became the Hearst ranch blacksmith. One of Steiner's jobs as a young man, age 12, was the drilling of holes in butter box hinges. He related that one day while doing this job, he accidentally caught his finger in the cogs of the drilling machine. As he freed his badly damaged hand Liggett urged him to "run home fast to your mother." His mother doctored the hand with camphor and ashes until his father came home and recommended cutting off the mangled finger. George protested so vigorously his father finally decided to doctor it with iodoform. "The finger," said George, "healed into eventual usefulness."

Young Steiner, a typical American boy of the period, when not kept busy with plenty of work, always found pranks to pull. Liggett's chickens were the target of one never-ending bit of amusement. With his friends, George drilled holes in grains of corn, attached threads to them, then threw them to the chickens as he held fast to the thread ends. Recalling his employment under Frankl in the late 1880's, Steiner said he was a kind old man who gave all the young lads who worked for him all the candy and other goodies they could eat as they worked.

In 1891 George Hearst died, leaving his estate to his wife, Phoebe Apperson Hearst who, with her husband's business managers, continued to direct rancho operations. In 1894 Captain Clark of the whaling station died and the station closed. Phoebe purchased the property from his heir, Hipolite Marshall.

In 1895, health failing and in fear of eminent death, Frankl began negotiations to settle his business affairs. Nina Hitchcock took over postmastership on February 13, and the American Exploration Company of New Jersey prepared to purchase the store and stock. However, Frankl died in June of 1896 before completion of the sale. The business was inherited by his nephew, Adolph Frankl, who continued to operate the store until legal entanglements were finally cleared in July of 1900 by McD. R. Venable and David Frankl.

The new owners of the Frankl store were promoters and developers of the Pine Mountain Quicksilver Mine located in the mountains east of San Simeon. They maintained the store as an office as well as a supply house for their mine, handling a complete line of merchandise from made-to-order clothes to heavy mining equipment.

Adolph Frankl continued to live in the area for several years and was especially active in the Masonic Lodge at Cambria, being Master in 1898. After Leopold Frankl's death Roy Summers, stepson of G. W. Lull of Cambria and husband to Mabel Estrada, a granddaughter of Julian Estrada of Rancho Santa Rosa, was made wharfinger at the Hearst pier.

About this time the Hearst management began a rental squeeze by slowly increasing lease fees on the dairy farms and on the subdivision lots until many of the lease holders were forced to abandon business. The dairies were the first to go. This, in turn, decreased business at the bay, making it doubly hard for the merchants to meet their obligations. Decreased dairy production on the rancho and a slump in mining curtailed port calls by the steamers who reduced their schedule to once a week. Their cargo was now supplied primarily by ranchers living south of Rancho Piedra Blanca.

When the demand for quicksilver decreased, curtailing mining activity in general, the Pine Mountain Quicksilver Mine closed as it was on the verge of bankruptcy. The Exploration Company sold the former Frankl property to L. V. Thorndyke, Jr., in 1904. Thorndyke was the son of Captain Lorin V. Thorndyke, keeper at Piedras Blancas lighthouse station. He had firsthand knowledge of the local people and conditions and also had a university education in business management. By revising all policies of management at the store, and increasing the scope of his investments, he was soon operating profitably.

A small abalone drying enterprise at the site of the whaling station, started in 1903 by a group of Japanese, was near collapse after one year of operation. So, when Thorndyke offered to buy the equipment and their lease, they were happy to sell.

Thorndyke soon had 20 Japanese working for him and quickly had the drying yard operating on a profitable basis. He used one boat with two expert Japanese divers working every favorable day from the first part of December until May or June. Eight men were employed on the boat while the rest remained ashore tending to the drying process. The divers were paid by the ton for the fresh abalone they secured, while the rest of the men worked on a monthly basis. In the beginning the abalone meat was removed from the shell while still on board the boat. Later, the law required removal from the shell be done on shore.

Abalone pearls were also much sought after. The proceeds from their sale was supposed to be divided as a bonus, half to Thorndyke and half to the men. According to Mr. Thorndyke, he had considerable difficulty in securing the pearls as the men who cleaned the abalone from the shells were exceedingly deft at locating and extracting the pearls, which they palmed, even though Thorndyke stood over them as they worked in an effort to guard against this practice.

The dried meat sold for $200 per ton and was shipped to San Francisco where it was reshipped to the Orient. Approximately three tons of meat were marketed each season. Such pearls as Thorndyke was able to recover usually netted more than the dried abalone. A really beautiful pearl would bring as much as $200 but the majority sold for an average of $3, some as low as 50 cents. Recounting his experience with these Japanese, Mr. Thorndyke said evidence of the theft of pearls during the cleaning process was noted through snatches of conversation he overheard between pearl buyers and his employees, as well as by the length of time the buyer spent with the men as they agreed upon a sale price. All night celebrations which followed these transactions, rendering the men unable to work the following day, were also proof of their surreptitious dealings. Nevertheless, if he wished to stay in business, punishment for the thefts was unthinkable, he said.

The Japanese method of preparation rendered the abalone meat clean and white when dry, as compared to the Chinese method which left it black. As told by Thorndyke, the black skin of the fresh animals was removed by soaking them in barrels of crushed salt for 24 hours, then dropping them momentarily into boiling water. Next, the abalone were placed on large strips of rough canvas and tossed vigorously about while a strong jet of water was played over them. Any remaining skin was removed with a stiff-bristled brush. The local Japanese used the dried abalone by grating it into their soups.

Purchases for the San Simeon store and the abalone business were often made by the freight carload or in 10-ton lots, which saved substantially on shipping charges. Rice for the Japanese crew was also purchased in these large quantities, as was salt for cleaning the abalone, dairy salt and flour.

After four years the higher rent demanded each year for the former whaling station site forced Thorndyke to abandon the abalone enterprise. Not long before he closed the business his diver, I. Yamamoto, quit and established his own yard at the mouth of Leffingwell Creek, the former site of the Leffingwell Pier near Cambria. In 1910 Yamamoto, with three of his companions, S. Kuroda, K. Satooka and T. Yokoyama, was drowned during a rough sea when their diving boat overturned near shore. The men, all excellent swimmers, were flung so violently against the rocks by the force of the waves they were unable to save themselves. All were buried in the local cemetery and Cambria citizens erected a monument at the site of their deaths.

Kakuchi, Thorndyke's second diver, after leaving San Simeon, joined an abalone enterprise operating in Cambria but soon went into business for himself at the site of the present veterans' building in Cayucos where he had 12 to 15 men and women working for him.

After taking over the operation of the store Thorndyke married Miss Maud Rogers of San Carpoforo Creek. They took over management of the Ferrari-Righetti Hotel next door to their store and Maud, whom he had known from childhood, took over the supervision, assisted by a sister and an aunt who did all the cooking. Meals were served to the customers at 25 cents each.

When Captain Thorndyke resigned from the lighthouse service in 1906 at age 75 "because he couldn't stand the noise" of the recently installed fog horn, he moved to San Simeon with his new wife, Margaret Jarmon, a sister of his former wife, and occupied a small cottage at the rear of the store. To keep the store in repair, Thorndyke, Jr., rebuilt the false front which was originally constructed with Cambria's Monterey pine, now badly weathered and termite eaten. The rest of the building was in good condition as it was built of another species of pine which grows in the Pine Mountain area.

By 1910 L. V. Thorndyke, Jr., was the only man still in business at the bay. Everyone else had been forced from business by increased rents and lack of customers. Steamer traffic with passenger service tapered off and the hotel was forced to close. In May of 1914 Thorndyke sold his property to Manuel Sebastian.

Sebastian continued to operate the store, aided during the first years following his purchase by a resurgence in mining activity and a lowering of high lease fees on Hearst properties, probably instigated by the increased demands of World War I, which encouraged a few dairy farmers to return to the area. Manuel Sebastian continued in business until he retired in 1948, selling to his son, J. C. "Pete" Sebastian, who retains ownership to the present day. The continuing success of this single business at San Simeon has not only been due to operator-ownership of the property, but to a flexible management. Owners have made the most of the limited market of the area, first by catering to steamship trade, whalers, dairymen and miners; later by catering to chance travelers and ranch hands; and finally, following the gift of Hearst Castle to the State, to a flourishing tourist economy.

The Sebastian Store stands as one of the last coastal remnants of busy shipping days when whale oil, butter, quicksilver, cattle, hogs and wheat comprised large and regular shipments to the San Francisco market. Linking the bygone era with today's kaleidoscopic whirl of tourist sightseers, the present owner endeavors to maintain a breath of the old charm while satisfying the continually changing demands of the new era. The old post office, still in operation, the cracker barrel atmosphere and the antiquities of the past on display retain the flavor of yesteryear.

Surrounding the Sebastian Store on Hearst land is what appears to be a small and prosperous group of residential homes, warehouses and an abandoned school house, remaining remnants of a past era. All nestle amid towering eucalyptus trees. The trees were first planted by Hearst in 1890 with the idea that the tall trunks of eucalyptus might be used to replace pier piling when needed. No trees of any kind were native to the bay property. The eucalyptus, however, were never used as originally intended but have been an efficient windbreak and provide an excellent source of firewood. Some of the existing wooden houses were built by George Hearst for his employees. Until a short time ago the curved roof home of Francisco "Pancho" Estrada, son of Julian Estrada, stood among the rest.

After the death of George Hearst in 1891, operations at the bay continued much as they had before until the death of Mrs. Hearst in 1919, when William Randolph Hearst became sole heir. W. R. Hearst built several Spanish style homes for his favorite employees, including a new home for Pancho Estrada. Additional warehouses were constructed to hold his many treasures accumulated by the ship load prior to and during the building of his "Castle" on the "Enchanted Hill."

Following the death of W. R. Hearst in 1951 the properties, now owned by several heirs, were placed into a corporation and Hearst pier was abandoned. A small tract of land, together with 800 feet of beach frontage and tideland at the junction of the state highway and access road to San Simeon, was donated to the County of San Luis Obispo in 1953 as the Phoebe Hearst Memorial Park for use as a public picnic and camp area. A new pier was constructed at this site by the county, primarily for use as a fishing pier as it does not extend far enough into deep water for boat use. In 1971 the Phoebe Hearst Memorial Park passed to state hands in a trade negotiated with the county, at which time the park became part of the State Park system.

In 1964 the last two men of the old regime retired: Randolph Apperson, ranch superintendent, and William W. Murray, president of the incorporated Hearst ranch properties. Following their retirement W. R. Hearst, Jr., unlike his father, was able to use his influence upon the corporation management for better public relations between the corporation and the local people. Access to beaches was provided where previously trespass over narrow beach frontage property had been severely punished.

A projected resurgence of activities within old bay property bounds is now under consideration for future development.

Scene typical of the beach landing of timber and lumber from a schooner anchored off shore along the Cambria-San Simeon coast. (Mary Hartzell collection)

The old lamp and its housing was removed and loaned to the Cambria Lions Club for display there.

Piedras Blancas Lighthouse as it appeared 80 years ago. (Paul Squibb collection)

One of three try pots used for rendering whale oil at San Simeon. Each held 500 gallons of rendered blubber.

Chapter 14

Piedras Blancas
Lighthouse Station

Before the establishment of a lighthouse at Piedras Blancas Point sea captains frequenting the shores of central California depended upon navigational charts, their own navigational ability which was often reputed to involve a sixth sense, and on their sighting of natural phenomena to guide them to their destination. Without shore stations to warn them by light and signal of the dangers of rock or shoal at night or in heavy fog, the early captains under sail, at the mercy of the winds, performed miracles as they glided safely into bays and coves which were frequently uncharted and unknown except to the most daring.

San Simeon Bay was a perfect refuge for the smaller trading schooners and brigs in times of heavy northwest wind or when fleeing from the Spanish patrol. The main danger was encountered when approaching the harbor. The rocky shore extended northwest and southeast. A captain misjudging his approach was in great danger of being blown toward shore where submerged rocks and the shore itself would soon destroy a ship entirely dependent upon wind for power.

Juan Rodriguez Cabrillo first sighted and named the gleaming white rocks north of San Simeon Bay as he sailed northward some distance from shore on his exploratory cruise of the California coast in 1542. Many historians believe he remained well off shore during much of his journey as his ship required strong winds to maneuver safely. Its style and inability to respond quickly in a light breeze prohibited close inspection of the dangerous rocky shore comprising much of the California coast line.

However, whether through the lenses of his telescope or by sending men ashore in small boats, Cabrillo saw several features of the land including Morro Rock and the estuary there. It is believed he detected the entrance to San Simeon Bay and sent boats ashore, though it was not charted until 300 years had passed. The white rocks, on the other hand, were noted as an aid to navigation, detectable from 18 miles at sea.

After the whaling station was located at San Simeon in 1864, Captain Joseph Clark maintained a crow's nest lookout at the site of the white rocks which served not only for the sighting of whales but, on occasion, aided in sighting ships in distress. At least once, the men at the lookout were able to rescue shipwrecked men when the unfortunate sailing vessel *Harlech Castle* ran ashore some distance to the north.

By 1872 shipping in and out of San Simeon Bay was relatively good business. Large quantities of lumber, farm produce and mining equipment formed the major part of the cargos. At this time the Pacific Lighthouse Board delegated a lighthouse for Piedras Blancas Point; and then, only on the urgent recommendation of Colonel R. S. Williamson, chief of the board and an officer in the United States Army.

Seventy thousand dollars were finally allotted for its erection, and Captain Ashley was appointed to superintend construction. He had previously proven his ability when he completed construction of a similarly designed lighthouse at Point Arena.

Work, however, did not begin until April of 1874 when material for the brick and steel tower was shipped directly from San Francisco on the *San Luis*, captained by Alexander, to the small Piedras Blancas dock (mentioned elsewhere), under contract with Goodall, Nelson and Perkins, prominent coastwise shippers of the day. Twenty-five to 30 men were employed in construction which was not completed until the following year.

The lighthouse station was built on land leased by the Army from Peter Gillis, who had purchased 1,414 acres of the Piedra Blanca Rancho from Juan Castro in 1867. During construction Gillis worked as a teamster and, apparently for the convenience of men working on the project and possibly with some hope of becoming the lighthouse keeper, he opened a federal post office at the site on April 5, 1875, which was officially known as Piedras Blancas Post Office. However, its life was short, closing on July 6 of the same year after operating only three months.

From the first establishment of a lighthouse system on the California coast by the Lighthouse Board under the supervision of the Army, it was manned by civilian personnel until 1939. At that time the United States Coast Guard took over operation under the newly enacted Lighthouse Act.

The tower of the Piedras Blancas lighthouse is the third of its kind to be constructed on the coast. It is located on base rock which appears to contain cinnabar. A double wall of brick with an airspace between keeps the structure from sweating and deteriorating in the moist sea air. Originally the tower reached a height of 94 feet to the focal plane and 110 feet to the top, making it a total of 150 feet above low water. The diameter at the base is 34 feet. The tower was designed with a circular iron stairway within which reached to the light. The stairway and its intermediate landing plates were supported by carriers resting on cast iron brackets. The brackets for the platforms and stairs were built into the wall while the brickwork was going up.

The original light was fitted with large glass prisms cut and polished in France. The light source was a Fresnel kerosene ardent vapor lamp with five wicks which consumed four to five tons of kerosene a year. The reflector was so cunningly cut, magnifying the light to such intensity that it could be seen on a clear night from the mast of a sailing vessel as much as 25 miles to sea, according to the *Pacific Coast Coast Pilot*.

The light was rotated by a clock mechanism to flash every 15 seconds, controlled by the measured fall of weights attached to cables and a crane in the center of the rotunda. The mechanism, also from France, was made by Henry Lapute in 1872. The lighthouse keepers cranked a drum, rewinding the weights every hour. Each evening when the mechanism was put in motion, the weights had to be readjusted in order to regulate the timing of the rotation. Three men were required to maintain the station, working on four-hour shifts during the night. Three large two-story houses were provided for the men and their families.

There is no record of a lighthouse keeper at the station before early 1876 when Captain Lorin Vincent Thorndyke was placed in charge. He served as its keeper until he retired in 1906 at the age of 75. His sons, Lorin V. and Emory, were born at the lighthouse. It is the recollections of Lorin, Jr., that have provided the information regarding actual lighthouse operation during the 30 years his father was in residence there. During these 30 years no shipwreck occurred, a credit to the efficiency of the warning system and the men in charge of the light.

Supplies were ordered once a year, brought by a government lighthouse tender approximately every twelfth month. Kerosene for the light, coal for the three families, flour and other staples and lighthouse supplies were delivered at a little dock built against the steep ocean cliff on the lee side of the point.

Other supplies were often ordered for delivery by a special government supply ship, scheduled to arrive every two or three months. The ship, according to the younger Thorndyke, could never be relied upon and many months would often pass between its visits. The captain of the ship, however, was an expert navigator and never hesitated to approach the station in a heavy fog, tying up at the dock and discharging cargo without ever having a mishap of any kind. Thorndyke said that, as a boy, he never ceased to marvel at the captain's skill in finding the landing no matter how dense the fog. Dress materials and household articles were usually ordered through this government boat, as well as some staples when Captain Thorndyke felt the supply might give out before the arrival of the annual tender.

At this time George Hearst was leasing rancho land to numerous Swiss dairymen. These were the neighbors of the station. Captain Thorndyke, unable to guess the arrival time of either the tender or the more frequent supply ship, occasionally found himself with a heavy surplus of flour and other commodities. These extra staples were often exchanged with the Swiss neighbors for young livestock which the Captain maintained on the land surrounding the lighthouse, and on property he owned further north along the coast and in San Carpoforo Creek canyon.

Mrs. Thorndyke died when her youngest son, Emory, was four years old. This left the responsibility of raising two boys upon the shoulders of the Captain. Captain Thorndyke was a native of Maine who first went to sea in a windjammer as a cabin boy and had circumnavigated the globe five times before becoming a coastwise sailor. He finally quit the sea to become captain at the lighthouse at Piedras Blancas. Soon after settling down he married Elizabeth Jarmon, a sister to Mrs. Thomas Evans, a near neighbor. Following the death of his wife, the children were given various responsibilities, one of which included the care of the San Carpoforo Creek property. At one time the two boys were sent to live there with neighbors while they attended school in the canyon and cared for the ranch. Lorin, often in poor health, remained with his father and assisted about the lighthouse as he grew older.

With the lighthouse situated about eight miles north of San Simeon Bay and the trail to the bay a very poor one, residents in the vicinity of the lighthouse seldom attempted the trip to San Simeon and the store located there, especially in the early days of the lighthouse. Occasionally a coastal trading schooner would come to the Piedras Blancas dock. These people, rather than cart their ranch produce, consisting primarily of butter, to the bay, would conduct their business at the lighthouse.

Young Thorndyke attended the Washington School a few miles to the north part of the time. After it closed he attended San Simeon School, using a horse and cart. The road over which he traveled wandered along the foothills from one ranch house to another. Before reaching San Simeon it passed through 14 gates, each made up of barbed wire strands. He had to open and close each of these 14 wire gates to and from school, mounting and dismounting from his cart 28 times each way.

As captain of the lighthouse station, Captain Thorndyke had first choice of watch. He always took the early evening shift from 6 p.m. to 10 p.m. in order to have an uninterrupted night at home with his family. The other men at the station alternated the two remaining shifts. Daylight hours were spent in repair and maintenance of the station. When the Captain went on duty in the evening it was his job to regulate the timing mechanism. Thorndyke, Jr., assisted him with this job. As the Captain made the adjustments the lad took off or added weight as his father called instructions. He also undertook the job of winding the mechanism by cranking the drum for the first course of the evening. Once adjusted, the timing remained perfect throughout the night. Once stopped, however, it had to be readjusted.

After the lighthouse was constructed, the whaling station continued to maintain a lookout and crews there until whaling was abandoned in 1894. The capture of a whale in the vicinity of the lighthouse brought all station hands out with their glasses to watch the excitement. The whalers kept two boats at the lighthouse dock, each with a crew of seven men. If they were fortunate in capturing a whale to the north of San Simeon Point, the tow to the flensing wharf and rendering vats was usually a short and easy one, the death blow being administered not far from the entrance to the bay.

For several summers during the 1880's guano was harvested from the rocks since it was this dung which, through countless centuries, had accumulated to make the rocks their glistening white. A schooner from San Francisco anchored off from the rocks during quiet tides. Men, without ever landing at the station, launched small boats which they drew along side the rocks. They scrambled about with shovels, scraping and transferring the guano into sacks which were loaded into the small boats for transfer to the waiting schooner. Both young Lorin and George Steiner, who visited at the lighthouse to play with him, recalled the very offensive odor which drifted ashore when the guano was disturbed. The major portion of the deposit was harvested in two or three years and the schooner ceased to call.

At the age of 75 Captain Thorndyke decided it was time to retire. Being in good health he could not think of a plausible excuse to attach to his resignation until the fog horn was installed in 1906. He used this installation as his complaint, saying that the noise it created was so great he could no longer work under the strain. According to Lorin, Jr., it was a very lame excuse, indeed, as it did not bother him particularly.

After retiring he decided to remarry, choosing for a wife his former wife's sister, Margaret Jarmon. They settled at San Simeon where, for several years, they assisted young Thorndyke and his wife at the store and hotel which he now owned.

Following Captain Thorndyke's resignation from the lighthouse service civilians continued to be in charge under the supervision of the Army, but records of these succeeding keepers have not been located. In 1939 the Coast Guard took over management of the station, at which time enlisted personnel replaced civilian employees.

In 1949 extensive remodeling of the lighthouse was undertaken. The old lamp and its housing were removed and loaned to the Cambria Lions Club for care and display in Cambria. It now stands near the Veterans' Memorial building on Pinedorado grounds. Approximately 40 feet of the old tower, including the overhanging catwalk, were removed during remodeling as it was deemed unsafe due to weathering and age.

In place of the old light an automatic electric drum aerorotating beacon with a 36-inch lens was installed. Operating in conjunction with a 1,000 watt electric bulb of 2,000 watt candle power, it is capable of casting a light beam a distance of 18 miles from its altitude of 142 feet above sea level. The fog signal, operating automatically in conjunction with the light, is heard when visibility drops to five miles. Emergency standby power operates both light and signal if commercial power fails.

In 1962 the three large two-story houses which served the station personnel for so many years were moved to make way for the present modern stucco buildings, four in number.

Station duties are few. The Coast Guard crew is rotated frequently as enlistment terms expire. Children of the young families in residence at the station attend school in Cambria, transported by school buses which serve the coastal area as far north as Pacific Valley in Monterey County, a far cry from the days of the cart and horse and the 14 wire gates.

Cattle of the Hearst Sunical Land and Cattle Corporation, now in charge of Piedra Blanca Rancho lands, roam the area around the station. Visitors, though not encouraged, are cordially welcomed and shown the interior of the old structure with its winding iron stairs and rotunda pit into which the weights of the old clock mechanism once descended. Some of the station personnel endeavor to learn a little about the history of the lighthouse structure and enjoy answering questions as they guide visitors during the regular visiting hours.

Chapter 15

Rancho San Simeon and Public Domain

Rancho San Simeon, unlike its neighboring ranchos, was granted to a Spanish Don who never occupied it. This land of rolling hills, well supplied with native grasses and springs, was first claimed by Mission San Miguel. It had poorly defined boundaries though San Simeon Creek was considered its southern border. From the creek it extended northward along the coast to the southern boundary of the lands claimed by Mission San Antonio, and eastward to an indefinite boundary limited only by the high ridges of the Santa Lucia Mountain range.

When Mission San Miguel was first founded in 1797 the lands surrounding it were observed to be fertile and appeared adequate for the raising of farm animals and grain. However, the padres soon learned that the water supply was entirely dependent on irregular seasonal rainfall. Weather conditions ranging from very hot summers to cold, late, dry winters did not guarantee sufficient moisture to support all the needs of the growing mission, either in grains or livestock. Unlike Mission San Antonio to the north, irrigation was not readily possible. The Salinas River beside which the mission was located did not flow continuously but disappeared underground for large portions of the year. So, the most practical solution was expansion toward the coast where rich lands with greater rainfall and permanently flowing streams could be utilized. Furthermore, the aboriginal Indians of the coast, adept at securing seafood from the rocky shores, had created regular trails over the Santa Lucia Mountains which had been used for centuries as trade routes to the

Indians of the Salinas River Valley and even as far east as the *Yokuta* of the San Joaquin Valley. At what date the padres began using the coast area is not known. Judging from contemporary accounts, it is altogether probable that contact with coastal smugglers was made as early as 1800, as the padres sought needed supplies in exchange for surplus produce and otter skins easily obtained by the Indians along the coast.

The first concerted effort to develop the coastal property began about 1810. According to researches of Father Engelhardt of Mission Santa Barbara, the first buildings and a corral were constructed there in that year. If either the creek or the rancho was named at this early date, it was not noted in the records; reference designated it simply as the ocean rancho.

The small corral, according to the account, measured 292 square feet, while the initial buildings, which consisted of an adobe house and granary, were each 75 feet long. If the measurement given for the corral is correct, it could only have been used as a holding pen for a very few head of saddle horses kept handy for immediate use. In 1814 two more rooms were added as additional living quarters. Whether these were for Indians, soldiers or other personnel is not noted.

In visualizing the life at this outpost, maintained exclusively as a business enterprise and primarily for farming and raising of fine saddle horses, we picture a small *rancheria* of Indians upon whose labors depended the success of the undertaking, together with one or more trustworthy Spanish subordinates of the mission who were entrusted with overseeing the labors and religion of the Indian neophytes.

Only 13 years had elapsed from the time the mission was founded until records indicate the coastal outpost was firmly established. In that short time few, if any, of the *Playano Salinan* Indians remained in their native camps along the shore. Many had succumbed quickly to the maladies of the white men, especially through early contact with the Spanish soldiers who were often of low repute and carriers of chronic diseases. These Indians may also have died off more rapidly than other nearby groups (as some of the earliest Spanish accounts noted) because of their poor physique and inability to cope with the rigors of life as compared (for instance) with the *Chumash* Indians to the south and the *Salinans* east of the Santa Lucias.

The neophytes who were placed at the San Simeon outpost were undoubtedly chosen from all the Indians of the San Miguel Mission (which included among its residents *Salinans* of the Salinas Valley, a very few coastal *Salinans,* and some *Yokuta* from the San Joaquin Valley) for their loyalty to the mission and their individual inclination toward industry. Only a very few *Chumash* were members of the mission, but some of this group, in all probability, were included with those sent to the coast as they were considered the most intelligent.

If one takes into account the size of the buildings, the amount of labor necessary to make the adobe brick and tile, to break up the adobe-like soil with their crude implements and to plant and harvest crops, it is clear that a tremendous amount of work was done at the outpost by the limited colony. In the beginning, brood mares were the principal animals kept on the rancho. These Spanish horses were in great demand by the trading vessels. The mares roamed the hills, requiring little attention except at roundup. The best of the young colts were broken to saddle and for occasional use in the field. Those not needed by the personnel of the mission were sold to Spanish colonizers and traded to the captains of the schooners who were glad to get them as the fine breed was in great demand in Hawaii.

No further report was made about the life at the rancho until December of 1830, when it was referred to for the first time as Rancho San Simeon. This report mentions the erection of another building, an adobe house measuring 85 by 31 feet. This is the third building known to have been erected on the rancho during mission occupancy. This report also mentions the harvest of grain during the preceding summer, and the raising of both tame horses and brood mares, 800 head of cattle, and a good producing fruit orchard.

One of the major complaints by the Spanish, and later by the Mexican governments, made against many of the missions was their failure to submit frequent reports concerning the "wild" Indians, and the produce and wealth of the mission establishments. The Spanish government, the Mexican government and the government of Alta California were all well aware that the mission fathers, as well as the Indians, were dealing extensively with unauthorized trading vessels but little could be done to control these activities which were so far from the centers of population and administration.

Undoubtedly one of the prime reasons for development of the San Simeon Rancho in preference to Santa Rosa Rancho, also owned by the Mission San Miguel, was its convenience to San Simeon Bay—a secluded and totally undeveloped but excellent harbor with a protected anchorage and gently sloping sandy beaches. The rapid growth of trade here has already been described in another chapter. Ships had little or no trouble when making landings and it was possible for them to secure not only hides and otter skins in large quantities but the fine horses, fresh fruits and garden vegetables raised at the outpost. Obviously the mission profited handsomely from these backdoor transactions and had no qualms when reporting small numbers of stock or produce on the San Simeon holdings.

Prior to the founding of the rancho sea otter were taken along the San Simeon coast by Russian and American vessels working in partnership with the Russians out of Sitka, Alaska. Early shipping records report these runs in which the vessels were, at that time, familiar with "every cove, inlet and bay" of the coast. Further evidence substantiating this early contact for the purpose of securing otter was found during excavation of an Indian site at Morro Bay in 1961, at which time a small Alaskan harpoon was unearthed, the only alien artifact discovered at the site. These harpoons have also been found at other sites along the coast as far south as Santa Barbara. Barnof of Sitka furnished the hunting ships with food supplies and Aleut hunters with skin canoes.

The early otter hunting records also substantiate early mission participation in this trade as they stated that the friars became the chief customers of these hunting vessels. They traded furs to them and sometimes actually outfitted boats themselves for hunting. Frequently large quantities of the goods obtained from the smugglers were profitably resold by the padres to the earliest Spanish settlers and *rancheros*.

Because cattle and horses ranged at will, knowing no boundaries either at the mission proper or at the coast ranchos, branding of cattle and horses was compulsory as it had been in Spain. San Miguel Mission marked all of its animals with its registered brand, a simple flattopped 3.

Soon after 1830 the Mexican government increased pressure for further civilian colonization, and a movement was started to deprive the missions of their control of the vast areas of land which, in the judgment of the government, was discouraging new settlers. In 1833 the Secularization Act was passed. Designed to bring an end to the all too powerful missions, it did away with the supreme power of the priests and put the missions on the same footing as parish churches. The properties of the missions were gradually placed under the supervision of government men for inventory, distribution to the Indians and disposal as land grants. Special laws and regulations were enacted for proper apportionment of the property. If these laws had been carried out as originally drafted, it is believed the complete ruin of the Indians and the tremendous influx of crime which followed secularization would probably never have occurred. It was during these years of distribution that some of the largest land grants were made.

San Miguel Mission was put under full secularization in 1838, and in 1839 Manuel Ortega was appointed majordomo of San Simeon Rancho overseeing the Indians living there. Ortega originally came from Mexico to Santa Barbara in 1832, where he married Andrea Cota. One of the first jobs he was given after arriving at San Simeon was to investigate an Indian complaint that outsiders were killing cattle on rancho lands for their hides.

Ortega was apparently unable to correct the situation or, in some other way he antagonized the Indians, for they soon registered another complaint. This time it was against Ortega, saying that he was not distributing the rancho property fairly as he was instructed to do. The complaint brought his immediate dismissal from the office he held, after which time the Indians received no further government-appointed supervision.

Following the appointment of Don José de Jésus Pico to Mission San Miguel in 1841 José Mariano Estrada was appointed majordomo at Mission San Antonio. After having served for some time in Monterey as *comandante* for the Mexican government, he established himself firmly at the mission with a family of two boys, José Ramon and Julian, and two girls, all of whom he was anxious to see settled and independent in the fertile San Luis Obispo area. He had already received Buena Vista Rancho near San Antonio Mission as a Spanish land grant for himself. Probably at the urging of Mariano Estrada, José Ramon, who was living on Rancho Buena Vista looking after its welfare, applied for Rancho San Simeon as a grant, which he received from Governor Juan B. Alvarado on December 1, 1842.

Rules for securing of a grant, once conceded by the governor, required the grantee to stock the land, plant an orchard and erect a dwelling. Rancho San Simeon already had an excellent orchard, buildings and farm land. Nothing was simpler than to claim as his own the mission stock which still roamed the hills, thus fulfilling the last provision needed to retain the grant.

Nevertheless, some conflict arose at this time. José Miguel Gomez, a curate who was first located at La Purisima Mission then transferred as overseer of affairs to San Miguel Mission, upon learning that the coastal rancho was no longer to be considered a part of the mission property, put in a request for it in his own name, asking Governor Alvarado for the grant. His claim was overridden, however, and the claim of José Ramon honored instead. Gomez, though angered by this turn of events, was unable to contest the governor's decision as the Estrada and Pico families had considerable "pull" in political circles at Monterey. However, the young curate did not relinquish his desires for Rancho San Simeon. In a few years, as the turn of events will indicate, he was able to buy it.

José Ramon Estrada, born at Monterey in 1811, received schooling under Corporal Miguel Archuleta from 1815 to 1820. Five years of instruction, according to present standards, would have afforded him little educational background with which to meet the problems of the world but at that time it was more education than the average Californian received. He had learned to read, write and do his figures. From his ninth birthday until his twenty-first he appears to have had little responsibility except for attendance of social functions. In 1832 he became interested in hunting sea otter, which were plentiful, offering adventure as well as a good income. Accordingly, he was licensed to take them in San Francisco Bay. With Castro, Ortega and others as partners, he hired Aleuts and equipment from the Russians. With the additional help of Indians from Mission San Jose they are said to have done a prosperous business for a time.

After two years he gave up the pursuit of otter in preference to a life in California politics. At this time he began courting his future wife, Maria Castro. Shortly after their marriage he was appointed *alcalde* of Monterey. While holding this office he became hotly entangled with Colonel Mariano Chico and subsequently lost his seat, this being the year of 1836. On December 27, 1837, he was appointed as a member of the *Diputacion* or Congress of California at Monterey and *Comisionado* and administrator at Santa Clara Mission. From 1841 through 1843 he was prefect of the First District of California, which included San Luis Obispo County, succeeding Tiburcio Castro, receiving the sizable sum of $2,000 a year. For a short time in 1842 he was in charge of the government of California during the absence of Alvarado.

The same year he received the grant of San Simeon he became a member of the *Junta,* a position he held until shortly before his death in 1845. Apparently due to ill health, José Ramon was absent from the assembly the last several meetings prior to the expiration of his term of office, which ended in 1845. When the term expired, he was not reelected to office.

Due to his position in the *Junta* and his established residences at Rancho Buena Vista and Santa Clara, his interest in Rancho San Simeon, in spite of his previously ardent desire for it, was limited to infrequent visits.

This rancho was small compared to the rancho received by José's brother as it contained a mere 4,468.81 acres. According to the Spanish description, it lay "between San Simeon Creek on the south, bordered by Rancho Santa Rosa; and Arroyo del Peñal on the north, bordered by Rancho de José de Jésus Pico; on the west by the ocean at high tide, and on the east by the Santa Lucia Mountains."

The official United States surveys of the coastal ranchos, conducted during the 1850's, limited the lands to specific boundaries and was at considerable variance with the Spanish descriptions. The original grant stated that Rancho San Simeon bordered Rancho Santa Rosa. The variance, however, created a gap between the two ranchos and placed the northern boundary of Rancho Santa Rosa at a point on the coast in the vicinity of a small stream later called Leffingwell Creek. Further inland its boundary was delineated by Santa Rosa Creek. This area between San Simeon Creek and the new boundary of Santa Rosa Rancho became public domain.

Prior to the government survey Rancho San Simeon was sold to Thomas A. Park (March 12, 1845) apparently in anticipation of the death of José Ramon, who died shortly after. Before Park could establish a residence on the property he, too, died. At his death George Bellomy was named administrator of his estate.

In Bancroft's *History of California* he refers at some length to a Captain Thomas B. Park, master of the schooner *California* and other ships that often put into port at San Simeon Bay during this early period. T. A. Park and T. B. Park appear to have died at the same time. It is possible Bancroft's reference is to the same man. The purchase of a small rancho by a sea captain who was ready to retire would not have been unlikely.

The estate of T. A. Park, or Rancho San Simeon, was offered for sale to the highest bidder. It was purchased for $1,400 by Henry A. Tefft, husband of Maria Josefa Dana of the noted Dana family of California, at public auction in San Luis Obispo on May 21, 1851. At this time there was a lien on the Rancho by William A. Streeter for the sum of $300, for which he held a trust deed. Tefft, a land speculator, paid off the trust deed the day following the purchase, bringing the cost of the Rancho to $1,700, an average price of 38 cents an acre. There is no record of livestock being included in any of the transactions up to this time. Livestock was often the most valuable part of a rancho and was generally sold separately or removed.

Tefft, only interested in making money by resale of his recent investment, soon found a buyer in José Miguel Gomez, the former curate, and his wife, Josefa. They paid $2,000 cash and gave Tefft a note for a balance of $500, making Tefft a nice little profit of $800.

The Gomez family moved to the rancho and lived there for five years during which time the government survey was concluded and the true rancho boundaries determined. They accumulated "1,200 horned cattle, 120 horses and mares (more or less), also 100 sheep and 100 hogs (more or less)" which they sold "together with the land, brand and *señal* (ear mark) as recorded in the San Luis Obispo County book of brands," for $1,600 to Jerome A. Limass on January 2, 1856. No explanation is forthcoming concerning the sale of Rancho San Simeon at this time nor the reason for the loss the Gomez family seems to have suffered though the size of the original grant was greatly reduced by the government survey.

Limass was another speculator and cattle dealer. By December 22, 1857, he had disposed of the cattle and other animals on the rancho and considered he was making a fine profit on the land when he sold it to Domingo Pujol for $5,000. The land now had a market value of $1.10 per acre.

Pujol was a young Spaniard, recently arrived in San Luis Obispo County. He was a well educated man and had wealth which he planned to use wisely for land investment. He made excellent connections in the county and soon courted and married Maria Ignacia Wilson, daughter of Captain John Wilson and his wife, Doña Ramona Carrillo Pacheco, who were part owners in Piedra Blanca Rancho as well as owners of other county property. Pujol was wealthy enough to buy and wait, and farseeing enough to know that with every passing year his land would become more valuable as the land hungry Americans were arriving daily. He stocked the rancho with cattle and affiliated himself with the San Francisco law firm of Saujurjo and Bolado. Separately and together these partners continued to busy themselves with buying and selling property in San Luis Obispo County. They made substantial loans to extravagant Spanish Dons, taking trust deeds to their rancho properties as security. At this time the Dons were busy trying to prove ownership of their ranchos according to United States law. This took hard, cold cash which few of the Dons had.

Soon after the transfer of Rancho San Simeon to José Ramon Estrada the Indians left, apparently to join activities on Santa Rosa Rancho which was owned by José's brother, Don Julian Estrada, who took an intense interest in his domain. After the Indians left, the mission buildings fell into disuse with the exception of that portion used as a residence by the Gomez family, and after they left it, together with the other buildings, continued to decay and fall apart helped by range animals which often used them for shelter.

Following the government survey finalized in 1859, Pujol transferred ownership of the rancho to the law firm for a credit of $8,000, though technically the rancho remained in his possession and he continued to run cattle on it. Eight years later, on April 30, 1867, it was sold by the firm to Ira VanGorden.

Mr. VanGorden and his family were residents of Arroyo Grande Valley at that time. They immediately moved to their new holdings where they erected a home from local and imported lumber. The adobe buildings, what little remained, became the site of their hog and cow pens. The transaction lists the sale as having been made for $10,000 but, according to an account given by the late Tom Stilts, who knew Ira VanGorden quite well, the transaction was not for cash but for 500 head of fat steers. In view of Pujol's previous interest in cattle, this may well have been true.

Ira VanGorden originally came to California in 1846 as a member of the Harlan Wagon Train, and was employed at Sutter's Mill at the time of gold discovery there. After working in the gold fields for a short time he moved, first to San Francisco, then to the San Joaquin Valley and finally to Arroyo Grande Valley before purchasing San Simeon Rancho. After settling on the rancho he became engrossed in his own affairs and did not aspire to public office as so many of his early neighbors did. Instead, he contented himself with the promotion of good roads into the area by serving on various road viewing boards from time to time. Shortly after purchasing the rancho, VanGorden and his wife, Mary Balaam, subdivided a large portion of it and offered small parcels for sale. A notice to that effect was placed in the San Luis Obispo *Pioneer* of February 29, 1868.

The first sale was made June 11, 1868, to George Dauskin, who paid $1,500 for 100 acres. This piece of land extended along the northern boundary of the property. The second sale was consumated July 7 of the same year. The purchase was for 80 acres by Henry Severance for a sum of $480. This sale bordered San Simeon Creek along the southern boundary of the rancho and was coincidental to several others which joined each other, and which were recorded at the same time. Uriah Slack purchased 120 acres for $720 the following week. November 10 and 11 other sales were made to William Arbuckle, bordering the public road (San Simeon Creek road) which intersected the land of Severance and Slack; and to Franklin Gross, whose purchase joined that of Arbuckle. At this time, averaging the sales, San Simeon Rancho had increased in value to $7.60 an acre, a far cry from the 38 cents an acre 17 years before.

Rancho San Simeon played little part in the actual promotion of industry or livelihood of the area prior to the formation of Cambria in 1866, but, while it lay relatively dormant, numerous settlers were pouring into the public domain behind San Simeon and Santa Rosa Ranchos and into the narrow corridor between them. It was these homestead settlers who laid the foundations for Cambria's birth as they created businesses and trades which led to the need for a town as a nearby center for supplies, transaction of their business and social contact.

Jeffrey Phelan was the first U. S. American on record to arrive. He took up public domain property in 1857, immediately following conclusion of the survey of Rancho San Simeon, though he had come to California many years before and had also been employed at Coloma when gold was discovered there.

In 1857 California land laws were vague and immigrants, finding land they wished to possess settled, first, as squatters. A pre-emption law was made in 1854 and remained the principal legal law by which land could be acquired for the next eight years. The first land Jeffrey Phelan secured was 160 acres which he purchased through these pre-emption graduation laws of the United States government for 12½ cents an acre. At this time large tracts were also allotted to the state for disposal for education and internal improvement projects. Some land was given free of charge to enterprising individuals and groups who promised to erect schools. Jeffrey Phelan acquired 320 acres under this law and built the first public school in the county, a small one-room cabin of hand hewn pine logs situated beside the horse and wagon trail which passed through his lands from San Luis Obispo to the Bay of San Simeon. The first teacher at this school was Miss Sarah Minerva Clark, daughter of a neighboring settler, Dr. E. A. Clark, who used the term "Dr." to indicate his degree of education.

Later, some settlers who were squatters, in order to hold their lands against encroachment by others, invoked the California Homestead Act of 1860-61, which was a state law protecting their squatter's rights but did not constitute final procurement of the property. In 1862 the federal government finally instituted the Homestead Act under which the squatter's homesteads were eventually secured.

Close on the heels of Jeffrey Phelan was James Mathers and his wife, Sarah, who arrived September 3, 1858. They chose property adjoining Phelan to the west, and north of Santa Rosa Creek. The Mathers lived as squatters for two years before they, too, took advantage of the state homestead act to protect their land. Carolan Mathers, his father, Newton, and his wife, Margaret, may have arrived simultaneously with James and Sarah, or at least soon afterward, as did Harrison Dart and his wife, Lovina, another daughter of Mr. Clark. Others were E. A. Clark, L. H. Clark and Franklin Riley and his wife, Hannah.

Carolan immediately became active in local affairs. He was named Justice of the Peace of San Simeon Township in 1860. As an untrained but "practical" surveyor he served officially on many primitive roads in the coastal north part of the county until R. R. Harris, a graduate surveyor, was appointed to the office. Carolan also established himself locally as a money lender, realtor and notary public becoming, what some deemed, an ambitious and obnoxious man of the community. However, in spite of his shortcomings, he was elected to the Board of Supervisors from the San Simeon District for 1865-66, and in 1867 he held the office of county assessor. James Mathers was less assuming though he, too, ran for Justice of the Peace of the district in 1862. He was elected but failed to receive the office as he could not post the necessary bond.

Franklin Riley arrived in 1858 and settled at the mouth of San Simeon Creek, filing for his homestead on December 29, 1860, in order to protect his squatter's rights on property extending one-half mile south along the coast and eastward for a half mile along the creek. Riley became involved in several mining adventures about the area, notably the coal mine which was discovered by William Leffingwell in 1863. Eventually Riley abandoned his homestead property and moved to the Morro Bay area where his name figured prominently as a founding pioneer.

The names of Warren C. and William C. Ricard, or Rickard (both spellings were used) are frequently seen in the business transactions of the early 1860's. It is to be noted that these two men had the same initials. When signing documents they often used only their initials, resulting in much confusion as to which Ricard was transacting what business. The brothers, for we can hardly assume them to be otherwise, jointly owned mining and land claims to the east in the San Marcos Creek area near Adelaida, operating a store there. They took up squatter's rights on the coast at Leffingwell Creek and opened another store which was simply called Rickard's Log Store (the first in the north coast area), and became involved in the coal mining enterprise with Leffingwell. For many years the indentation at the mouth of Leffingwell Creek was known as Rickard's Cove and the first wharf franchise issued for this site designated that the proposed construction was to be known as Ricard's Wharf.

William C. Ricard seems to have managed most of the coast business and Warren C. spent his time on the San Marcos Creek property. Reverses and over-investment eventually forced them to sell most of their interests, while other pieces were lost by attachment and sheriff's sale. Warren faded from the picture. In 1871 F. F. Letcher, P. A. Forrester and W. M. Gillespie acquired the log store. Leffingwell acquired the Ricard Wharf franchise in 1874 and built his pier, then called Leffingwell Pier, hiring William Ricard as wharfinger. William continued to live in a small cabin near the pier and to work for Leffingwell for several years, eventually leaving to live at San Diego.

William Leffingwell, to whom we have referred several times, arrived in 1858 with his wife, Eunice. and seven grown and nearly grown children, to settle on public domain joining San Simeon Rancho. He also acquired some coast land between San Simeon Creek and Santa Rosa Rancho but made his home on 160 acres joining Jeffrey Phelan in the pines.

Leffingwell had three hardworking grown sons, Adam, William, Jr., and Joseph, who, with their father, soon established a well organized ranch and started several businesses. The land was well timbered and with a good knowledge of saw mill operation, they set up a saw pit operated by horse power from which they supplied lumber to other settlers arriving in the area.

William, Sr., soon discovered an outcropping of coal on his beach property and used it to advantage in his blacksmith forge. It eventually attracted the attention of several people and with his neighbors as partners, he formed a coal mining company, the details of which are given in the chapter on mining. The demand for quality lumber and other supplies encouraged him to make further use of his beach holding by establishing a landing where top quality lumber and commodities could be floated ashore from ships anchored in deep water. In addition to the landing he built a small warehouse to store and protect goods until purchasers arrived from the hills to pick them up.

Young Joseph preferred to manage the ranch and cattle, free from the partnership with his father and brothers. He eventually bought land of his own for a dairy business at the junction of Santa Rosa Creek road and the coastal highway (recently included in Fiscalini property) and later became a partner with James M. Woods as half owner of the American Exchange Hotel in Cambria. Joseph and his wife, Margaret, continued to conduct most of their business apart from the rest of the family until his death, about 1880, when his widow and their two young children, John Henry and William Charles, moved to northern California. The property was subsequently placed under the management of other members of the Leffingwell clan. The dairy was rented to George Bright and part of his property was incorporated into what later became known as the Lester Smithers ranch.

William, Sr., continued to add to his property holdings through purchase from Jeffrey Phelan. In 1866, shortly after neighboring ranchers turned to grain raising and dairying, he built a wheat grist mill for grinding wheat into flour. The mill was powered by steam, as was the saw mill at this time. The grist mill was patronized by customers from the Salinas Valley as well as by the local ranchers for a period of about 15 years.

Every year, at assessment time, the assessors asked each man the nature of his business or occupation. It is interesting to note that the Leffingwell men responded according to the business uppermost in their minds in different years. They variously listed themselves as carpenters, millers, machinists and engineers.

Adam was killed August 4, 1882, by an explosion at the saw mill. Besides his wife, Emma, he left three young daughters, Laura Jane, Lena Ivy and Lorena Emma, and a stepson, Clayton Morss (Gison). Emma continued to oversee the maintenance of that portion of the ranch which belonged to her husband with the help of her son, Clayton, and to keep the books for the various other Leffingwell enterprises of which she was a third partner through the death of her husband. She had much strength of character, was admired by the community and was affectionately called Aunt Em by all who knew her.

For several years the Adam Leffiingwell home was at the site of the large cypress trees planted in the early 1870's on the south bank of Leffingwell Creek near the ocean. Five pines sheltered a two story dwelling, buggy shed, smoke house and chicken house. A picket fence surrounded the yard. Later the family moved to a home farther inland. The creek home was purchased by Phoebe Hearst, partially dismantled, and moved to Rancho San Simeon property which had been purchased by George Hearst.

William Leffingwell had four daughters: Caroline Amelia, Mary, Roxana Matilda and Cynthia. Two of the daughters married local ranchers, while Mary and Cynthia married men by the names of Thomas and Woodward and moved away.

Caroline married William M. Gillespie, who originally came to California by covered wagon in 1849. They built an adobe and log home on Leffingwell property overlooking the ocean where springs flowed from the hillside. William was employed by his father-in-law as a miller and at various other occupations on the property. They had seven children. The oldest son, George William, worked on the Hearst ranch for many years after 1875. He learned the blacksmith trade there from John Eubanks, then had his own shop in Cayucos for nine years, later returning to Cambria where he continued to blacksmith for another 18 years. He is noted for his friendship with Cambrian Senator Elmer S. Rigdon and his assistance in Rigdon's effort to have the coast north of Piedras Blancas surveyed for a highway to Monterey. His wife, Bertha Wittenberg, was the daughter of a local dairy pioneer of Piedra Blanca Rancho. George was a charter member of the Cambria chapter of the Native Sons of the Golden West and Bertha instituted El Pinal Parlor of the Native Daughters. They had two children who remained in the area: Muriel Soto of Cayucos and Evelyn, who married Donald Evans.

Other children of William and Caroline Gillespie were William Bradley Gillespie, Martha Cushing, Amelia Mable, Josie Tuttle, Bertha Rhodes and Harriet Jones.

Roxana Matilda Leffingwell (after a previous marriage to a Mr. Terrill, sometimes spelled Tyrell) married B. F. Mayfield, who owned San Simeon Rancho property adjoining William Leffingwell. Benjamin Franklin Mayfield was a native of Tennessee and a veteran of the Mexican War. He came to California as a miner about 1852 but soon turned to farming in Sonoma County, then to Cambria in 1868. Roxana had several children by her former marriage and seven children by Mayfield. Her daughter, Ida Terrill, married Amos Smithers and inherited what later became known as the "Smither's Ranch," that portion of the old Leffingwell property on which the saw mill and grist mill were located. The Smithers property has now been sold to Leimert and Company for subdivision as it joins the Happy Hill portion of Cambria. The Mayfield's seven children were Milton, Frank, Carrie, Fred, Solan, Ethel and Louise.

Ethel married the late Deville Bovee and lived on the upper part of what is now called the Stepladder Ranch, on Stilts Creek, a tributary to San Simeon Creek. Deville farmed the small flats on his property, supplied by spring water, furnishing

Cambria with an abundance of garden vegetables which he brought from the mountains by team and wagon twice a week. His watermelons and canteloupes were in big demand as well as corn, peppers, beans, tomatoes, potatoes and greens. He also met the steamer each week at San Simeon and sold all he could produce. After his wife died, Deville retired to San Luis Obispo to be near his sons who lived there. He was totally blind for a number of his later years though he lived alone and continued to garden and keep his own house until well past 90.

Solan Mayfield is remembered primarily for his ability as a caller at all the square dances.

In 1874 William Leffingwell, Sr., in partnership with J. C. Baker of Santa Rosa Creek, acquired Ricard's Cove and wharf franchise. They built the first pier there, which later became a "Leffingwell and Sons" enterprise. After the death of William, Sr., in 1884 at the age of 84, young William continued as head of the Leffingwell household and most of the business, including operation of the pier until 1894. He also cared for his aging mother, Eunice Leffingwell, who was noted as a spiritualist. Her grandchildren relate they often heard strange rapping and knocking sounds emanating from her room at night when visiting her. These strange sounds thoroughly frightened them. In 1889 Eunice died at age 79 and William fell heir to all the properties still in his mother's name. He eventually married May M. Woods and lived in Cambria in a house on upper Bridge Street built by his brother, Adam, shortly before his death.

Other portions of Leffingwell land are now owned by Tony Williams, himself a descendent of early settlers, descendents of the Phelan family and by the state, which has acquired the properties along the beach for state park use.

The original Jeffrey Phelan properties extending to the north and east of the Leffingwell lands were added to from time to time by additional homesteads filed in the names of several of Jeffrey's children. The major portion of the original ranch continues as an incorporated unit under the Phelan Land and Cattle Company, managed by Leo Nock, a descendent of Jeffrey.

During the early residence of the VanGorden family on San Simeon Rancho, the buildings of the San Miguel Mission outpost were completely obliterated through extensive farming over the site. The existence of the buildings and their purpose was long forgotten. In 1962 the site was rediscovered when pieces of mission-made tile were plowed out of the field by Lindy Bonomi, resident on the ranch. Further evidence was added by the discovery of pieces of Mexican stone *metates* and several brass buttons together with numerous Indian artifacts, floor and drainage tiles. Cultivation had all but obliterated the general plan of the building arrangement on a low rise overlooking San Simeon Creek a few hundred feet upstream from the old lagoon mouth. The buttons, in particular, were of interest because of their appearance and use along the coast as trade goods to mission Indians between the years of 1811 and 1820.

These buttons were originally ordered by Napoleon Bonaparte, together with blouses, for his armies. They bear the likeness of the legendery Phoenix bird and the motto: "Je renais de mas cendres." At sometime following their manufacture, probably at Napoleon's last imprisonment, delivery was cancelled. King Henri Christophe of Haiti, said to be an admirer of Napoleon, ordered a quantity of the blouses for his regiments. The shipment never reached Haiti but was pirated or otherwise diverted enroute. The blouses with buttons soon turned up along the Pacific coast as far north as Columbia, as barter goods to the Indians. Several of the same buttons were found at La Purisima Mission during excavation and restoration.

The western slopes and valleys of the rugged Santa Lucia mountain range, flanking the eastern border of the ranchos, became the camping ground for miners, settlers and adventurers in the 1860's and 1870's. This was public domain, open to squatters and prospecting. People arriving too late to stake out choice lands between the ranchos or touching their eastern boundaries settled in steep valleys and on rocky hills near springs, relying on their ability to survive under adverse circumstances, and trusting in a booming economy.

Rough miners, disappointed in early attempts to locate cinnabar claims near the rich discoveries of the 1860's in the Pine Mountain area, searched every outcropping they could find. They staked hundreds of claims, regardless of the holdings of early squatters and homesteaders. Each man, each family guarded the holding like a she-wolf. Trespassers were shot at without warning, whole families feuded over boundary lines, livestock and right-of-way. Some soon discovered their limited holdings were too poor to support them; others found the fight to hold their "rights" too dangerous. But others were determined to remain to the bitter end, which often involved petitions to county departments for legislative help and protection as well as court suits. Some lost their lives in shooting feuds, others became involved as witnesses. The Henry W. Martin family lost four children to diphtheria because the oldest boy witnessed a shooting. When subpoenaed to court in San Luis Obispo, he lodged in the only hotel room available in town. Unfortunately, a woman and her child had died in it the day before from diphtheria. In two weeks he was dead. In a month, three more children of the family had died of the dreaded disease.

Will and George Warren, both in their 90's, recall stories their parents told which involved many of their neighbors and themselves as they endeavored to hold their homesteads at the headwaters of San Simeon Creek. Once William Phillips hired a Hale boy in 1885 to run settlers off the mountain they were homesteading. He came home afoot one day after losing his horse to gunfire. At another time the Montañas, Guerras, Warrens and others were assembled at a neighbor's home when a shooting started. Some of the assembled quickly vacated the scene, not wishing to further risk their lives in a fight, others remained. Fortunately no one was killed though several found holes in their clothing afterward and Albert Warren received a bullet burn on one cheek.

Phillips also squabbled with several of his neighbors, sometimes seriously, though he eventually raised a fine family. Albert Warren once threatened to have him arrested but Phillips paid him $100 to drop his charges. James Lynch, who settled in the area in 1861, raised sheep in the Deer Flat area. Phillips squabbled with him and ran his sheep off the high bluffs, for which Lynch had him arrested. Cattlemen often resented sheep raisers and Lynch seems to have had other trouble for he hired Bill Bushten, who had gained a reputation as a professional gunman, to kill his enemy, Martin Hodges, who lived near the headwaters of Nacimiento River. Hodges was a big man and, as the story goes, he saw his assassin in time to hide behind a tree but his stomach protruded. Bushten nicked him. As Hodges pulled back, his rear came into view and received a bullet. Bushten galloped off without completing his job, and Hodges recovered from his wounds. Later, Lynch caught up with Hodges in Salinas and knifed him to death.

The Humphreys, who lived near the Jack Mountain area, were also involved in a series of shootings. William Humphrey is supposed to have killed Bushten. He also had feuds with the G. F. Beauchamp family which lived in the area. Hodges, before Lynch finished him, is reported to have killed a Mr. Hogan who was attempting to take up a homestead on property which Jeffrey Phelan claimed. And Beauchamp's brother, Charles, was killed by his falling horse while rustling cattle. Many more were involved in similar struggles, none of them willing to give an inch. But, the complete and interesting history of these lawless feuds is far too intricate for inclusion here.

Many descendents of these "back country" settlers are still in the area and are highly respected citizens of the community. Among the many who settled this section of the Santa Lucias and succeeded are the Williams, Porte, Montaña, Hale, Guerra, Martin, Paterson, Burnell, Bovee, Warren, Mathers, Peppard, Jack and Periera families.

As reversals and financial difficulties tormented various ranchers in the late 1870's many people of the San Simeon area put their properties up for sale. George Hearst, always ready to extend his holdings, slowly added them to his southern boundary until he finally owned most of Rancho San Simeon and some of the original public domain to the east.

When the financial depression of the 1930's endangered William Randolph Hearst's many business enterprises he was forced to sell various portions of his properties to remain solvent. By the late 1930's Rancho San Simeon and public domain properties, as well as his holdings on Rancho Santa Rosa had, again, been divided and sold into the hands of small ranchers.

At San Carpoforo Creek the Portolá Expedition turned inland as steep mountains extending into the sea barred further progress along the coast. (Overlooking the coast line at the mouth of the creek. Ragged Point in the background)

Cactus was planted near springs in double and triple rows about the circular palisade fences of the mountain corrals.

Home built by George Hearst for his top hand, Francisco "Pancho" Estrada, about 1876.

The buttons, in particular, were of interest.

A home on Center Street, 1900. Built on a tiny 25 by 50 foot lot. Mabel and Irma Music with their mother.

Original Grant, Lull and Co. Store. Built in 1865 and re-modeled in 1885, now the home of Mrs. Irma Jones.

Sebastian's store. Original built in 1872 by Grant, Lull and Co. Joined with Frankl store in 1878 to form present structure. (Photo by author)

Land to the left of San Simeon Creek was public domain of 1860. View to ocean with Stepladder ranch in foreground, formerly the Martin homestead on which the New Era School was located. Faint road at lower left corner was once a public road to ranches farther back to the southeast.

Hearst started personal development of his acreage in 1868. (Courtesy Mrs. Peter Fiscalini)

Chapter 16

Rancho Santa Rosa

Like Rancho San Simeon, Rancho Santa Rosa was once an outpost of Mission San Miguel. It had an abundance of wild forage for mission stock and numerous streams and springs which flowed throughout the year. In the fertile valleys through which Santa Rosa Creek and its tributaries wandered lived many deer, bear, fox and small animals such as the rabbit, squirrel and marsh rat. Oak, elderberry, sycamore and myrtle wood trees were plentiful in the canyons and along the streams while forage grasses and chaparral covered the drier hillsides and flats.

The northern end of the little valley through which Perry Creek flows was quite low and caused the formation of a shallow, broad lake called a *laguna* by the Spanish. It was fed not only by Perry Creek flowing from Harmony Valley but by the Green Valley stream and several other small streams caused by runoff from the surrounding hills to the west and northwest. During the summer the lake became a marsh clogged with tules and other water plants and was partially surrounded by willow.

The abundance of natural food and water encouraged the establishment of several large Indian camps which were inhabited for many hundred years before the first Spaniards arrived.

Unlike Rancho San Simeon, precipitous cliffs and rocky shores extended along its miles of ocean frontage providing only two small, sandy coves where small boats could be beached through the rough surf. Father Engelhardt, in his researches on the early history of Mission San Miguel and its holdings, has little to say about Rancho Santa Rosa except that it was held in conjunction with Rancho San Simeon, and probably was not separately developed. It played a minor role, being used exclusively as pasture land for wild herds of cattle and horses. There is implication that there might have been a building on the rancho, possibly a small adobe with thatched roof, used infrequently when cattle were branded or slaughtered. Mission records, however, do not verify this.

A network of Indian trails led from the rancho to the east, joining trails from the interior valleys and the mission. Mission produce was carried over them to the coast for trade, and bartered goods returned by the same routes. Droves of cattle raised along the flat lands near the Salinas River were undoubtedly herded from these interior mission lands to the coast in seasons of poor feed. The two coves were utilized as "drops" for hides to be picked up by schooners participating in illegal trade along the coast. The term "drop" was applied by the seamen as it described the manner in which the hides were delivered to the beach. After being hauled to the edge of the cliff above the landing cove they were actually dropped to the sand below. On Rancho Santa Rosa the drop was 75 to 100 feet.

Following secularization of mission properties, Rancho Santa Rosa was released for civilian occupancy at the same time as Rancho San Simeon. Don Julian Estrada, a younger brother of José Ramon, petitioned Governor Juan B. Alvarado for a grant of this rancho at the time the mission was secularized in 1838. Though he did not officially receive the grant until March 18, 1841, it appears that he was assured of ownership some time before. Don Julian was born at Monterey and soon after completion of his schooling he became interested in California government, eventually holding several offices of importance. His last, prior to acquisition of his ranch, was that *of comisionado* and administrator of Mission Santa Clara in 1837.

After petitioning for Rancho Santa Rosa Don Julian, a bachelor, spent some time on the ranch each year until the request for it became officially granted. During that time many of the Indians of the San Simeon *rancheria* are believed to have moved to the more southern rancho and joined with another group previously kept there by the mission. Many of them had cattle as their share in the division of mission property. They brought these with them. Also, during this time, Don Julian chose a site on the eastern slope of a hill bordering the *laguna* on the west where he began construction of an adobe home and the planting of fruit trees, required for retaining the grant.

The Indian and horse trail connecting San Luis Obispo with San Simeon passed through Santa Rosa Rancho along the bank of the *laguna* skirting it on the east side by way of some low lying hills. Continuing north, it followed the overflow of the *laguna* to Santa Rosa Creek.

The grant contained, roughly, three Spanish leagues and was casually designated as being bounded on the north by Santa Rosa Creek, on the east by the high mountains, on the south by Encinalitas Creek and Puerto Suelo, and on the west by the ocean. Don Julian had no idea where the eastern boundary line really was but assumed that the grant extended to the summit of the Santa Lucia mountains, and since no one else claimed the land between Santa Rosa and San Simeon Creeks, he visualized that land as part of his holdings as well.

None of the coastal grants given to the Dons at this time were occupied except for a few Indians. The area was considered a remote wilderness, too primitive for the society loving Spanish to use as permanent residences.

After building his adobe and making arrangements with the Indians for care of the rancho Don Julian left to continue residence in Monterey, near friends and relatives, returning infrequently to preside over the round-ups and slaughters. Back at Monterey he courted and married Nicolasa Gajiola in 1842. Now, relatively wealthy due to a prosperous rancho, he continued to live at Monterey spending and entertaining lavishly, looking upon himself as a lordly person. In spite of many shortcomings, Don Julian had a kind and generous heart and a deep sense of responsibility toward his relations and in-laws, a failing which caused him much financial grief in later years.

Though his rancho was not as large as many, the size seemed limitless to the Don. When his wife's brothers offered to move to his holdings to supervise the Indians and the rancho during his absence, he graciously accepted the offer and suggested they make their homes there. Guadalupe, Felipe, Valentine and José Antonio Gajiola all moved in. They established themselves in the higher mountains with flocks of sheep which were more suited to the rough terrain than cattle.

Following annexation of the territory of California to the United States Don Julian moved to San Luis Obispo as his friends and cousins were also obtaining lands in the area and making this town their home. He soon developed an interest in town government and in his rancho. He now made frequent trips to the rancho, probably overseeing additional improvement to his adobe home. Soon an influx of Spanish settlers took up holdings and moved into the adjacent mountains to the east. Several of the Dons now moved to their ranchos in order to protect them from encrouchment as well as to avoid much of the lawlessness suddenly rampant about San Luis Obispo.

Don Julian persuaded his wife and family to move to his holdings as permanent residents in 1849. The Indians proved trustworthy. They had continued to maintain the garden, orchard, vineyard and fields, as well as the rancho work. Some of the squaws were soon trained for domestic jobs, leaving Nicolasa free to supervise the household and education of her growing family, and to entertain frequent visitors which they made it a point to have.

Tutors were hired for the children, and the home was offered as a center for religious and political activities of the area. Visiting priests were encouraged to come often to attend to the affairs of marriage, baptism and death, and the religious training of the family, relatives, hired hands and Indians. Elections for the district after California became a state were also held there.

The Estradas continued to live at the rancho in a style comparable to their previous life at Monterey. Like other Dons, Julian considered velvet and lace, brocade cloth, and silver and gold trim as every day attire. He did no actual work other than tally his cattle at roundup time and the hides at slaughter. When riding about his rancho he wore a *sombrero* heavily trimmed with silver and gold; with trappings for the saddle and horse also heavily adorned by the same metals, and with jewels. He was so fond of pomp that, even when riding over his own estate, he was flanked by runners and mounted horsemen who proceeded ahead of him and followed behind.

It is said in various accounts left by his neighbors that little pretext was needed for Julian to have a *fiesta* with displays of horsemanship, bear and bull fights, dancing and eating. Such special occasions lasted for days, with people making long and arduous journeys by horseback and *carreta* to attend them.

Don Julian's favorite form of entertainment, like other county Dons, was the staging of a bear and bull fight. The bears, which were numerous, were ferocious fighters. The bear would be tied to a stout oak tree and several bulls driven up to it; the bear was then freed and the fight was on. Weddings, deaths, and passing visitors all gave occasion for gaiety and feasting. The lesser ones, without dancing and *fiesta*, were none the less gay, with contests among the ranch hands and the inevitable bear and bull fights.

Most of the food was produced on the rancho. It consisted primarily of corn, barley and wheat. These grains were pounded and ground into flour on stone *metates*, or in mortars, by the Indian women for making bread and *tortillas*. *Frijoles*, red peppers, garlic and onions were the chief garden foods. Cattle, sheep and wild game furnished an abundance of meat. Fruit trees, especially pears, provided preserves for great occasions. In season these were supplemented by fresh grapes.

Some ranchos were fortunate in obtaining large millstones which had been used at the missions for grinding grains. In using them a long pole was attached horizontally to the upper part of the millstone's turning post. The stone was revolved by pushing against it, either by hand or by a horse harnessed to it.

Twice a year extended activity involving rancho management occurred. These were the time of branding and counting stock, and the time of slaughter and preparation of hides and by-products for trade with the schooners. It took many long days of hard riding to gather the wild cattle and horses from the unfenced lands into scattered corrals which dotted the mountain rancho and unclaimed lands. Animals from all the ranchos ranged over the lands and often mingled together. At this time *vaqueros* from neighboring ranchos joined with those of Rancho

Santa Rosa and as the herded animals were sorted and counted the calves were branded by running iron and the ears cut according to the marks of the cows they tailed.

Reminders of these exciting days are still found in the hills and mountains of the Santa Lucias. The cactus (*Opuntia megacantha*) was utilized by the Indians as food previous to the discovery of America, and widely adopted by the Spanish and Mexicans for its fruit or *tuñas*. The young fleshy limbs of this cactus, which grows tall, branching and rank without attention, were found to provide excellent feed for stock in times of drought. The heavy growth, especially of those varieties with spines, also made good fence material which discouraged both bears and cattle. Probably first utilized in Alta California by the missions, this cactus was planted in double and triple rows about the circular palisade fences of the mountain corrals used at roundup time. It soon grew to form an impenetrable hedge 10 or more feet high, capable of holding the wild Spanish cattle and bands of equally wild horses called *mañada* animals. Repairs to the cactus stockade were seldom necessary.

Sites were carefully chosen near springs flanked by elevated points and hills which formed a natural channel to the corral where a watch for approaching *vaqueros* hazing the animals in for branding was maintained. High gates swung on sturdy posts.

When the lands in the mountain area were divided into small ranches, most of the cactus corrals fell into disuse and were forgotten. Imported American stock was raised in place of the wild, lanky hide-producing Spanish breed; and the new cattle were kept under fence with special pens and corrals constructed close by the barns and homes.

In many instances the cactus of these early round corrals still continues to grow, though the circular form is often obliterated by its own superfluous growth; trees and shrubs filling the richly fertilized center. One corral, however, is still maintained in a fairly good state by yearly use. Kept trim and in repair, it is located several miles from the coast at the eastern extremity of the Walter Warren ranch at the headwaters of San Simeon Creek. When the Warrens round up cattle in the back country, they herd them to this corral for branding, cutting and sale.

Two gates, side by side, open into the corral, each from a separate field. Sometimes when cattle are gathered for market they are held here for inspection, after which they are driven to ranch headquarters and loaded into waiting trucks.

Remnants of another cactus corral are to be found near the base of Scott Rock, a short distance from Cambria, overlooking Santa Rosa Valley. Unused for many years, this corral is overgrown with poison oak, trees and the cactus itself. Its original outline may still be detected and it, too, is located near a spring. Other such corrals, all beyond use, are found northward near the crest of the Santa Lucia range.

Relaxed on a high slope overlooking such a corral, a dreamer can visualize the flying dust rising from numerous wild, longhorned, fast-legged cattle as faster horses and equally wild Spanish, Mexican and Indian *vaqueros* come galloping in behind, funneling toward the corral whose rounded walls prevent bunching and trampling. One can almost hear the whoops and yells of the approaching men over the bellowing and snorting of bulls and cows, for bulls and cows they all were. The Spanish left all male calves to grow unaltered. They did not make steers of them as is done today for the creation of better meat.

The work of branding was dangerous and rough. Undoubtedly more than one *vaquero* or his horse felt the vicious thrust of a long, sharp horn as he nimbly worked about inside the enclosure, *reata* circling and flying, needle-sharp Spanish spurs jangling.

With the fall of night the dreamer may again visualize the brightly burning camp fire, freshly slaughtered beef broiling; *sombreros* laid aside, *panchos* on the ground, and the dirty, sweating, swarthy men relaxing till the pre-dawn of another day. Sounds of the night echo as the penned cattle bellow and paw, stymied by the strong thorny limbs of the sturdy cactus.

Many canyons of this back country are steep. The mountains reach upward, often ending in rocky crags. The trees and brush are thick. Ferreting out the wily cattle was a month-long job for strong horses and enduring men.

The second great activity on the ranch was the time of slaughter, or *matanza,* when the herds were thinned and the hides prepared for trade. The activity was confined to the hands of the rancho but meant fast work and long hours until the various phases of the job were done, for upon this event hinged the entire income of the rancho. Indian riders, called stickers or *navajadores,* went dashing over the range with long sharp knives. They usually rode in groups of three. Coming upon an animal with the Julian Estrada brand, two of the riders would haze the animal while the third, riding at full speed, with one wild plunge of the knife severed the spinal cord or cut the jugular vein. Following the stickers were the strippers, or *peladores,* who skinned the animals, taking the hides with them. On the heels of the strippers were the butchers, or *tasajoras.* This job was relegated to the Indian women who cut the meat from the carcasses into strips for jerky, and gathered the fat for rendering into tallow.

The hides were taken, sometimes to the beach and sometimes to headquarters, where they were scraped clean of clinging meat and fat, salted and stretched to dry. After drying they were folded once and stacked in bales ready for shipping. The tallow was rendered in large iron kettles and poured into skin pouches which held 25 pounds or the Spanish *arroba.* Horn and the hair of horses butchered at this same time were also saved and shipped with the hides. Large packs of dogs were maintained by each rancho. These dogs acted as scavengers after the slaughter and cleaned great quantities of the carcasses left behind.

Hospitality was the keynote of all the ranchos. Passing strangers, whether they stopped at the rancho adobe or merely passed through the land, were welcome to eat their fill of meat as the Don had little regard for the death of his cattle as long as the hide was preserved for him. Complying with this rule of hospitality, the vagrant butcher left the hide carefully skinned and spread on limb or bush where it could dry and eventually be found for return to its owner.

Most of the Indians lived apart from the Estrada home on a *rancheria* about one mile to the east beside a stream flowing down from the hills and through Green Valley. They gathered much of their own food, killing wild animals and harvesting native seeds and roots. Each fall, after the first heavy rains, the *laguna* became their hunting ground as rising water flushed out the wood rats that lived there. These were hunted with bow and arrow, both for pleasure and for food. It has been estimated that approximately 75 Indians lived there before 1864.

Prior to the acquisition of California by the United States as a territory in 1847, many American adventurers came seeking land and wealth which some of them obtained by marrying the daughters of already wealthy Spanish families. Those who were not so fortunate soon found employment or participated in the gold rush of 1849. Following the gold rush, these early arrivals who had not already settled on a place of their own, together with many disappointed late arrivals, fanned out into various parts of the state seeking land which would provide a home and income. Many drifted to San Luis Obispo County. These men, sometimes with families, settled the mountains east of the high mountain crest declared by the Dons to be rancho boundaries.

After the state was formed the United States government required the Dons to furnish legitimate proof of land ownership, together with clarification of rancho boundaries by approved government surveyors. The cost of proof and survey had to be borne by the land owner. As soon as government surveys were started, land grabbers followed in their wake. Most of the families who had settled in the mountains east of the rancho had their hands full trying to prove up on their pre-emption claims and were often too poor to resettle on new lands opened through surveys nearer the ocean.

Fees for the expensive job of proving title to the large tracts of land had to be paid in cash, an item neither Don Julian nor other grant owners had readily at hand. Heretofore hard cash, fluctuations in the market price, or the changing political scene outside of the immediate area interested them very little. Living was by credit, to be paid for in hides at the next arrival of the schooner. These Dons were not business men.

In order to meet the increasing costs which also included land and personal property taxes, previously unknown, as well as court and survey fees, Julian Estrada was forced to borrow money. This he did from Domingo Pujol, a young Spaniard, well educated and wealthy, recently arrived in the country. As security he gave Pujol a deed of trust to his entire rancho which, according to the survey when completed in 1858, contained 13,183 acres whose boundaries were well within those previously claimed by Julian. The loan, amounting to $7,900, was for a six-month period with an interest rate of two per cent compounded monthly, or approximately 27 per cent per year. Julian must have been gambling heavily on a large return from his hides, a gamble which he apparently lost for, after a lapse of nine months, Pujol foreclosed by offering to buy the rancho for $12,000, a sum which little more than covered the loan and accrued interest. Generously, Pujol offered to allow Don Julian to retain 1,500 acres surrounding his home. The transaction was concluded immediately but was not recorded until May 17, 1862. This sale led to an interesting complication a few years later. While to all intents and purposes the 1,500 acres belonged to Don Julian, he did not receive clear title to them until six years had elapsed.

At the conclusion of the survey the Gajiola brothers found themselves living on land outside of the rancho. To protect their interests it became necessary for them to file homestead under the California Homestead Act. Up to this time they had taken an interest in local political and governmental affairs though Guadalupe was the only one of the four to vote in the first county election held February 18, 1850, at which time 46 votes were cast from the entire county. Valentine was elected Justice of the Peace for the "Coasta" District (as the north county coastal area was first called) in 1856. Felipe worked for the sheriff's office in 1859, and José Antonio assisted at the elections held in the Coasta District at the Estrada adobe.

Rufus Burnett Olmsted was the first American to settle in Green Valley. He located at the eastern edge of the rancho midway between the north and south extremities. The Olmsteds were living on the Foster ranch at the head of San Marcos Creek, caring for homestead property belonging to Rufus' father-in-law, Judge A. T. Foster of San Jose, when the Santa Rosa Rancho survey was completed. Advised by the Judge concerning the location of the new boundaries of the rancho, Olmsted located a homestead adjoining the border immediately after Don Julian received his rancho patent in May of 1859 and, according to the tax rolls of the county, placed William Prindle on the land to hold it until he could arrange to move there with his family. Olmsted finally arrived in December of 1860 with his wife, Juliette Foster, and a family of six children, several of whom were nearly grown. At the time of their arrival Prindle had partially erected a log house, though it still lacked a roof and other refinements.

The family had barely encamped when they were approached by Don Julian, accompanied by much pomp and ceremony, and informed that they were on private property and must leave immediately. Olmsted, thoroughly acquainted with the survey lines, explained his rights and refused to move. Apparently resigned to his new neighbors, Don Julian gave no further trouble and on occasion was moved to visit them, especially when he learned they raised fine watermelons, a delicacy of which he was very fond. Each visit from the Don cost quantities of melons because of the large number of Mexicans and Indians who always accompanied him and who could not be refused a share in the harvest. In appreciation of his generosity, Don Julian once staged a special *fiesta* for Mr. Olmsted.

Jerry Johnson and James Monroe Buffum, both bachelors, settled at the northwest border of the rancho on Santa Rosa Creek in 1859. The property was registered to Buffum with Jerry, interested primarily in horses, remaining as a ranch hand, working not only on the Buffum land but occasionally for Don Julian. They were the nearest American neighbors the Olmsteds had for some time though they were not really considered neighbors by Mrs. Olmsted as there were no women with whom she could visit. Buffum, Johnson, the Olmsteds, Gajiolas and Estradas were the only residents for miles around except for Indians and A. M. Hardie, another bachelor who was living in Green Valley in 1860, though not as a property owner.

Rufus Olmsted was very much interested in the development of schools and the teaching of children who were arriving in the valley with new settlers. His only public office was Justice of the Peace in 1865 which, according to members of his family, was a difficult job. Cattle thieves were his worst offenders. These he could not punish because of recriminations enacted by their Mexican outlaw friends and relatives. On occasion he was also called upon to serve on the board of road reviewers in the area between San Simeon and Santa Rosa Creeks. Also, for several years he kept the mining records of the area. Shortly before his death in 1869 he spent a great deal of his own time prospecting, much to the discomfort of his wife who remained at home assuming much of the burden of ranch operation.

Buffum was also interested in promoting schools and roads and often worked with Olmsted on these matters. He was first noted publicly as serving as precinct inspector in 1862 at the Estrada adobe; he was elected county tax assessor in 1869, appointed assistant road master for the San Simeon and Santa Rosa roads in 1870, and overseer of the newly formed Road District 8. He was also an active member of the Odd Fellows after the formation of the Cambria lodge, and served for several years as a member of the County Board of Equalization, dying in 1889 at the age of 65.

By 1866 Jerry Johnson had acquired a farm of his own. He also opened a livery stable in Cambria which he operated for several years, then in later years tended bar at a local saloon.

Hardie was never interested in ranching but did become keenly interested in local mining and mine development and became foreman of the Sunderland Mine for several years. In 1868 he was appointed superintendent of the San Simeon Road District. After the formation of the little town of Cayucos 13 miles to the south, he moved there and became a prominent citizen of the town. Hardie Park in Cayucos was named for him.

Early rancho stock, including cattle, horses and sheep, were of Spanish breed introduced by the mission fathers. As American settlers came into the country they brought American stock which was considered of much better quality and produced more meat. Early tax assessments were very specific regarding the number of stock and the breed of each. American breeds were often assessed for twice the value of the Spanish breeds. The Board of Equalization had many complaints about the high tax rates on these animals and the land on which they grazed.

Rancho Santa Rosa was given an assessed value of $1 per acre in 1859. Stock cattle were assessed at $10 a head; tame cows at $16; work oxen of which there were many, at $20; tame mares at $25; *mañada* or wild horses and mares at $10 each; sheep at $2; goats at $1.50, and hogs at $3. Taxes for 1859 were set at $2.05 per $100 of assessed value. Considering the large number of cattle and horses, as well as other animals on the rancho, the number of acres, and his loan indebtedness, it is no wonder that Julian Estrada appealed for readjustment of his taxes. By 1861 many adjustments had been made. Spanish cattle were noted as being valued at $2 a head while American cattle were valued at $3. Similar adjustments were made for other animals. The value of the ranch was lowered to 40 cents an acre, much more in keeping with the income then derived from the land.

Following the loss of most of his rancho to Domingo Pujol, Don Julian still continued to live on a lavish scale. At this time, too, more of his relatives were dependent on him, among them the Gajiola brothers for they had given up their ranches and were following the less secure pursuit of prospecting. With other Spanish-Americans they located and established several mining claims but received little if any gain from them. In November of 1862 Don Julian again found it necessary to borrow heavily. He accepted a loan from Morris Cohen and Nathan Goldtree for $1,332, due and payable in one year, plus interest.

Apparently Julian made some effort to repay this debt for Cohen and Goldtree did not foreclose, but the following winter was a most unfortunate one for Julian as well as every other land owner in the area. It did not rain enough to produce a blade of grass. Only one shower fell in November of 1863 and not another drop of rain came until the following April of 1864. That winter the worst drought on record caused Don Julian and his neighbors to lose every head of cattle and almost every horse they owned.

Rather than see the animals die slowly of starvation, it is said large numbers were driven over the cliffs to the sea and rocks below where the waves washed away the carcasses. When a buyer could be found, the cattle were sold at 10 cents a head. Large numbers were butchered to save the hides, but labor was scarce for at this time, or possibly the previous year (ranchers whose parents related the event, are not sure) an epidemic killed all but three of the Indians living on Rancho Santa Rosa in the space of three weeks.

According to Anne Morrison in her *History of San Luis Obispo County,* the Indians died of smallpox. County records fail to substantiate this claim. Had there been such a devastating epidemic as smallpox in the county some record, though slight, would certainly have been made of it for smallpox was the one epidemic of which everyone was most fearful. At this time smallpox was prevalent in other parts of the state, but statements are to be found in which the county was actually praised for its efficient efforts in keeping the disease out of the area. On the other hand, diphtheria was another matter. It was widespread, causing death from one end of the county to the other. It was more probable the Indians died of this disease, or even measles. More than one writer has blamed the mass deaths, not so much on the disease as on the Indian method of treatment.

Obviously, few people, if any, were interested in risking contagion by devoting their efforts to the care of sick Indians; therefore, they were left to treat themselves in their own manner. Unfamiliar with the proper treatment of diseases of the white man, the Indians resorted to their age-old method: profuse sweating followed by a plunge into cold water. This treatment undoubtedly hastened their death at this time by inducing pneumonia as a complication.

During the drought many ranchers subsisted on seafoods of various kinds, including seaweeds. The Olmsted sons gathered clams from the beaches at Morro Bay which they brought home on foot, carrying the shelled clam meat in sacks on their backs. Mr. Olmsted walked to San Simeon Bay, a distance of 12 miles, whenever a schooner came into port. He would purchase flour or any other food commodity if it could be obtained. He, too, carried his purchases home on his back, as others did.

In an effort to save some of the horses and cattle when feed was nearly gone, Olmsted and other ranchers drove many of them deep into the mountains above San Carpoforo Creek in the hope they would find sufficient forage to survive. However, when feed was again plentiful, only 16 animals could be found.

Not only was food scarce, but other commodities were very high and almost unobtainable due to the Civil War. Calico was 50 cents a yard when available, and other things in proportion. Mrs. Olmsted used drilling sack for clothing, a heavy coarse fabric her husband had purchased the year before for farm use. Oak bark was used to dye the material a dark brown. Many other makeshift items were improvised before relief came.

In the fall of 1864 the rains fell in abundance but, without cattle, the ranchers were forced to turn to farming as a quick return on their investment. Prior to this time efforts had been made to interest the ranchers in the raising of wheat and other grains for trade. The idea had never taken hold. Eventually the ranchers realized the drought was a blessing, an outgrowth of the enforced turn of events. It rid the county of the rangy, long-horned Spanish cattle which had little economic value, establishing the profitable American cattle for dairying and farming.

Immediately following the drought George Hearst, realizing the financial and economic losses which had been sustained by the Dons, began avid acquisition of all the coastal rancho lands he could buy at a very low price. Not knowing that Don Julian had already sold the major portion of his rancho to Domingo Pujol, he thought he was getting an enormous bargain when Don Julian accepted his offer of $3,000 for his property. A deed was made and filed in which the sale of 13,183 acres was made to Hearst, excepting 160 acres about the house. Don Julian had never mastered the English language. Whether he knew the full context of the deed drafted by Hearst lawyers is a moot question. He may have proceeded without fully reading the deed on the assumption that Hearst knew he was buying only the 1,500 acres to which Julian still laid claim.

After the deed was recorded, Hearst discovered he actually owned no part of the ranch. Not only the portion rightfully purchased by Pujol but the 1,500 acres theoretically belonging to Julian were still in Pujol's name, no deed of transfer having been completed. It took three court battles before Hearst was finally convinced that he did not have a case. Meanwhile, local newspapers were not hesitant to make scathing remarks about

Hearst and his tactics. Later Hearst bought 1,340 acres from Don Julian, leaving the Don his home and a few adjacent acres.

In the meantime Pujol hired a Mr. Ward of San Luis Obispo to survey and plot the subdivision of his part of the rancho into ranches of varying sizes. He began the sale of this land in September 1866. John H. Myers was his first customer, purchasing 195 acres at the northwestern extremity of the rancho. This land, now part of Cambria, is known as Park Hill. Another portion became the property of the Pacific Steam Saw Mill and is now a part of the Fiscalini ranch in the heart of Cambria.

In October of 1866 George E. Long bought 2,094 acres; Miles C. Marks, 640 acres, and George W. Armstrong, 296 acres. In November Nathan Fletcher and Sam Pollard purchased lands. The following May William H. Freer, Charles Roberts, George Long, Mary Ivans and Peter Whittaker bought other portions. The rest of the rancho remained unsold until 1874 when Pujol incorporated it into the law firm of which he was a member. Future sales were then transacted by that firm. In February of 1874 Elijah Morris purchased property. In October the Oceanic Mining Company became interested and bought its first portion consisting of 112 acres, and again in February, 1875, the company purchased another 83 acres. Also purchasing in 1875 were S. L. Whittaker, John C. Hill and George Campbell, and John and James Taylor. In 1876 Robert Perry and David Morrow bought rancho land. Finally, in 1879, two of the law firm partners took over 437 acres; Joseph Johnson bought the last piece.

Hearst started personal development of his acreage in 1868, gradually buying up other pieces as people were willing to sell. He eventually owned about 3,000 acres of the original grant. Here he indulged in the raising and breeding of fine race horses during the 1870's. Later he rented the property out as dairy land and had a ditch constructed to drain the *laguna*. For years this ditch was known as the Walker Ditch.

Don Julian was the only one of the north coast Dons who was deeply interested in his rancho as a home for himself and his family. As a family man he was more concerned for the happiness of those near and dear to him than for his own glory through political activity in the state or county, though in the beginning he participated in the formation of the early government of the county and was most concerned that the people have a full voice in county affairs, as evidenced by the generous donation of his home as a polling place and his own time at each election when he endeavored to see that the people voted.

He was elected as the county's first assessor and registrar in February, 1850, offices he held for two years, after which he devoted almost his entire time to his home and the north coast area until 1860 when he was again elected to office as county supervisor, an office he held of several years by commuting frequently on horseback rather than spend several days each month in San Luis Obispo. As a consequence, he was often forced to be absent from meetings due to bad weather or rancho activities which, more often than not, consisted of his continued lavish entertainment of numerous visitors in almost constant attendance at the adobe. Many of Cambria's first citizens were house guests at the adobe before locating and building their own homes in the village.

Until a Catholic church was established in Cambria about 1872, the adobe was the center of Catholic religious activities for the entire coast area north of Morro Bay. It was the scene of many marriages as well as baptisms. Even after establishment of the church and Don Julian's death, the home continued to be used for occasional church functions until abandoned to George Hearst in 1876. The late Anna Steiner was probably the last to be baptized there.

Don Julian died in 1871, not yet 60 years old, still proud but a ruined man reduced to near poverty. He left his wife, Nicolasa, age 48, and seven children: Guadalupe, age 10; Elvira, 13; Francisco, 17; Mariano, 19; Luisa de Avila, 21; Isabel, 23, and Rosamel, 25. Francisco took over the management of the 160-acre holding and cared for his mother and the family which still remained at home until 1876. At that time the rest of the ranch was sold to Hearst and Francisco took employment on Rancho Piedra Blanca. Hearst provided a home for him at San Simeon where he was a highly respected ranch employee. Later, William Randolph Hearst built a new Spanish style home for him in which he lived until his death.

The Estrada adobe soon fell into ruin, and in 1900 only remnants of the walls remained, none being over four feet high. Earlier a number of the tile were removed from the adobe by George Hearst, hastening its destruction. When W. R. Hearst finally built the Spanish style home for Francisco, these same Indian-made tile were used on its roof. In 1907 the horses of the Sandercock firm of San Luis Obispo were kept in the Estrada corral while the company did roadwork on the highway which, at this time, passed to the southwest of the old home site. Finally, at the request of W. R. Hearst, the remaining ruins of the adobe were leveled, horses and Fresno scrapers being used to clear the area. Still later, new and larger corrals were built on the site for overnight holding of cattle being driven to the Goldfield railroad siding near San Luis Obispo for shipment.

In 1962 relocation of Highway One placed the road almost directly over the site of the old Estrada home. Prior to and during road grading Paul Squibb and his wife, Louise, of Cambria were fortunate in salvaging a number of artifacts from the site including an old French perfume bottle, a tin candle holder, pottery fragments, pieces of cut glassware, roof tiles, Indian artifacts and broken toys, all reminiscent of the years gone by.

Several years previously numerous Indian graves were discovered on the present Ioppini ranch of Green Valley near the site of the early Indian *rancheria*. Grave goods included rosaries, crucifix and glass beads. These burials, for the most part, are believed to have been made at about the same time and it is also believed they were the Santa Rosa *rancheria* Indians who died during the 1862 or 1863 epidemic.

George Hearst indulged in raising fine horses on Rancho Santa Rosa. Horse barns and corrals built during the 1870's. (Courtesy Mrs. Peter Fiscalini)

Bibliography

Academy of the Pacific Coast, History Publication, Vol. 1, No. 3.

Andrews, Mrs. Lela Martin, personal correspondence.

Angel, Myron, *History of San Luis Obispo County,* Thompson and West, 1883.

Bancroft, Hubert Howe, *History of California,* Vols. 1-5, 1886.

Britton and Rey, *Maps of California,* 1853 and 1857.

Budker, P., *Whales and Whaling,* MacMillan, 1959.

California Coast Pilot for years 1869 and 1889.

California Highways and Public Works, Official Journal, Division of Highways, State of California, Vol. 29.

California Historical Society Quarterly, Vol. 1, 1922-23; Vol. for 1927, pgs. 254-8.

Calif. State Mining Bureau, *Quicksilver Resources of California,* Bull. 78, 1918.

Cambria Cemetery; various private cemeteries on ranches surrounding Cambria.

Cambria Courier, weekly newspaper of Cambria, 1916-17.

Cambrian, weekly newspaper of Cambria, 1954-1973.

Chapman, Charles E., *History of California: the Spanish period,* MacMillan Co., 1926.

Coast and Geodetic Survey. A Summary of the Years 1807-1957, Government Printing Office.

Cooper, deGuy, *Visit to San Simeon,* 1875, Bancroft Library.

Costanso, Don Miguel, *Dairy of,* from the Spanish, 1879.

Courier, unpublished *log book of Schooner,* 1825-29, Bancroft Library.

Courter, John P., Jr., *History of Mission San Miguel,* Chas. A. Black, San Luis Obispo, 1914 (?)

Coy, Owen C., *Guide to the County Archives of California.* Calif. State Printing Office, Sacramento, 1919.

Crespi, Fr. Juan, *Dairy of,* 1769, from the Spanish.

Dana, Richard Henry, *Two Years Before the Mast,* Dodd, Ed., 1946.

Davidson, G., 1869 *Pacific Coast Coast Pilot.*

Davis, Wm. Heath, 75 *Years in California,* 1774-1847, John Howell, 1929, S. F.

Eddy, William M., *Official California Map of* 1853.

Encyclopaedia Britannica, Edition of 1956.

Engelhardt, Fr. Zephyrin, *Mission San Miguel,* Santa Barbara Mission Publication, 1929.

Engelhardt, Fr. Zephyrin, *Mission San Antonio,* Santa Barbara Mission Publication, 1929.

Engelhardt, Fr. Zephyrin, *Mission San Luis Obispo,* Santa Barbara Mission Publication, 1933.

Font, Pedro, Diary of, Translation by Herbert E. Bolton, 1931.

Forbes, Alexander, *History of Upper and Lower California,* 1839.

Frickstad, Walter, *A Century of California Post Offices,* 1848-1954, Philatelic Research Society, 1955.

General Services Administration, National Archives and Records Service, Washington, D. C. Postal information by personal correspondence.

Geodetic Survey Maps: Quadrangles of *San Simeon, Adelaide, Piedra Blanca,. Cayucos, Pebblestone - Shut-in, Cambria, Cypress Mountain* and *Lime Mountain,* 1957.

Gift, George W., *Settler's Guide, Circulars and laws to pre-emption claims in California,* 1854.

Gleason, J. D., *Islands and Ports of California,* Sea Publication, 1950, L. A.

Goode, Geo. B., *Fisheries and Fishery Industry of the United States,* Sec. 1, 1884.

Grimes, Captain Eleah, *Unpublished log book,* date unknown, Bancroft Library.

Guinn, Prof. J. M., *History and Biographical Record of the Central Coast,* 1902.

Hafely, Helen, personal correspondence regarding the Evans, Gillis and Van-Gorden families, 1964.

Handbook and Directory of Southern California, 1875.

Hansen, Gladys C., *The Chinese in California,* Richard Able and Co., 1970.

Harmony Valley Creamery Association, *Association Records.*

Hayes Emigrations Notes, 1860-61.

Heizer, R. F., *The California Indians,* University of California Press, 1960.

Holt, Alfred, *American Place Names,* Thomas Y. Crowell Co., N. Y., 1938.

Kane, Joseph Nathan, *The American Counties,* Scarecrow Press, 196?.

Langsdorff, Freiherr Gerog Heinrich von, *Voyages and Travels,* an original manuscript, date unknown, Bancroft Library.

Lucas, Kay, *Dead Mens' Chests,* Travel Magazine, Feb. 1964.

Mentor, Log Book of Schooner, unpublished, 1824-25, Bancroft Library.

Mission San Luis Obispo *early birth and death records.*

Mofras, Eugene Duflot de, *Map of the Pacific Coast,* 1842-44, Bancroft Library.

Montgomery, David H., *Leading Facts of American History,* Ginn and Co., 1893.

Morrison, Anne, *History of San Luis Obispo County,* L. A. Historic Record Co., 1917.

National Geographic Magazine, Nov. 1959.

Ng, Pearl, *Writings on the Chinese in California,* (thesis) U. C., Jan. 1939.

Oceanic Quicksilver Mine, *original documents,* courtesy Mr. and Mrs. Henry Curti, Cambria, Ca.

Older, Mr. and Mrs. Fremont, *Life of George Hearst, California Pioneer,* Private Edition, 1933.

Olmsted, Rufus B., *unpublished mining record book for Cambria area,* 1860's.

Olmsted, Miss Frances, personal correspondence regarding the Olmsted family, 1962-64.

Pico, Don José de Jésus, *Acontecimientos,* 1840, unpublished, Bancroft Library.

Pioneer, San Luis Obispo weekly newspaper, 1867-69.

Portolá, Diary of Gaspar de, in original Spanish of 1769.
Sacramento Daily Union, March 14, 1855.
San Francisco Chronicle, Jan.-March, 1874.
San Luis Obispo County *Board of Equalization Minutes,* 1852 - -.
San Luis Obispo County *Board of Supervisors Minutes,* 1850 - -.
San Luis Obispo County *Incorporation Records,* 1850 - -.
San Luis Obispo County record books for: *Brands, Deaths, Homesteads, Marriages, Mortgages, Patents, Pre-emption claims, Tax Assessments, Wills of Probate* and numerous other miscellaneous records.
San Luis Obispo Independent Order of Odd Fellows, early *cemetery burial records.*
San Luis Obispo, *papers of the Junta,* 1847-1850.
Santa Rosa Catholic Church Cemetery.
Scammon, Charles M., *Mammals of the Northwestern Coast of North America,* Shore Whale Fishing, J. Carmany, 1874., S. F.
Shaler, Captain William, *unpublished personal papers* relating to his voyage along the California coast in 1805, Bancroft Library.
Sexton, Lucy Foster, *The Foster Family, California Pioneers of* 1849, a private publication of 1889 borrowed from Foster family descendents by author.
Smith, David E., and Frederick J. Teggart, *A Summary and Translation of the Portolá Expedition.* University of California Press, 1909.
Squibb, Paul, unpublished *Comparative Translation of diaries kept by members of the Portolá Expedition,* 1964.
Starks, Edwin C., *History of California Shore Whaling,* Fish and Game Bulletin No. 6, 1922.
State Lands Commission Records, State Lands Division, Sacramento, Ca.
State Water Resources Board, *Bulletin 18.*
Stewart, George R., *American Place Names,* Oxford University Press, 1970.
Swanberg, W. A., *Citizen Hearst,* Scribner, 1961
Times World Atlas, reference names, use of the name Cambria.
Tribune, San Luis Obispo weekly newspaper, 1869-89.
Waltz, Marcus L., *Chronicles of Cambria Pioneers,* published by the Cambrian, Nov. 30, 1946.
White, James T., *White's Conspectus of American Biography.* James T. White & Co., Publishers, N. Y., 1937.
White, Michael C., *unpublished manuscript* written about 1850, Bancroft Library.
Wineman, Mrs. Isabelle Paterson, personal correspondence regarding Paterson family and early events of Cambria, 1963-64.

Index

211

These tandem wagons, hitched to a four-horse team of fine matched greys
said to have been purchased by Bob Warren from Wm. Leffingwell, are
loaded with four-foot lengths of firewood for the Oceanic Mine. Bob War-
ren, brother of Will and George, is seated.

New Hesperian School, 1907.

Cambria town band of 1880's ready for Fourth of July parade. (Courtesy SLO Co. Museum, Helen Ballard collection)